THE WRITINGS OF CHUANG TZU

ISBN-10:1-940849-52-7
ISBN-13:978-1-940849-52-2
www.bigfontbooks.com

THE WRITINGS OF CHUANG TZU

TRANSLATED BY JAMES LEGGE

ANCIENT WISDOM PUBLICATION

WOODLAND, CALIFORNIA

Contents

Hsiâo-yâo Yû, or 'Enjoyment in Untroubled Ease.'

1. In the Northern Ocean there is a fish, the name of which is Khwan,-- I do not know how many lî in size. It changes into a bird with the name of Phang, the back of which is (also)-- I do not know how many lî in extent. When this bird rouses itself and flies, its wings are like clouds all round the sky. When the sea is moved (so as to bear it along), it prepares to remove to the Southern Ocean. The Southern Ocean is the Pool of Heaven.

There is the (book called) Khî Hsieh,-- a record of marvels. We have in it these words:-- 'When the phang is removing to the Southern Ocean it flaps (its wings) on the water for 3000 lî. Then it ascends on a whirlwind 90,000 lî, and it rests only at the end of six months.' (But similar to this is the movement of the breezes which we call) the horses of the fields, of the dust (which quivers in the sunbeams), and of living things as they are blown against one another by the air. Is its azure the proper colour of the sky? Or is it occasioned by its distance and illimitable extent? If one were looking down (from above), the very same appearance would just meet his view.

2. And moreover, (to speak of) the accumulation of water;-- if it be not great, it will not have strength to support a large boat. Upset a cup of water in a cavity, and a straw will float on it as if it were a boat. Place a cup in it, and it will stick fast;-- the water is shallow and the boat is large. (So it is with) the accumulation of wind; if it be not great, it will not have strength to support great wings. Therefore (the phang ascended to) the height of 90,000 lî, and there was such a mass of wind beneath it; thenceforth the accumulation of wind was sufficient. As it seemed to bear the blue sky on its back, and there was nothing to obstruct or arrest its course, it could pursue its way to the South.

A cicada and a little dove laughed at it, saying, 'We make an effort and fly towards an elm or sapanwood tree; and sometimes before we reach it, we can do no more but drop to the ground. Of what use is it for this (creature) to rise 90,000 lî, and make for the South?' He who goes to the grassy suburbs, returning to the third meal (of the day), will have his belly as full as when he set out; he who goes to a distance of 100 lî will have to pound his grain where he stops for the night; he who goes a thousand lî, will have to carry with him provisions for three months. What should these two small creatures know about the matter? The knowledge of that which is small does not reach to that which is great; (the experience of) a few years does not reach to that of many. How do we know that it is so? The mushroom of a morning does not know (what takes place between) the beginning and end of a month; the short-lived cicada does not know (what takes place between) the spring and autumn. These are instances of a short term of life. In the south of Khû there is the (tree) called Ming-ling, whose spring is 500 years, and its autumn the same; in high antiquity there was that called Tâ-khun, whose spring was 8000 years, and its autumn the same. And Phang Tsu is the one man renowned to the present day for his length of life:-- if all men were (to wish) to match him, would they not be miserable?

3. In the questions put by Thang to Kî we have similar statements:-- 'In the bare and barren north there is the dark and vast ocean,-- the Pool of Heaven. In it there is a fish, several thousand lî in breadth, while no one knows its length. Its name is the khwan. There is (also) a bird named the phang; its back is like the Thâi mountain, while its wings are like clouds all round the sky. On a whirlwind it mounts upwards as on the whorls of a goat's horn for 90,000 lî1, till, far removed from the cloudy vapours, it bears on its back the blue sky, and then it shapes its course for the South, and proceeds to the ocean there.' A quail by the side of a marsh laughed at it, and said, 'Where is it going to? I spring up with a bound, and come down again when I have reached but a few fathoms, and then fly about among the brushwood and bushes; and this is the perfection of flying. Where is that creature going to?' This shows the difference between the small and the great.

Thus it is that men, whose wisdom is sufficient for the duties of some one office, or whose conduct will secure harmony in some one district, or whose virtue is befitting a ruler so that they could efficiently govern some one state, are sure to look on themselves in this manner (like the quail), and yet Yung-tsze of Sung would have smiled and laughed at them. (This Yung-tsze), though the whole world should have praised him, would not for that have stimulated himself to greater endeavour, and though the whole world should have condemned him, would not have exercised any more repression of his course; so fixed was he in the difference between the internal (judgment of himself) and the external (judgment of others), so distinctly had he marked out the bounding limit of glory and disgrace. Here, however, he stopped. His place in the world indeed had become indifferent to him, but still he had not planted himself firmly (in the right position).

---

1   The li also known as the Chinese mile, is a traditional Chinese unit of distance. The li has varied considerably over time but was usually about a third as long as the English mile and now has a standardized length of a half-kilometer (500 meters or 1,640 feet).

There was Lieh-tsze, who rode on the wind and pursued his way, with an admirable indifference (to all external things), returning, however, after fifteen days, (to his place). In regard to the things that (are supposed to) contribute to happiness, he was free from all endeavours to obtain them; but though he had not to walk, there was still something for which he had to wait. But suppose one who mounts on (the ether of) heaven and earth in its normal operation, and drives along the six elemental energies of the changing (seasons), thus enjoying himself in the illimitable,-- what has he to wait for? Therefore it is said, 'The Perfect man has no (thought of) self; the Spirit-like man, none of merit; the Sagely-minded man, none of fame.'

4. Yâo, proposing to resign the throne to Hsü Yû, said, 'When the sun and moon have come forth, if the torches have not been put out, would it not be difficult for them to give light? When the seasonal rains are coming down, if we still keep watering the ground, will not our toil be labour lost for all the good it will do? Do you, Master, stand forth (as sovereign), and the kinadorn will (at once) be well governed. If I still (continue to) preside over it, I must look on myself as vainly occupying the place;-- I beg to resign the throne to you.' Hsü Yû said, 'You, Sir, govern the kingdom, and the kingdom is well governed. If I in these circumstances take your place, shall I not be doing so for the sake of the name? But the name is but the guest of the reality;-- shall I be playing the part of the guest? The tailor-bird makes its nest in the deep forest, but only uses a single branch; the mole drinks from the Ho, but only takes what fills its belly. Return and rest in being ruler,-- I will have nothing to do with the throne. Though the cook were not attending to his kitchen, the representative of the dead and the officer of prayer would not leave their cups and stands to take his place.'

5. Kien Wû asked Lien Shû, saying, 'I heard Khieh-yü talking words which were great, but had nothing corresponding to them (in reality);-- once gone, they could not be brought back. I was frightened by them;-- they were like the Milky Way which cannot be traced to its beginning or end. They had no connexion with one another, and were not akin to the experiences of men.' 'What were his words?' asked Lien Shû, and the other replied, (He said) that 'Far away on the hill of Kû-shih there dwelt a Spirit-like man whose flesh and skin were (smooth) as ice and (white) as snow; that his manner was elegant and delicate as that of a virgin; that he did not eat any of the five grains, but inhaled the wind and drank the dew; that he mounted on the clouds, drove along the flying dragons, rambling and enjoying himself beyond the four seas; that by the concentration of his spirit-like powers he could save men from disease and pestilence, and secure every year a plentiful harvest.' These words appeared to me wild and incoherent and I did not believe them. 'So it is,' said Lien Shû.

'The blind have no perception of the beauty of elegant figures, nor the deaf of the sound of bells and drums. But is it only the bodily senses of which deafness and blindness can be predicated ? There is also a similar defect in the intelligence; and of this your words supply an illustration in yourself. That man, with those attributes, though all things were one mass of confusion, and he heard in that condition the whole world crying out to him to be rectified, would not have to address himself laboriously to the task, as if it were his business to rectify the world. Nothing could hurt that man; the greatest floods, reaching to the sky, could not drown him, nor would he feel the fervour of the greatest heats melting metals and stones till they flowed, and scorching all the ground and hills. From the dust and chaff of himself, he could still mould and fashion Yâos and Shuns;-- how should he be willing to occupy himself with things?'

6. A man of Sung, who dealt in the ceremonial caps (of Yin), went with them to Yüeh, the people of which cut off their hair and tattooed their bodies, so that they had no use for them. Yâo ruled the people of the kingdom, and maintained a perfect government within the four seas. Having gone to see the four (Perfect) Ones on the distant hill of Kû-shih, when (he returned to his capital) on the south of the Fan water, his throne appeared no more to his deep-sunk oblivious eyes.

7. Hui-tsze told Kwang-tsze, saying, 'The king of Wei sent me some seeds of a large calabash, which I sowed. The fruit, when fully grown, could contain five piculs (of anything). I used it to contain water, but it was so heavy that I could not lift it by myself. I cut it in two to make the parts into drinking vessels; but the dried shells were too wide and unstable and would not hold (the liquor); nothing but large useless things! Because of their uselessness I knocked them to pieces.' Kwang-tsze replied, 'You were indeed stupid, my master, in the use of what was large. There was a man of Sung who was skilful at making a salve which kept the hands from getting chapped; and (his family) for generations had made the bleaching of cocoon-silk their business. A stranger heard of it, and proposed to buy the art of the preparation for a hundred ounces of silver. The kindred all came together, and considered the proposal. "We have," said they, "been bleaching cocoon-silk for generations, and have only gained a little money. Now in one morning we can sell to this man our art for a hundred ounces;-- let him have it." The stranger accordingly got it and went away with it to give counsel to the king of Wû, who was then engaged in hostilities with Yüeh. The king gave him the command of his fleet, and in the winter he had an engagement with that of Yüeh, on which he inflicted a great defeat, and was invested with a portion of territory taken from Yüeh. The keeping the hands from getting chapped was the same in both cases; but in the one case it led to the investiture (of

the possessor of the salve), and in the other it had only enabled its owners to continue their bleaching. The difference of result was owing to the different use made of the art. Now you, Sir, had calabashes large enough to hold five piculs;-- why did you not think of making large bottle-gourds of them, by means of which you could have floated over rivers and lakes, instead of giving yourself the sorrow of finding that they were useless for holding anything. Your mind, my master, would seem to have been closed against all intelligence!'

Hui-tsze said to Kwang-tsze, 'I have a large tree, which men call the Ailantus. Its trunk swells out to a large size, but is not fit for a carpenter to apply his line to it; its smaller branches are knotted and crooked, so that the disk and square cannot be used on them. Though planted on the wayside, a builder would not turn his head to look at it. Now your words, Sir, are great, but of no use;-- all unite in putting them away from them.' Kwang-tsze replied, 'Have you never seen a wildcat or a weasel? There it lies, crouching and low, till the wanderer approaches; east and west it leaps about, avoiding neither what is high nor what is low, till it is caught in a trap, or dies in a net. Again there is the Yak, so large that it is like a cloud hanging in the sky. It is large indeed, but it cannot catch mice. You, Sir, have a large tree and are troubled because it is of no use;-- why do you not plant it in a tract where there is nothing else, or in a wide and barren wild? There you might saunter idly by its side, or in the enjoyment of untroubled ease sleep beneath it. Neither bill nor axe would shorten its existence; there would be nothing to injure it. What is there in its uselessness to cause you distress?'

Khî Wû Lun, or 'The Adjustment of Controversies.'

1. Nan-kwo Tsze-khî was seated, leaning forward on his stool. He was looking up to heaven and breathed gently, seeming to be in a trance, and to have lost all consciousness of any companion. (His disciple), Yen Khang Tsze-yû, who was in attendance and standing before him, said, 'What is this? Can the body be made to become thus like a withered tree, and the mind to become like slaked lime? His appearance as he leans forward on the stool to-day is such as I never saw him have before in the same position.' Tsze-khî said, 'Yen, you do well to ask such a question, I had just now lost myself; but how should you understand it? You may have heard the notes of Man, but have not heard those of Earth; you may have heard the notes of Earth, but have not heard those of Heaven.'

Tsze-yû said, 'I venture to ask from you a description of all these.' The reply was, 'When the breath of the Great Mass (of nature) comes strongly, it is called Wind. Sometimes it does not come so; but when it does, then from a myriad apertures there issues its excited noise;-- have you not heard it in a prolonged gale? Take the projecting bluff of a mountain forest;-- in the great trees, a hundred spans round, the apertures and cavities are like the nostrils, or the mouth, or the ears; now square, now round like a cup or a mortar; here like a wet footprint, and there like a large puddle. (The sounds issuing from them are like) those of fretted water, of the arrowy whizz, of the stern command, of the inhaling of the breath, of the shout, of the gruff note, of the deep wail, of the sad and piping note. The first notes are slight, and those that follow deeper, but in harmony with them. Gentle winds produce a small response; violent winds a great one. When the fierce gusts have passed away, all the apertures are empty (and still);-- have you not seen this in the bending and quivering of the branches and leaves?'

Tsze-yû said, 'The notes of Earth then are simply those which come from its myriad apertures; and the notes of Man may just be compared to those which (are brought from the tubes of) bamboo;-- allow me to ask about the notes of Heaven.' Tsze-khî replied, 'When (the wind) blows, (the sounds from) the myriad apertures are different, and (its cessation) makes them stop of themselves. Both of these things arise from (the wind and the apertures) themselves:-- should there be any other agency that excites them?'

2. Great knowledge is wide and comprehensive; small knowledge is partial and restricted. Great speech is exact and complete; small speech is (merely) so much talk. When we sleep, the soul communicates with (what is external to us); when we awake, the body is set free. Our intercourse with others then leads to various activity, and daily there is the striving of mind with mind. There are hesitancies; deep difficulties; reservations; small apprehensions causing restless distress, and great apprehensions producing endless fears. Where their utterances are like arrows from a bow, we have those who feel it their charge to pronounce what is right and what is wrong; where they are given out like the conditions of a covenant, we have those who maintain their views, determined to overcome. (The weakness of their arguments), like the decay (of things) in autumn and winter, shows the failing (of the minds of some) from day to day; or it is like their water which, once voided, cannot be gathered up again. Then their ideas seem as if fast bound with cords, showing that the mind is become like an old and dry moat, and that it is nigh to death, and cannot be restored to vigour and brightness.

Joy and anger, sadness and pleasure, anticipation and regret, fickleness and fixedness, vehemence and indolence, eagerness and tardiness;-- (all these moods), like music from an empty tube, or mushrooms from the warm moisture, day and night succeed to one another and come before us, and we do not know whence they sprout. Let us stop! Let us stop! Can we expect to find out suddenly how they are produced?

If there were not (the views of) another, I should not have mine; if there were not I (with my views), his would be uncalled for:-- this is nearly a true statement of the case, but we do not know what it is that makes it be so. It might seem as if there would be a true Governor concerned in it, but we do not find any trace (of his presence and acting). That such an One could act so I believe; but we do not see His form. He has affections, but He has no form.

Given the body, with its hundred parts, its nine openings, and its six viscera, all complete in their places, which do I love the most? Do you love them all equally? or do you love some more than others? Is it not the case that they all perform the part of your servants and waiting women? All of them being such, are they not incompetent to rule one another? or do they take it in turns to be now ruler and now servants? There must be a true Ruler (among them) whether by searching you can find out His character or not, there is neither advantage nor hurt, so far as the truth of His operation is concerned. When once we have received the bodily form complete, its parts do not fail to perform their functions till the end comes. In conflict with things or in harmony with them, they pursue their course to the end, with the speed of a galloping horse which cannot be stopped;-- is it not sad? To be constantly toiling all one's life-time, without seeing the fruit of one's labour, and to be weary and worn out with his labour, without knowing where he is going to:-- is it not a deplorable case? Men may say, 'But it is not death;' yet of what advantage is this? When the body is decomposed, the mind will be the same along with it:-- must not the case be pronounced very deplorable? Is the life of man indeed enveloped in such darkness? Is it I alone to whom it appears so? And does it not appear to be so to other men?

3. If we were to follow the judgments of the predetermined mind, who would be left alone and without a teacher? Not only would it be so with those who know the sequences (of knowledge and feeling) and make their own selection among them, but it would be so as well with the stupid and unthinking. For one who has not this determined mind, to have his affir-mations and negations is like the case described in the saying, 'He went to Yüeh to-day, and arrived at it yesterday.' It would be making what was not a fact to be a fact. But even the spirit-like Yü could not have known how to do this, and how should one like me be able to do it?

But speech is not like the blowing (of the wind); the speaker has (a meaning in) his words. If, however, what he says, be indeterminate (as from a mind not made up), does he then really speak or not? He thinks that his words are different from the chirpings of fledgelings; but is there any distinction between them or not? But how can the Tâo be so obscured, that there should be 'a True' and 'a False' in it? How can speech be so obscured that there should be 'the Right' and 'the Wrong' about them? Where shall the Tâo go to that it will not be found? Where shall speech be found that it will be inappropriate? Tâo becomes obscured through the small comprehension (of the mind), and speech comes to be obscure through the vain-gloriousness (of the speaker). So it is that we have the contentions between the Literati and the Mohists, the one side affirming what the other denies, and vice versa. If we would decide on their several affirmations and denials, no plan is like bringing the (proper) light (of the mind) to bear on them.

All subjects may be looked at from (two points of view),-- from that and from this. If I look at a thing from another's point of view, I do not see it; only as I know it myself, do I know it. Hence it is said, 'That view comes from this; and this view is a consequence of that:'-- which is the theory that that view and this--(the opposite views)-- produce each the other. Although it be so, there is affirmed now life and now death; now death and now life; now the admissibility of a thing and now its inadmis-sibility; now its inadmissibility and now its admissibility. (The disputants) now affirm and now deny; now deny and now affirm. Therefore the sagely man does not pursue this method, but views things in the light of (his) Heaven (-ly nature), and hence forms his judgment of what is right.

This view is the same as that, and that view is the same as this. But that view involves both a right and a wrong; and this view involves also a right and a wrong:-- are there indeed, or are there not the two views, that and this? They have not found their point of correspondency which is called the pivot of the Tâo. As soon as one finds this pivot, he stands in the centre of the ring (of thought), where he can respond without end to the changing views;-- without end to those affirming, and without end to those denying. Therefore I said, 'There is nothing like the proper light (of the mind).'

4. By means of a finger (of my own) to illustrate that the finger (of another) is not a finger is not so good a plan as to illustrate that it is not so by means of what is (acknowledged to be) not a finger; and by means of (what I call) a horse to illustrate that (what another calls) a horse is not so, is not so good a plan as to illustrate that it is not a horse, by means of what is (acknowledged to be) not a horse. (All things in) heaven and earth may be (dealt with as) a finger; (each of) their myriads may be (dealt with as) a horse. Does a thing seem so to me? (I say that) it is so. Does it seem not so to me? (I say that) it is not so. A path is formed by (constant) treading on the ground. A thing is called by its name through the (constant) application of the name to it. How is it so? It is so because it is so. How is it not so? It is not so, because it is not so. Everything has its inherent character and its proper capability. There is nothing which has not these. Therefore, this being so, if we take a stalk of grain and a (large) pillar, a loathsome (leper) and (a beauty like) Hsî Shih, things large and things insecure, things crafty and things strange;-- they may in the light of the Tâo all be reduced to the same category (of opinion about them).

It was separation that led to completion; from completion ensued dissolution. But all things, without regard to their completion and dis- solution, may again be comprehended in their unity;-- it is only the far reaching in thought who know how to comprehend them in this unity. This being so, let us give up our devotion to our own views, and occupy ourselves with the ordinary views. These ordinary views are grounded on the use of things. (The study of that) use leads to the comprehensive judgment, and that judgment secures the success (of the inquiry). That success gained, we are near (to the object of our search), and there we stop. When we stop, and yet we do not know how it is so, we have what is called the Tâo.

When we toil our spirits and intelligence, obstinately determined (to establish our own view), and do not know the agreement (which underlies it and the views of others), we have what is called 'In the morning three.' What is meant by that 'In the morning three?' A keeper of monkeys, in giving them out their acorns, (once) said, 'In the morning I will give you three (measures) and in the evening four.' This made them all angry, and he said, 'Very well. In the morning I will give you four and in the evening three.' His two proposals were substantially the same, but the result of the one was to make the creatures angry, and of the other to make them pleased:-- an illustration of the point I am insisting on. Therefore the sagely man brings together a dispute in its affirmations and denials, and rests in the equal fashioning of Heaven. Both sides of the question are admissible.

5. Among the men of old their knowledge reached the extreme point. What was that extreme point? Some held that at first there was not anything. This is the extreme point, the utmost point to which nothing can be added. A second class held that there was something, but without any responsive recognition of it (on the part of men).

A third class held that there was such recognition, but there had not begun to be any expression of different opinions about it.

It was through the definite expression of different opinions about it that there ensued injury to (the doctrine of) the Tîo. It was this injury to the (doctrine of the) Tîo which led to the formation of (partial) preferences. Was it indeed after such preferences were formed that the injury came? or did the injury precede the rise of such preferences? If the injury arose after their formation, Kîo's method of playing on the lute was natural. If the injury arose before their formation, there would have been no such playing on the lute as Kâo's.

Kâo Wan's playing on the lute, Shih Kwang's indicating time with his staff, and Hui-tsze's (giving his views), while leaning against a dryandra tree (were all extraordinary). The knowledge of the three men (in their several arts) was nearly perfect, and therefore they practised them to the end of their lives. They loved them because they were different from those of others. They loved them and wished to make them known to others. But as they could not be made clear, though they tried to make them so, they ended with the obscure (discussions) about 'the hard' and 'the white.' And their sons, moreover, with all the threads of their fathers' compositions, yet to the end of their lives accomplished nothing. If they, proceeding in this way, could be said to have succeeded, then am I also successful; if they cannot be pronounced successful, neither I nor any other can succeed.

Therefore the scintillations of light from the midst of confusion and perplexity are indeed valued by the sagely man; but not to use one's own views and to take his position on the ordinary views is what is called using the (proper) light.

6. But here now are some other sayings:-- I do not know whether they are of the same character as those which I have already given, or of a different character. Whether they be of the same character or not when looked at along with them, they have a character of their own, which cannot be distinguished from the others. But though this be the case, let me try to explain myself.

There was a beginning. There was a beginning before that beginning. There was a beginning previous to that beginning before there was the beginning.

There was existence; there had been no existence. There was no existence before the beginning of that no existence. There was no existence previous to the no existence before there was the beginning of the no existence. If suddenly there was nonexistence, we do not know whether it was really anything existing, or really not existing. Now I have said what I have said, but I do not know whether what I have said be really anything to the point or not.

Under heaven there is nothing greater than the tip of an autumn down, and the Thâi mountain is small. There is no one more long-lived than a child which dies prematurely, and Phang Tsû did not live out his time. Heaven, Earth, and I were produced together, and all things and I are one. Since they are one, can there be speech about them? But since they are spoken of as one, must there not be room for speech? One and Speech are two; two and one are three. Going on from this (in our enumeration), the most skilful reckoner cannot reach (the end of the necessary numbers), and how much less can ordinary people do so! Therefore from non-existence we proceed to existence till we arrive at three; proceeding from existence to existence, to how many should we reach? Let us abjure such procedure, and simply rest here.

7. The Tâo at first met with no responsive recognition. Speech at first had no constant forms of expression. Because of this there came the demarcations (of different views). Let me describe those demarcations:-- they are the Left and the Right; the Relations and their Obligations; Classifications and their Distinctions; Emulations and Contentions. These are what are called 'the Eight Qualities.' Outside the limits of the world of men, the sage occupies his thoughts, but does not discuss about

anything; inside those limits he occupies his thoughts, but does not pass any judgments. In the Khun Khiû, which embraces the history of the former kings, the sage indicates his judgments, but does not argue (in vindication of them). Thus it is that he separates his characters from one another without appearing to do so, and argues without the form of argument. How does he do so? The sage cherishes his views in his own breast, while men generally state theirs argumentatively, to show them to others. Hence we have the saying, 'Disputation is a proof of not seeing clearly.'

The Great Tâo does not admit of being praised. The Great Argument does not require words. Great Benevolence is not (officiously) benevolent. Great Disinterestedness does not vaunt its humility. Great Courage is not seen in stubborn bravery.

The Tâo that is displayed is not the Tâo. Words that are argumentative do not reach the point. Benevolence that is constantly exercised does not accomplish its object. Disinterestedness that vaunts its purity is not genuine. Courage that is most stubborn is ineffectual. These five seem to be round (and complete), but they tend to become square (and immovable). Therefore the knowledge that stops at what it does not know is the greatest. Who knows the argument that needs no words, and the Way that is not to be trodden?

He who is able to know this has what is called 'The Heavenly Treasure-house.' He may pour into it without its being filled; he may pour from it without its being exhausted; and all the while he does not know whence (the supply) comes. This is what is called 'The Store of Light.'

Therefore of old Yâo asked Shun, saying, 'I wish to smite (the rulers of) Tsung, Kwei, and Hsü-âo. Even when standing in my court, I cannot get them out of my mind. How is it so?' Shun replied, 'Those three rulers live (in their little states) as if they were among the mugwort and other brushwood;-- how is it that you cannot get them out of your mind? Formerly, ten suns came out together, and all things were illuminated by them;-- how much should (your) virtue exceed (all) suns!'

8. Nieh Khüeh asked Wang Î, saying, 'Do you know, Sir, what all creatures agree in approving and affirming?' 'How should I know it?' was the reply. 'Do you know what it is that you do not know?' asked the other again, and he got the same reply. He asked a third time,-- 'Then are all creatures thus without knowledge?' and Wang Î answered as before, (adding however), 'Notwithstanding, I will try and explain my meaning. How do you know that when I say "I know it," I really (am showing that) I do not know it, and that when I say "I do not know it," I really am showing

that I do know it.' And let me ask you some questions:-- 'If a man sleep in a damp place, he will have a pain in his loins, and half his body will be as if it were dead; but will it be so with an eel? If he be living in a tree, he will be frightened and all in a tremble; but will it be so with a monkey? And does any one of the three know his right place ? Men eat animals that have been fed on grain and grass; deer feed on the thick-set grass; centipedes enjoy small snakes; owls and crows delight in mice; but does any one of the four know the right taste? The dog-headed monkey finds its mate in the female gibbon; the elk and the axis deer cohabit; and the eel enjoys itself with other fishes. Mâo Tshiang and Lî Kî were accounted by men to be most beautiful, but when fishes saw them, they dived deep in the water from them; when birds, they flew from them aloft; and when deer saw them, they separated and fled away. But did any of these four know which in the world is the right female attraction? As I look at the matter, the first principles of benevolence and righteousness and the paths of approval and disapproval are inextricably mixed and confused together:-- how is it possible that I should know how to discriminate among them?'

Nieh Khüeh said (further), 'Since you, Sir, do not know what is advantageous and what is hurtful, is the Perfect man also in the same way without the knowledge of them?' Wang Î replied, 'The Perfect man is spirit-like. Great lakes might be boiling about him, and he would not feel their heat; the Ho and the Han might be frozen tip, and he would not feel the cold; the hurrying thunderbolts might split the mountains, and the wind shake the ocean, without being able to make him afraid. Being such, he mounts on the clouds of the air, rides on the sun and moon, and rambles at ease beyond the four seas. Neither death nor life makes any change in him, and how much less should the considerations of advantage and injury do so!'

9. Khü Tshiâo-tsze asked Khang-wû Tsze, saying, 'I heard the Master (speaking of such language as the following):-- "The sagely man does not occupy himself with worldly affairs. He does not put himself in the way of what is profitable, nor try to avoid what is hurtful; he has no pleasure in seeking (for anything from any one); he does not care to be found in (any established) Way; he speaks without speaking; he does not speak when he speaks; thus finding his enjoyment outside the dust and dirt (of the world)." The Master considered all this to be a shoreless flow of mere words, and I consider it to describe the course of the Mysterious Way.-- What do you, Sir, think of it?' Khang-wû Tsze replied, 'The hearing of such words would have perplexed even Hwang-Tî, and how should Khiû be competent to understand them? And you, moreover, are too hasty in forming your estimate (of their meaning). You see the egg, and (imme-

diately) look out for the cock (that is to be hatched from it); you see the bow, and (immediately) look out for the dove (that is to be brought down by it) being roasted. I will try to explain the thing to you in a rough way; do you in the same way listen to me.

'How could any one stand by the side of the sun and moon, and hold under his arm all space and all time? (Such language only means that the sagely man) keeps his mouth shut, and puts aside questions that are uncertain and dark; making his inferior capacities unite with him in honouring (the One Lord). Men in general bustle about and toil; the sagely man seems stupid and to know nothing. He blends ten thousand years together in the one (conception of time); the myriad things all pursue their spontaneous course, and they are all before him as doing so.

'How do I know that the love of life is not a delusion? and that the dislike of death is not like a young person's losing his way, and not knowing that he is (really) going home? Lî Kî was a daughter of the border Warden of Âi. When (the ruler of) the state of Tsin first got possession of her, she wept till the tears wetted all the front of her dress. But when she came to the place of the king, shared with him his luxurious couch, and ate his grain-and-grass-fed meat, then she regretted that she had wept. How do I know that the dead do not repent of their former craving for life?

'Those who dream of (the pleasures of) drinking may in the morning wail and weep; those who dream of wailing and weeping may in the morning be going out to hunt. When they were dreaming they did not know it was a dream; in their dream they may even have tried to interpret it; but when they awoke they knew that it was a dream. And there is the great awaking, after which we shall know that this life was a great dream. All the while, the stupid think they are awake, and with nice discrimination insist on their knowledge; now playing the part of rulers, and now of grooms. Bigoted was that Khiû! He and you are both dreaming. I who say that you are dreaming am dreaming myself. These words seem very strange; but if after ten thousand ages we once meet with a great sage who knows how to explain them, it will be as if we met him (unexpectedly) some morning or evening.

10. 'Since you made me enter into this discussion with you, if you have got the better of me and not I of you, are you indeed right, and I indeed wrong? If I have got the better of you and not you of me, am I indeed right and you indeed wrong? Is the one of us right and the other wrong? are we both right or both wrong? Since we cannot come to a mutual and common understanding, men will certainly continue in darkness on the subject.

'Whom shall I employ to adjudicate in the matter? If I employ one who agrees with you, how can he, agreeing with you, do so correctly? And the same may be said, if I employ one who agrees with me. It will be the same if I employ one who differs from us both or one who agrees with us both. In this way I and you and those others would all not be able to come to a mutual understanding; and shall we then wait for that (great sage)? (We need not do so.) To wait on others to learn how conflicting opinions are changed is simply like not so waiting at all. The harmonising of them is to be found in the invisible operation of Heaven, and by following this on into the unlimited past. It is by this method that we can complete our years (without our minds being disturbed).

'What is meant by harmonising (conflicting opinions) in the invisible operation of Heaven? There is the affirmation and the denial of it; and there is the assertion of an opinion and the rejection of it. If the affirmation be according to the reality of the fact, it is certainly different from the denial of it:-- there can be no dispute about that. If the assertion of an opinion be correct, it is certainly different from its rejection:-- neither can there be any dispute about that. Let us forget the lapse of time; let us forget the conflict of opinions. Let us make our appeal to the Infinite, and take up our position there.'

11. The Penumbra asked the Shadow, saying, 'Formerly you were walking on, and now you have stopped; formerly you were sitting, and now you have risen up:-- how is it that you are so without stability?' The Shadow replied, 'I wait for the movements of something else to do what I do, and that something else on which I wait waits further on another to do as it does. My waiting,-- is it for the scales of a snake, or the wings of a cicada? How should I know why I do one thing, or do not do another?

'Formerly, I, Kwang Kâu, dreamt that I was a butterfly, a butterfly flying about, feeling that it was enjoying itself. I did not know that it was Kâu. Suddenly I awoke, and was myself again, the veritable Kâu. I did not know whether it had formerly been Kâu dreaming that he was a butterfly, or it was now a butterfly dreaming that it was Kâu. But between Kâu and a butterfly there must be a difference. This is a case of what is called the Transformation of Things.'

Yang Shang Kû, or 'Nourishing the Lord of Life.'

1. There is a limit to our life, but to knowledge there is no limit. With what is limited to pursue after what is unlimited is a perilous thing; and when, knowing this, we still seek the increase of our knowledge, the peril cannot be averted. There should not be the practice of what is good with any thought of the fame (which it will bring), nor of what is evil with any approximation to the punishment (which it will incur):-- an accordance with the Central Element (of our nature) is the regular way to preserve the body, to maintain the life, to nourish our parents, and to complete our term of years.

2. His cook was cutting up an ox for the ruler Wan-hui. Whenever he applied his hand, leaned forward with his shoulder, planted his foot, and employed the pressure of his knee, in the audible ripping off of the skin, and slicing operation of the knife, the sounds were all in regular cadence. Movements and sounds proceeded as in the dance of 'the Mulberry Forest' and the blended notes of 'the King Shâu.' The ruler said, 'Ah! Admirable! That your art should have become so perfect!' (Having finished his operation), the cook laid down his knife, and replied to the remark, 'What your servant loves is the method of the Tâo, something in advance of any art. When I first began to cut up an ox, I saw nothing but the (entire) carcass.

After three years I ceased to see it as a whole. Now I deal with it in a spirit-like manner, and do not look at it with my eyes. The use of my senses is discarded, and my spirit acts as it wills. Observing the natural lines, (my knife) slips through the great crevices and slides through the great cavities, taking advantage of the facilities thus presented. My art avoids the membranous ligatures, and much more the great bones.

'A good cook changes his knife every year;-- (it may have been injured) in cutting; an ordinary cook changes his every month;-- (it may have been) broken. Now my knife has been in use for nineteen years; it has cut up several thousand oxen, and yet its edge is as sharp as if it had newly come from the whetstone. There are the interstices of the joints, and the edge of the knife has no (appreciable) thickness; when that which is so thin enters where the interstice is, how easily it moves along! The blade has more than room enough. Nevertheless, whenever I come to a complicated joint, and see that there will be some difficulty, I proceed anxiously and with caution, not allowing my eyes to wander from the place, and moving my hand slowly. Then by a very slight movement of the knife, the part is quickly separated, and drops like (a clod of) earth to the ground. Then standing up with the knife in my hand, I look all round, and in a leisurely manner, with an air of satisfaction, wipe it clean, and put it in its sheath.' The ruler Wan- hui said, 'Excellent! I have heard the words of my cook, and learned from them the nourishment of (our) life.'

3. When Kung-wan Hsien saw the Master of the Left, he was startled, and said, 'What sort of man is this? How is it he has but one foot? Is it from Heaven? or from Man?' Then he added, 'It must be from Heaven, and not from Man. Heaven's making of this man caused him to have but one foot. In the person of man, each foot has its marrow. By this I know that his peculiarity is from Heaven, and not from Man. A pheasant of the marshes has to take ten steps to pick up a mouthful of food, and thirty steps to get a drink, but it does not seek to be nourished in a coop. Though its spirit would (there) enjoy a royal abundance, it does not think (such confinement) good.'

4. When Lâo Tan died, Khin Shih went to condole (with his son), but after crying out three times, he came out. The disciples said to him, 'Were you not a friend of the Master?' 'I was,' he replied, and they said, 'Is it proper then to offer your condolences merely as you have done?' He said, 'It is. At first I thought he was the man of men, and now I do not think so. When I entered a little ago and expressed my condolences, there were the old men wailing as if they had lost a son, and the young men wailing as if they had lost their mother. In his attracting and uniting them to himself in such a way there must have been that which made them involuntarily express their words (of condolence), and involuntarily wail, as they were doing. And this was a hiding from himself of his Heaven (-nature), and an excessive indulgence of his (human) feelings;-- a forgetting of what he had received (in being born); what the ancients called the punishment due to neglecting the Heaven (-nature). When the Master came, it was at the proper time; when he went away, it was the simple sequence (of his coming). Quiet acquiescence in what happens at its proper time, and quietly submitting (to its ceasing) afford no occasion for grief or for joy. The ancients described (death) as the loosening of the cord on which God suspended (the life). What we can point to are the faggots that have been consumed; but the fire is transmitted (elsewhere), and we know not that it is over and ended.

Zan Kien Shih, or 'Man in the World, Associated with other Men.'

1. Yen Hui went to see Kung-nî, and asked leave to take his departure. 'Where are you going to?' asked the Master. 'I will go to Wei' was the reply. 'And with what object?' 'I have heard that the ruler of Wei is in the vigour of his years, and consults none but himself as to his course. He deals with his state as if it were a light matter, and has no perception of his errors. He thinks lightly of his people's dying; the dead are lying all over the country as if no smaller space could contain them; on the plains and about the marshes, they are as thick as heaps of fuel. The people know not where to turn to. I have heard you, Master, say, "Leave the state that is well governed; go to the state where disorder prevails." At the door of a physician there are many who are ill. I wish through what I have heard (from you) to think out some methods (of dealing with Wei), if peradventure the evils of the state may be cured.'

Kung-nî said, 'Alas! The risk is that you will go only to suffer in the punishment (of yourself)! The right method (in such a case) will not admit of any admixture. With such admixture, the one method will become many methods. Their multiplication will embarrass you. That embarrassment will make you anxious. However anxious you may be, you will not save (yourself). The perfect men of old first had (what they wanted to do) in themselves, and afterwards they found (the response to it) in others. If what they wanted in themselves was not fixed, what leisure had they to go and interfere with the proceedings of any tyrannous man?

'Moreover, do you know how virtue is liable to be dissipated, and how wisdom proceeds to display itself? Virtue is dissipated in (the pursuit of) the name for it, and wisdom seeks to display itself in the striving with others. In the pursuit of the name men overthrow one another; wisdom becomes a weapon of contention. Both these things are instruments of evil, and should not be allowed to have free course in one's conduct. Supposing one's virtue to be great and his sincerity firm, if he do not comprehend the spirit of those (whom he wishes to influence); and supposing he is free from the disposition to strive for reputation, if he do not comprehend their minds;-- when in such a case he forcibly insists on benevolence and righteousness, setting them forth in the strongest and most direct language, before the tyrant, then he, hating (his reprover's) possession of those excellences, will put him down as doing him injury. He who injures others is sure to be injured by them in return. You indeed will hardly escape being injured by the man (to whom you go)!

'Further, if perchance he takes pleasure in men of worth and hates those of an opposite character, what is the use of your seeking to make yourself out to be different (from such men about him)? Before you have begun to announce (your views), he, as king and ruler, will take advantage of you, and immediately contend with you for victory. Your eyes will be dazed and full of perplexity; you will try to look pleased with him; you will frame your words with care; your demeanour will be conformed to his; you will confirm him in his views. In this way you will be adding fire to fire, and water to water, increasing, as we may express it, the evils (which you deplore). To these signs of deferring to him at the first there will be no end. You will be in danger, seeing he does not believe you, of making your words more strong, and you are sure to die at the hands of such a tyrant.

'And formerly Kieh killed Kwan Lung-fang, and Kâu killed the prince Pî-kan. Both of these cultivated their persons, bending down in sympathy with the lower people to comfort them suffering (as they did) from their oppressors, and on their account opposing their superiors. On this account, because they so ordered their conduct, their rulers compassed their destruction:-- such regard had they for their own fame. (Again), Yâo anciently attacked (the states of) Tshung-kih and Hsü-âo, and Yü attacked the ruler of Hû. Those states were left empty, and with no one to continue their population, the people being exterminated. They had engaged in war without ceasing; their craving for whatever they could get was insatiable. And this (ruler of Wei) is, like them, one who craves after fame and greater substance;-- have you not heard it? Those sages were not able to overcome the thirst for fame and substance;-- how much less will you be able to do so! Nevertheless you must have some ground (for the course which you wish to take); pray try and tell it to me.'

Yen Hui said, 'May I go, doing so in uprightness and humility, using also every endeavour to be uniform (in my plans of operation)?' 'No, indeed!' was the reply. 'How can you do so? This man makes a display of being filled to overflowing (with virtue), and has great self-conceit. His feelings are not to be determined from his countenance. Ordinary men do not (venture to) oppose him, and he proceeds from the way in which he affects them to seek still more the satisfaction of his own mind. He may be described as unaffected by the (small lessons of) virtue brought to bear on him from day to day; and how much less will he be so by your great lessons? He will be obstinate, and refuse to be converted. He may outwardly agree with you, but inwardly there will be no self-condemnation;-- how can you (go to him in this way and be successful)?'

(Yen Hui) rejoined, 'Well then; while inwardly maintaining my straightforward intention, I will outwardly seem to bend to him. I will deliver (my lessons), and substantiate them by appealing to antiquity.

Inwardly maintaining my straightforward intention, I shall be a co-worker with Heaven. When I thus speak of being a co-worker with Heaven, it is because I know that (the sovereign, whom we style) the son of Heaven, and myself, are equally regarded by Heaven as Its sons. And should I then, as if my words were only my own, be seeking to find whether men approved of them, or disapproved of them? In this way men will pronounce me a (sincere and simple) boy. This is what is called being a co-worker with Heaven.

'Outwardly bending (to the ruler), I shall be a co-worker with other men. To carry (the memorandum tablet to court), to kneel, and to bend the body reverentially:-- these are the observances of ministers. They all employ them, and should I presume not to do so? Doing what other men do, they would have no occasion to blame me. This is what is called being a fellow-worker with other men.

'Fully declaring my sentiments and substantiating them by appealing to antiquity, I shall be a co-worker with the ancients. Although the words in which I convey my lessons may really be condemnatory (of the ruler), they will be those of antiquity, and not my own. In this way, though straightforward, I shall be free from blame. This is what is called being a co-worker with antiquity. May I go to Wei in this way, and be successful?' 'No indeed!' said Kung-nî. 'How can you do so? You have too many plans of proceeding, and have not spied out (the ruler's character). Though you firmly adhere to your plans, you may be held free from transgression, but this will be all the result. How can you (in this way) produce the transformation (which you desire)? All this only shows (in you) the mind of a teacher!'

2. Yen Hui said, 'I can go no farther; I venture to ask the method from you.' Kung-nî replied, 'It is fasting, (as) I will tell you. (But) when you have the method, will you find it easy to practise it? He who thinks it easy will be disapproved of by the bright Heaven.' Hui said, 'My family is poor. For months together we have no spirituous drink, nor do we taste the proscribed food or any strong-smelling vegetables;-- can this be regarded as fasting?' The reply was, 'It is the fasting appropriate to sacrificing, but it is not the fasting of the mind.' 'I venture to ask what that fasting of the mind is,' said Hui, and Kung-nî answered, 'Maintain a perfect unity in every movement of your will, You will not wait for the hearing of your ears about it, but for the hearing of your mind. You will not wait even for the hearing of your mind, but for the hearing of the spirit. Let the hearing

(of the ears) rest with the ears. Let the mind rest in the verification (of the rightness of what is in the will). But the spirit is free from all pre-occupation and so waits for (the appearance of) things. Where the (proper) course is, there is freedom from all pre-occupation;-- such freedom is the fasting of the mind.' Hui said, 'Before it was possible for me to employ (this method), there I was, the Hui that I am; now, that I can employ it, the Hui that I was has passed away. Can I be said to have obtained this freedom from pre-occupation?' The Master replied, 'Entirely. I tell you that you can enter and be at ease in the enclosure (where he is), and not come into collision with the reputation (which belongs to him). If he listen to your counsels, let him hear your notes; if he will not listen, be silent. Open no (other) door; employ no other medicine; dwell with him (as with a friend) in the same apartment, and as if you had no other option, and you will not be far from success in your object. Not to move a step is easy; to walk without treading on the ground is difficult. In acting after the manner of men, it is easy to fall into hypocrisy; in acting after the manner of Heaven, it is difficult to play the hypocrite. I have heard of flying with wings; I have not heard of flying without them. I have heard of the knowledge of the wise; I have not heard of the knowledge of the unwise. Look at that aperture (left in the wall);-- the empty apartment is filled with light through it. Felicitous influences rest (in the mind thus emblemed), as in their proper resting place. Even when they do not so rest, we have what is called (the body) seated and (the mind) galloping abroad. The information that comes through the ears and eyes is comprehended internally, and the knowledge of the mind becomes something external:-- (when this is the case), the spiritual intelligences will come, and take up their dwelling with us, and how much more will other men do so! All things thus undergo a transforming influence. This was the hinge on which Yü and Shun moved; it was this which Fû-hsî and Kî-khü practised all their lives: how much more should other men follow the same rule!'

3. Tsze-kâo, duke of Sheh, being about to proceed on a mission to Khî, asked Kung-nî, saying, 'The king is sending me, Kû-liang, on a mission which is very important. Khî will probably treat me as his commissioner with great respect, but it will not be in a hurry (to attend to the business). Even an ordinary man cannot be readily moved (to action), and how much less the prince of a state! I am very full of apprehension. You, Sir, once said to me that of all things, great or small, there were few which, if not conducted in the proper way, could be brought to a happy conclusion; that, if the thing were not successful, there was sure to be the evil of being dealt with after the manner of men; that, if it were successful, there was sure to be the evil of constant anxiety; and that, whether it succeeded or not, it was only the virtuous man who could secure its not being followed by evil. In my diet I take what is coarse, and do not seek delicacies,-- a

man whose cookery does not require him to be using cooling drinks. This morning I received my charge, and in the evening I am drinking iced water;-- am I not feeling the internal heat (and discomfort)? Such is my state before I have actually engaged in the affair;-- I am already suffering from conflicting anxieties. And if the thing do not succeed, (the king) is sure to deal with me after the manner of men. The evil is twofold; as a minister, I am not able to bear the burden (of the mission). Can you, Sir, tell me something (to help me in the case)?'

Kung-nî replied, 'In all things under heaven there are two great cautionary considerations:-- the one is the requirement implanted (in the nature); the other is the conviction of what is right. The love of a son for his parents is the implanted requirement, and can never be separated from his heart; the service of his ruler by a minister is what is right, and from its obligation there is no escaping anywhere between heaven and earth. These are what are called the great cautionary considerations. Therefore a son finds his rest in serving his parents without reference to or choice of place; and this is the height of filial duty.

In the same way a subject finds his rest in serving his ruler, without reference to or choice of the business; and this is the fullest discharge of loyalty. When men are simply obeying (the dictates of) their hearts, the considerations of grief and joy are not readily set before them. They know that there is no alternative to their acting as they do, and rest in it as what is appointed; and this is the highest achievement of virtue.

He who is in the position of a minister or of a son has indeed to do what he cannot but do. Occupied with the details of the business (in hand), and forgetful of his own person, what leisure has he to think of his pleasure in living or his dislike of death? You, my master, may well proceed on your mission.

'But let me repeat to you what I have heard:-- In all intercourse (between states), if they are near to each other, there should be mutual friendliness, verified by deeds; if they are far apart, there must be sincere adherence to truth in their messages. Those messages will be transmitted by internuncios. But to convey messages which express the complacence or the dissatisfaction of the two parties is the most difficult thing in the world. If they be those of mutual complacence, there is sure to be an overflow of expressions of satisfaction; if of mutual dissatisfaction, an overflow of expressions of dislike. But all extravagance leads to reckless language, and such language fails to command belief. When this distrust arises, woe to the internuncio! Hence the Rules for Speech say, "Transmit the message exactly as it stands; do not transmit it with any overflow of language; so is (the internuncio) likely to keep himself whole."

4. 'Moreover, skilful wrestlers begin with open trials of strength, but always end with masked attempts (to gain the victory); as their excitement grows excessive, they display much wonderful dexterity. Parties drinking according to the rules at first observe good order, but always end with disorder; as their excitement grows excessive, their fun becomes uproarious. In all things it is so. People are at first sincere, but always end with becoming rude; at the commencement things are treated as trivial, but as the end draws near, they assume great proportions. Words are (like) the waves acted on by the wind; the real point of the matters (discussed by them) is lost. The wind and waves are easily set in motion; the success of the matter of which the real point is lost is easily put in peril. Hence quarrels are occasioned by nothing so much as by artful words and one-sided speeches. The breath comes angrily, as when a beast, driven to death, wildly bellows forth its rage. On this animosities arise on both sides. Hasty examination (of the case) eagerly proceeds, and revengeful thoughts arise in their minds;-- they do not know how. Since they do not know how such thoughts arise, who knows how they will end? Hence the Rules for Speech say, "Let not an internuncius depart from his instructions. Let him not urge on a settlement. If he go beyond the regular rules, he will complicate matters. Departing from his instructions and urging on a settlement imperils negotiations. A good settlement is proved by its lasting long, and a bad settlement cannot be altered;-- ought he not to be careful?"

'Further still, let your mind find its enjoyment in the circumstances of your position; nourish the central course which you pursue, by a reference to your unavoidable obligations. This is the highest object for you to pursue; what else can you do to fulfil the charge (of your father and ruler). The best thing you can do is to be prepared to sacrifice your life; and this is the most difficult thing to do.'

5. Yen Ho, being about to undertake the office of Teacher of the eldest son of duke Ling of Wei, consulted Kü Po-yü. 'Here,' said he, 'is this (young) man, whose natural disposition is as bad as it could be. If I allow him to proceed in a bad way, it will be at the peril of our state; if I insist on his proceeding in a right way, it will be at the peril of my own person. His wisdom is just sufficient to know the errors of other men, but he does not know how he errs himself. What am I to do in such a case?' Kü Po-yü replied,'Good indeed is your question! Be on your guard; be careful; see that you keep yourself correct! Your best plan will be, with your person to seek association with him, and with your mind to try to be in harmony with him; and yet there are dangers connected with both of these things. While seeking to keep near to him, do not enter into his pursuits; while cultivating a harmony of mind with him, do not show how

superior you are to him. If in your personal association you enter into his pursuits, you will fall with him and be ruined, you will tumble down with a crash. If in maintaining a harmony with his mind, you show how different you are from him, he will think you do so for the reputation and the name, and regard you as a creature of evil omen. If you find him to be a mere boy, be you with him as another boy; if you find him one of those who will not have their ground marked out in the ordinary way, do you humour him in this characteristic; if you find him to be free from lofty airs, show yourself to be the same;-- (ever) leading him on so as to keep him free from faults.

'Do you not know (the fate of) the praying mantis? It angrily stretches out its arms, to arrest the progress of the carriage, unconscious of its inability for such a task, but showing how much it thinks of its own powers. Be on your guard; be careful. If you cherish a boastful confidence in your own excellence, and place yourself in collision with him, you are likely to incur the fate (of the mantis).

'Do you not know how those who keep tigers proceed? They do not dare to supply them with living creatures, because of the rage which their killing of them will excite. They do not (even) dare to give them their food whole, because of the rage which their rending of it will excite. They watch till their hunger is appeased, (dealing with them) from their knowledge of their natural ferocity. Tigers are different from men, but they fawn on those who feed them, and do so in accordance with their nature. When any of these are killed by them, it is because they have gone against that nature.

'Those again who are fond of horses preserve their dung in baskets, and their urine in jars. If musquitoes and gadflies light on them, and the grooms brush them suddenly away, the horses break their bits, injure (the ornaments on) their heads, and smash those on their breasts. The more care that is taken of them, the more does their fondness (for their attendants) disappear. Ought not caution to be exercised (in the management of them)?

6. A (master) mechanic, called Shih, on his way to Khî, came to Khü-yüan, where he saw an oak-tree, which was used as the altar for the spirits of the land. It was so large that an ox standing behind it could not be seen. It measured a hundred spans round, and rose up eighty cubits on the hill before it threw out any branches, after which there were ten or so, from each of which a boat could be hollowed out. People came to see it in crowds as in a market place, but the mechanic did not look round at it, but held on his way without stopping. One of his workmen, however,

looked long and admiringly at it, and then ran on to his master, and said to him, 'Since I followed you with my axe and bill, I have never seen such a beautiful mass of timber as this. Why would you, Sir, not look round at it, but went on without stopping?' 'Have done,' said Mr. Shih, 'and do not speak about it. It is quite useless. A boat made from its wood would sink; a coffin or shell would quickly rot; an article of furniture would soon go to pieces; a door would be covered with the exuding sap; a pillar would be riddled by insects; the material of it is good for nothing, and hence it is that it has attained to so great an age.'

When Mr. Shih was returning, the altar-oak appeared to him in a dream, and said, 'What other tree will you compare with me? Will you compare me to one of your ornamental trees? There are hawthorns, pear-trees, orange-trees, pummelo-trees, gourds and other low fruit-bearing plants. When their fruits are ripe, they are knocked down from them, and thrown among the dirt. The large branches are broken, and the smaller are torn away. So it is that their productive ability makes their lives bitter to them; they do not complete their natural term of existence, but come to a premature end in the middle of their time, bringing on themselves the destructive treatment which they ordinarily receive. It is so with all things. I have sought to discover how it was that I was so useless;-- I had long done so, till (the effort) nearly caused my death; and now I have learned it:-- it has been of the greatest use to me. Suppose that I had possessed useful properties, should I have become of the great size that I am? And moreover you and I are both things;-- how should one thing thus pass its judgment on another? how is it that you a useless man know all this about me a useless tree?' When Mr. Shih awoke, he kept thinking about his dream, but the workman said, 'Being so taken with its uselessness, how is it that it yet acts here as the altar for the spirits of the land?' 'Be still,' was the master's reply, 'and do not say a word. It simply happened to grow here; and thus those who do not know it do not speak ill of it as an evil thing. If it were not used as the altar, would it be in danger of being cut down? Moreover, the reason of its being preserved is different from that of the preservation of things generally; is not your explaining it from the sentiment which you have expressed wide of the mark?'

7. Nan-po Tsze-khî in rambling about the Heights of Shang, saw a large and extraordinary tree. The teams of a thousand chariots might be sheltered under it, and its shade would cover them all! Tsze-khî said, 'What a tree is this! It must contain an extraordinary amount of timber! When he looked up, however, at its smaller branches, they were so twisted and crooked that they could not be made into rafters and beams; when he looked down to its root, its stem was divided into so many rounded portions that neither coffin nor shell could be made from

them. He licked one of its leaves, and his mouth felt torn and wounded. The smell of it would make a man frantic, as if intoxicated, for more than three whole days together. 'This, indeed,' said he, 'is a tree good for nothing, and it is thus that it has attained to such a size. Ah! and spirit-like men acknowledge this worthlessness (and its result).'

In Sung there is the district of King-shih, in which catalpae, cypresses, and mulberry trees grow well. Those of them which are a span or two or rather more in circumference are cut down by persons who want to make posts to which to tie their monkeys; those which are three or four spans round are cut down by persons who want beams forr their lofty and famous houses; and those of seven or eight spans are cut down by noblemen and rich merchants who want single planks for the sides of their coffins. The trees in consequence do not complete their natural term of life, and come to a premature end in the middle of their growth under the axe and bill;-- this is the evil that befalls them from their supplying good timber.

In the same way the Kieh (book) specifies oxen that have white foreheads, pigs that have turned-up snouts, and men that are suffering from piles, and forbids their being sacrificed to the Ho. The wizards know them by these peculiarities and consider them to be inauspicious, but spirit-like men consider them on this account to be very fortunate.

8. There was the deformed object Shû. His chin seemed to hide his navel; his shoulders were higher than the crown of his head; the knot of his hair pointed to the sky; his five viscera were all compressed into the upper part of his body, and his two thigh bones were like ribs. By sharpening needles and washing clothes he was able to make a living. By sifting rice and cleaning it, he was able to support ten individuals.

When the government was calling ut soldiers, this poor Shû would bare his arms among the others; when it had any great service to be undertaken, because of his constant ailments, none of the work was assigned to him; when it was giving out grain to the sick, he received three kung, and ten bundles of firewood. If this poor man, so deformed in body, was still able to support himself, and complete his term of life, how much more may they do so, whose deformity is that of their faculties!

9. When Confucius went to Khû, Khieh-yû, the madman of Khû, as he was wandering about, passed by his door, and said, '0 Phoenix, 0 Phoenix, how is your virtue degenerated! The future is not to be waited for; the past is not to be sought again! When good order prevails in the world, the sage tries to accomplish all his service; when disorder prevails, he may preserve his life; at the present time, it is enough if he simply

escape being punished. Happiness is lighter than a feather, but no one knows how to support it; calamity is heavier than the earth, and yet no one knows how to avoid it. Give over! give over approaching men with the lessons of your virtue! You are in peril! you are in peril, hurrying on where you have marked out the ground against your advance! I avoid publicity, I avoid publicity, that my path may not be injured. I pursue my course, now going backwards, now crookedly, that my feet may not be hurt.

'The mountain by its trees weakens itself. The grease which ministers to the fire fries itself. The cinnamon tree can be eaten, and therefore it is cut down. The varnish tree is useful, and therefore incisions are made in it. All men know the advantage of being useful, but no one knows the advantage of being useless.'

Teh Khung Fû, or 'The Seal of Virtue Complete.'

1. In Lû there was a Wang Thâi who had lost both his feet; while his disciples who followed and went about with him were as numerous as those of Kung-nî. Khang Kî asked Kung-nî about him, saying, 'Though Wang Thâi is a cripple, the disciples who follow him about divide Lû equally with you, Master. When he stands, he does not teach them; when he sits, he does not discourse to them. But they go to him empty, and come back full. Is there indeed such a thing as instruction without words? and while the body is imperfect, may the mind be complete? What sort of man is he?'

Kung-nî replied, 'This master is a sage. I have only been too late in going to him. I will make him my teacher; and how much more should those do so who are not equal to me! Why should only the state of Lû follow him? I will lead on all under heaven with me to do so.' Khang Kî rejoined, 'He is a man who has lost his feet, and yet he is known as the venerable Wang;-- he must be very different from ordinary men. What is the peculiar way in which he employs his mind?' The reply was, 'Death and life are great considerations, but they could work no change in him. Though heaven and earth were to be overturned and fall, they would occasion him no loss. His judgment is fixed regarding that in which there is no element of falsehood; and, while other things change, he changes not. The transformations of things are to him the developments prescribed for them, and he keeps fast hold of the author of them.'

Khang Kî said, 'What do you mean?' 'When we look at things,' said Kung-nî, 'as they differ, we see them to be different, (as for instance) the liver and the gall, or Khû and Yüeh; when we look at them, as they agree, we see them all to be a unity. So it is with this (Wang Thâi). He takes no knowledge of the things for which his ears and eyes are the appropriate organs, but his mind delights itself in the harmony of (all excellent) qualities. He looks at the unity which belongs to things, and does not perceive where they have suffered loss. He looks on the loss of his feet as only the loss of so much earth.'

Khang Kî said, 'He is entirely occupied with his (proper) self. By his knowledge he has discovered (the nature of) his mind, and to that he holds as what is unchangeable; but how is it that men make so much of him?' The reply was, 'Men do not look into running water as a mirror, but into still water;-- it is only the still water that can arrest them all, and keep them (in the contemplation of their real selves). Of things which are what they are by the influence of the earth, it is only the pine and cypress which are the best instances;-- in winter as in summer brightly green. Of those which were what they were by the influence of Heaven, the most correct examples were Yâo and Shun; fortunate in (thus) maintaining their own life correct, and so as to correct the lives of others.

'As a verification of the (power of) the original endowment, when it has been preserved, take the result of fearlessness,-- how the heroic spirit of a single brave soldier has been thrown into an army of nine hosts. If a man only seeking for fame and able in this way to secure it can produce such an effect, how much more (may we look for a greater result) from one whose rule is over heaven and earth, and holds all things in his treasury, who simply has his lodging in the six members of his body, whom his ears and eyes serve but as conveying emblematic images of things, who comprehends all his knowledge in a unity, and whose mind never dies! If such a man were to choose a day on which he would ascend far on high, men would (seek to) follow him there. But how should he be willing to occupy himself with other men?'

2. Shan-thû Kiâ was (another) man who had lost a his feet. Along with Tsze-khân of Kang he studied under the master Po-hwan Wû-zan. Tsze-khân said to him (one day), 'If I go out first, do you remain behind; and if you go out first, I will remain behind.' Next day they were again sitting together on the same mat in the hall, when Tsze-khân spoke the same words to him, adding, 'Now I am about to go out; will you stay behind or not? Moreover, when you see one of official rank (like myself), you do not try to get out of his way;-- do you consider yourself equal to one of official rank?' Shan-thû Kiâ replied, 'In our Master's school is there indeed such recognition required of official rank? You are one, Sir, whose pleasure is in your official rank, and would therefore take precedence of other men. I have heard that when a mirror is bright, the dust does not rest on it; when dust rests on it the mirror is not bright. When one dwells long with a man of ability and virtue, he comes to be without error. There now is our teacher whom you have chosen to make you greater than you are; and when you still talk in this way, are you not in error?' Tsze-khan rejoined, 'A (shattered) object as you are, you would still strive to make yourself out as good as Yâo!

If I may form an estimate of your virtue, might it not be sufficient to lead you to the examination of yourself?' The other said, 'Most criminals, in describing their offences, would make it out that they ought not to have lost (their feet) for them; few would describe them so as to make it appear that they should not have preserved their feet. They are only the virtuous who know that such a calamity was unavoidable, and therefore rest in it as what was appointed for them. When men stand before (an archer like) Î with his bent bow, if they are in the middle of his field, that is the place where they should be hit; and if they be not hit, that also was appointed. There are many with their feet entire who laugh at me because I have lost my feet, which makes me feel vexed and angry. But when I go to our teacher, I throw off that feeling, and return (to a better mood);-- he has washed, without my knowing it, the other from me by (his instructions in) what is good. I have attended him now for nineteen years, and have not known that I am without my feet. Now, you, Sir, and I have for the object of our study the (virtue) which is internal, and not an adjunct of the body, and yet you are continually directing your attention to my external body;-- are you not wrong in this?' Tsze-khân felt uneasy, altered his manner and looks, and said, 'You need not, Sir, say anything more about it.'

3. In Lû there was a cripple, called Shû-shan the Toeless, who came on his heels to see Kung-nî. Kung-nî said to him, 'By your want of circumspection in the past, Sir, you have incurred such a calamity;-- of what use is your coming to me now?' Toeless said, 'Through my ignorance of my proper business and taking too little care of my body, I came to lose my feet. But now I am come to you, still possessing what is more honourable than my feet, and which therefore I am anxious to preserve entire. There is nothing which Heaven does not cover, and nothing which Earth does not sustain; you, Master, were regarded by me as doing the part of Heaven and Earth;-- how could I know that you would receive me in such a way?' Confucius rejoined, 'I am but a poor creature. But why, my master, do you not come inside, where I will try to tell you what I have learned?' When Toeless had gone out, Confucius said, 'Be stimulated to effort, my disciples. This toeless cripple is still anxious to learn to make up for the evil of his former conduct;-- how much more should those be so whose conduct has been unchallenged!'

Mr. Toeless, however, told Lâo Tan (of the interview), saying, 'Khung Khiû, I apprehend, has not yet attained to be a Perfect man. What has he to do with keeping a crowd of disciples around him? He is seeking to have the reputation of being an extraordinary and marvellous man, and does not know that the Perfect man considers this to be as handcuffs and fetters to him.' Lâo Tan said, 'Why did you not simply lead him to see the unity of life and death, and that the admissible and inadmissible belong to one category, so freeing him from his fetters? Would this be possible?' Toeless said, 'It is the punishment inflicted on him by Heaven. How can he be freed from it?'

4. Duke Âi of Lû asked Kung-nî, saying, 'There was an ugly man in Wei, called Ai-thâi Tho. His father-in-law, who lived with him, thought

so much of him that he could not be away from him. His wife, when she saw him (ugly as he was), represented to her parents, saying, "I had more than ten times rather be his concubine than the wife of any other man." He was never heard to take the lead in discussion, but always seemed to be of the same opinion with others. He had not the position of a ruler, so as to be able to save men from death. He had no revenues, so as to be able to satisfy men's craving for food. He was ugly enough, moreover, to scare the whole world. He agreed with men instead of trying to lead them to adopt his views; his knowledge did not go beyond his immediate neighbourhood. And yet his father-in-law and his wife were of one mind about him in his presence (as I have said);-- he must have been different from other men. I called him, and saw him. Certainly he was ugly enough to scare the whole world. He had not lived with me, however, for many months, when I was drawn to the man; and before he had been with me a full year, I had confidence in him. The state being without a chief minister, I (was minded) to commit the government to him. He responded to my proposal sorrowfully, and looked undecided as if he would fain have declined it. I was ashamed of myself (as inferior to him), but finally gave the government into his hands. In a little time, however, he left me and went away. I was sorry and felt that I had sustained a loss, and as if there were no other to share the pleasures of the kingdom with me. What sort of man was he?'

Kung-nî said, 'Once when I was sent on a mission to Khû, I saw some pigs sucking at their dead mother. After a little they looked with rapid glances, when they all left her, and ran away. They felt that she did not see them, and that she was no longer like themselves. What they had loved in their mother was not her bodily figure, but what had given animation to her figure. When a man dies in battle, they do not at his interment employ the usual appendages of plumes: as to supplying shoes to one who has lost his feet, there is no reason why he should care for them;-- in neither case is there the proper reason for their use. The members of the royal harem do not pare their nails nor pierce their ears; when a man is newly married, he remains (for a time) absent from his official duties, and unoccupied with them. That their bodies might be perfect was sufficient to make them thus dealt with;-- how much greater results should be expected from men whose mental gifts are perfect! This Âi-thâi Tho was believed by men, though he did not speak a word; and was loved by them, though he did no special service for them. He made men appoint him to the government of their states, afraid only that he would not accept the appointment. He must have been a man whose powers were perfect, though his realisation of them was not manifested in his person.

Duke Âi said, 'What is meant by saying that his powers were complete?' Kung-nî replied, 'Death and life, preservation and ruin, failure and success, poverty and wealth, superiority and inferiority, blame and praise, hunger and thirst, cold and heat;-- these are the changes of circumstances, the operation of our appointed lot. Day and night they succeed to one another before us, but there is no wisdom able to discover to what they owe their origination. They are not sufficient therefore to disturb the harmony (of the nature), and are not allowed to enter into the treasury of intelligence. To cause this harmony and satisfaction ever to be diffused, while the feeling of pleasure is not lost from the mind; to allow no break to arise in this state day or night, so that it is always spring-time in his relations with external things; in all his experiences to realise in his mind what is appropriate to each season (of the year):-- these are the characteristics of him whose powers are perfect.'

'And what do you mean by the realisation of these powers not being manifested in the person?' (pursued further the duke). The reply was, 'There is nothing so level as the surface of a pool of still water. It may serve as an example of what I mean. All within its circuit is preserved (in peace), and there comes to it no agitation from without. The virtuous efficacy is the perfect cultivation of the harmony (of the nature).

Though the realisation of this be not manifested in the person, things cannot separate themselves (from its influence).'

Some days afterwards duke Âi told this conversation to Min-tsze, saying, 'Formerly it seemed to me the work of the sovereign to stand in court with his face to the south, to rule the kingdom, and to pay good heed to the accounts of the people concerned, lest any should come to a (miserable) death;-- this I considered to be the sum (of his duty). Now that I have heard that description of the Perfect man, I fear that my idea is not the real one, and that, by employing myself too lightly, I may cause the ruin of my state. I and Khung Khiû are not on the footing of ruler and subject, but on that of a virtuous friendship.'

5. A person who had no lips, whose legs were bent so that he could only walk on his toes, and who was (otherwise) deformed, addressed his counsels to duke Ling of Wei, who was so pleased with him, that he looked on a perfectly formed man as having a lean and small neck in comparison with him. Another who had a large goitre like an earthenware jar addressed his counsels to duke Hwan of Khî, who was so pleased with him that he looked on a perfectly formed man as having a neck lean and small in comparison with him. So it is that when one's virtue is extraordinary, (any deficiency in) his bodily form may be forgotten. When men do not forget what is (easily) forgotten, and forget what is not (easily) forgotten, we have a case of real oblivion. Therefore the sagely man has that in

which his mind finds its enjoyment, and (looks on) wisdom as (but) the shoots from an old stump; agreements with others are to him but so much glue ; kindnesses are (but the arts of) intercourse; and great skill is (but as) merchants' wares. The sagely man lays no plans;-- of what use would wisdom be to him? He has no cutting and hacking to do;-- of what use would glue be to him? He has lost nothing;-- of what use would arts of intercourse be to him? He has no goods to dispose of;-- what need has he to play the merchant? (The want of) these four things are the nourishment of (his) Heavenly (nature); that nourishment is its Heavenly food. Since he receives this food from Heaven, what need has he for anything of man's (devising)? He has the bodily form of man, but not the passions and desires of (other) men. He has the form of man, and therefore he is a man. Being without the passions and desires of men, their approvings and disapprovings are not to be found in him.

How insignificant and small is (the body) by which he belongs to humanity! How grand and great is he in the unique perfection of his Heavenly (nature)!

Hui-tsze said to Kwang-tsze, 'Can a man indeed be without desires and passions?' The reply was, 'He can.'

'But on what grounds do you call him a man, who is thus without passions and desires?' Kwang-tsze said, 'The Tâo gives him his personal appearance (and powers); Heaven gives him his bodily form; how should we not call him a man?' Hui-tsze rejoined, 'Since you call him a man, how can he be without passions and desires?' The reply was, 'You are misunderstanding what I mean by passions and desires. What I mean when I say that he is without these is, that this man does not by his likings and dislikings do any inward harm to his body;-- he always pursues his course without effort, and does not (try to) increase his (store of) life.' Hui-tsze rejoined, 'If there were not that increasing of (the amount) of life, how would he get his body?' Kwang-tsze said, 'The Tâo gives him his personal appearance (and powers); Heaven gives him his bodily form; and he does not by his likings and dislikings do any internal harm to his body. But now you, Sir, deal with your spirit as if it were something external to you, and subject your vital powers to toil. You sing (your ditties), leaning against a tree; you go to sleep, grasping the stump of a rotten dryandra tree. Heaven selected for you the bodily form (of a man), and you babble about what is strong and what is white.'

1. He who knows the part which the Heavenly (in him) plays, and knows (also) that which the Human (in him ought to) play, has reached the perfection (of knowledge). He who knows the part which the Heavenly plays (knows) that it is naturally born with him; he who knows the part which the Human ought to play (proceeds) with the knowledge which he possesses to nourish it in the direction of what he does not (yet) know:-- to complete one's natural term of years and not come to an untimely end in the middle of his course is the fulness of knowledge. Although it be so, there is an evil (attending this condition). Such knowledge still awaits the confirmation of it as correct; it does so because it is not yet determined. How do we know that what we call the Heavenly (in us) is not the Human? and that what we call the Human is not the Heavenly? There must be the True man, and then there is the True knowledge.

2. What is meant by 'the True Man?' The True men of old did not reject (the views of) the few; they did not seek to accomplish (their ends) like heroes (before others); they did not lay plans to attain those ends. Being such, though they might make mistakes, they had no occasion for repentance; though they might succeed, they had no self-complacency. Being such, they could ascend the loftiest heights without fear; they could pass through water without being made wet by it; they could go into fire without being burnt; so it was that by their knowledge they ascended to and reached the Tâo.

The True men of old did not dream when they slept, had no anxiety when they awoke, and did not care that their food should be pleasant. Their breathing came deep and silently. The breathing of the true man comes (even) from his heels, while men generally breathe (only) from their throats. When men are defeated in argument, their words come from their gullets as if they were vomiting. Where lusts and desires are deep, the springs of the Heavenly are shallow.

The True men of old knew nothing of the love of life or of the hatred of death. Entrance into life occasioned them no joy; the exit from it awakened no resistance. Composedly they went and came. They did not forget what their beginning bad been, and they did not inquire into what their end would be. They accepted (their life) and rejoiced in it; they forgot (all fear of death), and returned (to their state before life). Thus there was in them what is called the want of any mind to resist the Tâo, and of all attempts by means of the Human to assist the Heavenly. Such were they who are called the True men.

3. Being such, their minds were free from all thought; their demeanour was still and unmoved; their foreheads beamed simplicity. Whatever

coldness came from them was like that of autumn; whatever warmth
came from them was like that of spring. Their joy and anger assimilated
to what we see in the four seasons. They did in regard to all things what
was suitable, and no one could know how far their action would go.
Therefore the sagely man might, in his conduct of war, destroy a state
without losing the hearts of the people; his benefits and favours might
extend to a myriad generations without his being a lover of men. Hence
he who tries to share his joys with others is not a sagely man; he who
manifests affection is not benevolent; he who observes times and seasons
(to regulate his conduct) is not a man of wisdom; he to whom profit and
injury are not the same is not a superior man; he who acts for the sake of
the name of doing so, and loses his (proper) self is not the (right) scholar;
and he who throws away his person in a way which is not the true (way)
cannot command the service of others. Such men as Hû Pû- kieh, Wû
Kwang, Po-î, Shû-khî, the count of Kî, Hsü-yü, Kî Thâ, and Shan-thû Tî,
all did service for other men, and sought to secure for them what they
desired, not seeking their own pleasure.

4. The True men of old presented the aspect of judging others aright,
but without being partisans; of feeling their own insufficiency, but being
without flattery or cringing. Their peculiarities were natural to them, but
they were not obstinately attached to them; their humility was evident,
but there was nothing of unreality or display about it. Their placidity and
satisfaction had the appearance of joy; their every movement seemed
to be a necessity to them. Their accumulated attractiveness drew men's
looks to them; their blandness fixed men's attachment to their virtue. They
seemed to accommodate themselves to the (manners of their age), but
with a certain severity; their haughty indifference was beyond its control.
Unceasing seemed their endeavours to keep (their mouths) shut; when
they looked down, they had forgotten what they wished to say.

They considered punishments to be the substance (of government,
and they never incurred it); ceremonies to be its supporting wings (and
they always observed them); wisdom (to indicate) the time (for action,
and they always selected it); and virtue to be accordance (with others), and
they were all- accordant. Considering punishments to be the substance
(of government), yet their generosity appeared in the (manner of their)
infliction of death. Considering ceremonies to be its supporting wings,
they pursued by means of them their course in the world. Considering
wisdom to indicate the time (for action), they felt it necessary to employ
it in (the direction of) affairs. Considering virtue to be accordance (with
others), they sought to ascend its height along with all who had feet (to
climb it). (Such were they), and yet men really thought that they did what
they did by earnest effort.

5. In this way they were one and the same in all their likings and dislikings. Where they liked, they were the same; where they did not like, they were the same. In the former case where they liked, they were fellow-workers with the Heavenly (in them); in the latter where they disliked, they were co-workers with the Human in them. The one of these elements (in their nature) did not overcome the other. Such were those who are called the True men.

Death and life are ordained, just as we have the constant succession of night and day;-- in both cases from Heaven. Men have no power to do anything in reference to them;-- such is the constitution of things. There are those who specially regard Heaven as their father, and they still love It (distant as It is);-- how much more should they love That which stands out (Superior and Alone)! Some specially regard their ruler as superior to themselves, and will give their bodies to die for him; how much more should they do so for That which is their true (Ruler)! When the springs are dried up, the fishes collect together on the land. Than that they should moisten one another there by the damp about them, and keep one another wet by their slime, it would be better for them to forget one another in the rivers and lakes. And when men praise Yâo and condemn Kieh, it would be better to forget them both, and seek the renovation of the Tâo.

6. There is the great Mass (of nature);-- I find the support of my body on it; my life is spent in toil on it; my old age seeks ease on it; at death I find rest in it;-- what makes my life a good makes my death also a good. If you hide away a boat in the ravine of a hill, and hide away the hill in a lake, you will say that (the boat) is secure; but at midnight there shall come a strong man and carry it off on his back, while you in the dark know nothing about it. You may hide away anything, whether small or great, in the most suitable place, and yet it shall disappear from it. But if you could hide the world in the world, so that there was nowhere to which it could be removed, this would be the grand reality of the ever-during Thing. When the body of man comes from its special mould, there is even then occasion for joy; but this body undergoes a myriad transformations, and does not immediately reach its perfection;-- does it not thus afford occasion for joys incalculable? Therefore the sagely man enjoys himself in that from which there is no possibility of separation, and by which all things are preserved. He considers early death or old age, his beginning and his ending, all to be good, and in this other men imitate him;-- how much more will they do so in regard to That Itself on which all things depend, and from which every transformation arises!

7. This is the Tâo;-- there is in It emotion and sincerity, but It does nothing and has no bodily form. It may be handed down (by the teacher),

but may not be received (by his scholars). It may be apprehended (by the mind), but It cannot be seen. It has Its root and ground (of existence) in Itself. Before there were heaven and earth, from of old, there It was, securely existing. From It came the mysterious existences of spirits, from It the mysterious existence of God. It produced heaven; It produced earth. It was before the Thâi-kî, and yet could not be considered high; It was below all space, and yet could not be considered deep. It was produced before heaven and earth, and yet could not be considered to have existed long; It was older than the highest antiquity, and yet could not be considered old.

Shih-wei got It, and by It adjusted heaven and earth. Fû-hsî got It, and by It penetrated to the mystery of the maternity of the primary matter. The Wei-tâu got It, and from all antiquity has made no eccentric movement. The Sun and Moon got It, and from all antiquity have not intermitted (their bright shining). Khan-pei got It, and by It became lord of Khwan-lun. Fang-î got It, and by It enjoyed himself in the Great River. Kien Wû got It, and by It dwelt on mount Thâi. Hwang-Tî got It, and by It ascended the cloudysky. Kwan-hsü got It, and by It dwelt in the Dark Palace. Yü-khiang got It, and by It was set on the North Pole. Hsî Wang-mû got It, and by It had her seat in (the palace of) Shâo-kwang. No one knows Its beginning; no one knows Its end. Phang Tsû got It, and lived on from the time of the lord of Yü to that of the Five Chiefs. Fû Yüeh got It, and by It became chief minister to Wû-ting, (who thus) in a trice became master of the kingdom. (After his death), Fû Yüeh mounted to the eastern portion of the Milky Way, where, riding on Sagittarius and Scorpio, he took his place among the stars.

8. Nan-po Tsze-khwei asked Nü Yü, saying, 'You are old, Sir, while your complexion is like that of a child;--how is it so?' The reply was, 'I have become acquainted with the Tâo.' The other said, 'Can I learn the Tâo?' Nü Yü said, 'No. How can you? You, Sir, are not the man to do so. There was Pû-liang Î who had the abilities of a sagely man, but not the Tâo, while I had the Tâo, but not the abilities. I wished, however, to teach him, if, peradventure, he might become the sagely man indeed. If he should not do so, it was easy (I thought) for one possessing the TAo of the sagely man to communicate it to another possessing his abilities. Accordingly, I proceeded to do so, but with deliberation. After three days, he was able to banish from his mind all worldly (matters). This accomplished, I continued my intercourse with him in the same way; and in seven days he was able to banish from his mind all thought of men and things. This accomplished, and my instructions continued, after nine days, he was able to count his life as foreign to himself. This accomplished, his mind was afterwards clear as the morning; and after this he was able to see his own individuality. That individuality perceived, he was able to banish all

thought of Past or Present. Freed from this, he was able to penetrate to (the truth that there is no difference between) life and death;-- (how) the destruction of life is not dying, and the communication of other life is not living. (The Tâo) is a thing which accompanies all other things and meets them, which is present when they are overthrown and when they obtain their completion. Its name is Tranquillity amid all Disturbances, meaning that such Disturbances lead to Its Perfection.'

'And how did you, being alone (without any teacher), learn all this?' 'I learned it,' was the reply, 'from the son of Fû-mo; he learned it from the grandson of Lo-sung; he learned it from Shan-ming; he learned it from Nieh-hsü; he, from Hsü-yî; he, from Wû-âo; he, from Hsüan-ming; he, from Tshan-liâo; and he learned it from Î-shih.'

9. Tsze-sze, Tsze-yü, Tsze-lî, and Tsze-lâi, these four men, were talking together, when some one said,

'Who can suppose the head to be made from nothing, the spine from life, and the rump-bone from death? Who knows how death and birth, living on and disappearing, compose the one body?-- I would be friends with him.' The four men looked at one another and laughed, but no one seized with his mind the drift of the questions. All, however, were friends together.

Not long after Tsze-yü fell ill, and Tsze-sze went to inquire for him. 'How great,' said (the sufferer), 'is the Creator! That He should have made me the deformed object that I am!' He was a crooked hunchback; his five viscera were squeezed into the upper part of his body; his chin bent over his navel; his shoulder was higher than his crown; on his crown was an ulcer pointing to the sky; his breath came and went in gasps:-- yet he was easy in his mind, and made no trouble of his condition. He limped to a well, looked at himself in it, and said, 'Alas that the Creator should have made me the deformed object that I am!' Tsze said, 'Do you dislike your condition?' He replied, 'No, why should I dislike it? If He were to transform my left arm into a cock, I should be watching with it the time of the night; if He were to transform my right arm into a cross-bow, I should then be looking for a hsiâo to (bring down and) roast; if He were to transform my rump-bone into a wheel, and my spirit into a horse, I should then be mounting it, and would not change it for another steed. Moreover, when we have got (what we are to do), there is the time (of life) in which to do it; when we lose that (at death), submission (is what is required). When we rest in what the time requires, and manifest that submission, neither joy nor sorrow can find entrance (to the mind). This would be what the ancients called loosing the cord by which (the life) is suspended. But one hung up cannot loose himself;-- he is held fast by his bonds. And that creatures cannot overcome Heaven (the inevitable) is a long-acknowledged fact;-- why should I hate my condition?'

10. Before long Tsze-lâi fell ill, and lay gasping at the point of death, while his wife and children stood around him wailing. Tsze-lî went to ask for him, and said to them, 'Hush! Get out of the way! Do not disturb him as he is passing through his change.' Then, leaning against the door, he said (to the dying man), 'Great indeed is the Creator! What will He now make you to become? Where will He take you to? Will He make you the liver of a rat, or the arm of an insect? Tsze-lâi replied, 'Wherever a parent tells a son to go, east, west, south, or north, he simply follows the command. The Yin and Yang are more to a man than his parents are. If they are hastening my death, and I do not quietly submit to them, I shall be obstinate and rebellious. There is the great Mass (of nature);-- I find the support of my body in it; my life is spent in toil on it; my old age seeks ease on it; at death I find rest on it:-- what has made my life a good will make my death also a good.

'Here now is a great founder, casting his metal. If the metal were to leap up (in the pot), and say, "I must be made into a (sword like the) Mo-yeh," the great founder would be sure to regard it as uncanny. So, again, when a form is being fashioned in the mould of the womb, if it were to say, "I must become a man; I must become a man," the Creator would be sure to regard it as uncanny. When we once understand that heaven and earth are a great melting-pot, and the Creator a great founder, where can we have to go to that shall not be right for us? We are born as from a quiet sleep, and we die to a calm awaking.'

11. Tsze-sang Hû, Mang Tsze-fan, and Tsze-khin Kang, these three men, were friends together. (One of them said), 'Who can associate together without any (thought of) such association, or act together without any (evidence of) such co-operation? Who can mount up into the sky and enjoy himself amidst the mists, disporting beyond the utmost limits (of things), and forgetting all others as if this were living, and would have no end?' The three men looked at one another and laughed, not perceiving the drift of the questions; and they continued to associate together as friends.

Suddenly, after a time, Tsze-sang Hû died. Before he was buried, Confucius heard of the event, and sent Tsze-kung to go and see if he could render any assistance. One of the survivors had composed a ditty, and the other was playing on his lute. Then they sang together in unison, 'Ah! come, Sang Hû! ah! come, Sang Hû! Your being true you've got again, While we, as men, still here remain Ohone!'

Tsze-kung hastened forward to them, and said, 'I venture to ask whether it be according to the rules to be singing thus in the presence of the corpse?' The two men looked at each other, and laughed, saying, 'What does this man know about the idea that underlies (our) rules?' Tsze-kung returned to Confucius, and reported to him, saying, 'What sort of men are those? They had made none of the usual preparations, and treated the body as a thing foreign to them. They were singing in the presence of the corpse, and there was no change in their countenances. I cannot describe them;-- what sort of men are they?' Confucius replied, 'Those men occupy and enjoy themselves in what is outside the (common) ways (of the world), while I occupy and enjoy myself in what lies within those ways. There is no common ground for those of such different ways; and when I sent you to condole with those men, I was acting stupidly. They, moreover, make man to be the fellow of the Creator, and seek their enjoyment in the formless condition of heaven and earth. They consider life to be an appendage attached, an excrescence annexed to them, and death to be a separation of the appendage and a dispersion of the contents of the excrescence. With these views, how should they know wherein death and life are to be found, or what is first and what is last? They borrow different substances, and pretend that the common form of the body is composed of them. They dismiss the thought of (its inward constituents like) the liver and gall, and (its outward constituents), the ears and eyes. Again and again they end and they begin, having no knowledge of first principles. They occupy themselves ignorantly and vaguely with what (they say) lies outside the dust and dirt (of the world), and seek their enjoyment in the business of doing nothing. How should they confusedly address themselves to the ceremonies practised by the common people, and exhibit themselves as doing so to the ears and eyes of the multitude?'

Tsze-kung said, 'Yes, but why do you, Master, act according to the (common) ways (of the world)?' The reply was, 'I am in this under the condemning sentence of Heaven. Nevertheless, I will share with you (what I have attained to).' Tsze-kung rejoined, 'I venture to ask the method which you pursue;' and Confucius said, 'Fishes breed and grow in the water; man developes in the Tâo. Growing in the water, the fishes cleave the pools, and their nourishment is supplied to them. Developing in the Tâo, men do nothing, and the enjoyment of their life is secured. Hence it is said, "Fishes forget one another in the rivers and lakes; men forget one another in the arts of the Tâo."'

Tsze-kung said, 'I venture to ask about the man who stands aloof from others.' The reply was, 'He stands aloof from other men, but he is in accord with Heaven! Hence it is said, "The small man of Heaven is the superior man among men; the superior man among men is the small man of Heaven!'"

12. Yen Hui asked Kung-nî, saying, 'When the mother of Mang-sun Tshâi died, in all his wailing for her he did not shed a tear; in the core of his heart he felt no distress; during all the mourning rites, he exhibited no sorrow. Without these three things, he (was considered to have) discharged his mourning well;-- is it that in the state of Lû one who has not the reality may yet get the reputation of having it? I think the matter very strange.' Kung-nî said, 'That Mang-sun carried out (his views) to the utmost. He was advanced in knowledge; but (in this case) it was not possible for him to appear to be negligent (in his ceremonial observances), but he succeeded in being really so to himself. Mang-sun does not know either what purposes life serves, or what death serves; he does not know which should be first sought, and which last. If he is to be transformed into something else, he will simply await the transformation which he does not yet know. This is all he does. And moreover, when one is about to undergo his change, how does he know that it has not taken place? And when he is not about to undergo his change, how does he know that it has taken place? Take the case of me and you:-- are we in a dream from which we have not begun to awake?

'Moreover, Mang-sun presented in his body the appearance of being agitated, but in his mind he was conscious of no loss. The death was to him like the issuing from one's dwelling at dawn, and no (more terrible) reality. He was more awake than others were. When they wailed, he also wailed, having in himself the reason why he did so. And we all have our individuality which makes us what we are as compared together; but how do we know that we determine in any case correctly that individuality? Moreover you dream that you are a bird, and seem to be soaring to the sky; or that you are a fish, and seem to be diving in the deep. But you do not know whether we that are now speaking are awake or in a dream. It is not the meeting with what is pleasurable that produces the smile; it is not the smile suddenly produced that produces the arrangement (of the person). When one rests in what has been arranged, and puts away all thought of the transformation, he is in unity with the mysterious Heaven.'

13. Î-r Tsze having gone to see Hsü Yü, the latter said to him, 'What benefit have you received from Yâo?' The reply was, 'Yâo says to me, You must yourself labour at benevolence and righteousness, and be able to tell clearly which is right and which wrong (in conflicting statements).' Hsü Yû rejoined, 'Why then have you come to me? Since Yâo has put on you the brand of his benevolence and righteousness, and cut off your nose with his right and wrong, how will you be able to wander in the way of aimless

enjoyment, of unregulated contemplation, and the ever-changing forms
(of dispute)?' Î-r Tsze said, 'That may be; but I should like to skirt along
its hedges.' 'But,' said the other, 'it cannot be. Eyes without pupils can see
nothing of the beauty of the eyebrows, eyes, and other features; the blind
have nothing to do with the green, yellow, and variegated colours of the
sacrificial robes.' Î-r Tsze rejoined, 'Yet, when Wû-kwang lost his beauty,
Kü-liang his strength, and Hwang-Tî his wisdom, they all (recovered
them) under the moulding (of your system);-- how do you know that
the Maker will not obliterate the marks of my branding, and supply my
dismemberment, so that, again perfect in my form, I may follow you as
my teacher?' Hsü Yû said, 'Ah! that cannot yet be known. I will tell you
the rudiments. 0 my Master! 0 my Master! He gives to all things their
blended qualities, and does not count it any righteousness; His favours
reach to all generations, and He does not count it any benevolence; He is
more ancient than the highest antiquity, and does not count Himself old;
He overspreads heaven and supports the earth; He carves and fashions
all bodily forms, and does not consider it any act of skill;-- this is He in
whom I find my enjoyment.'

14. Yen Hui said, 'I am making progress.' Kung-nî replied, 'What do
you mean?' 'I have ceased to think of benevolence and righteousness,'
was the reply. 'Very well; but that is not enough.'

Another day, Hui again saw Kung-nî, and said, 'I am making progress.'
'What do you mean?' 'I have lost all thought of ceremonies and music.'
'Very well, but that is not enough.'

A third day, Hui again saw (the Master), and said, 'I am making progress.' 'What do you mean?' 'I sit and forget everything.' Kung-nî changed
countenance, and said, 'What do you mean by saying that you sit and
forget (everything)?' Yen Hui replied, 'My connexion with the body and
its parts is dissolved; my perceptive organs are discarded. Thus leaving
my material form, and bidding farewell to my knowledge, I am become
one with the Great Pervader. This I call sitting and forgetting all things.'
Kung-nî said, 'One (with that Pervader), you are free from all likings; so
transformed, you are become impermanent. You have, indeed, become
superior to me! I must ask leave to follow in your steps.'

15. Tsze-yü and Tsze-sang were friends. (Once), when it had rained
continuously for ten days, Tsze-yü said, 'I fear that Tsze-sang may be in
distress.' So he wrapped up some rice, and went to give it to him to eat.
When he came to Tsze-sang's door, there issued from it sounds between
singing and wailing; a lute was struck, and there came the words, '0
Father! 0 Mother! 0 Heaven! 0 Men!' The voice could not sustain itself,

and the line was hurriedly pronounced. Tsze-yü entered and said, 'Why are you singing, Sir, this line of poetry in such a way?' The other replied, 'I was thinking, and thinking in vain, how it was that I was brought to such extremity. Would my parents have wished me to be so poor? Heaven overspreads all without any partial feeling, and so does Earth sustain all;-- Would Heaven and Earth make me so poor with any unkindly feeling? I was trying to find out who had done it, and I could not do so. But here I am in this extremity!-- it is what was appointed for me!'

Ying Tî Wang, or 'The Normal Course for Rulers and Kings.'

1. Nieh Khüeh put four questions to Wang Î, not one of which did he know (how to answer). On this Nieh Khüeh leaped up, and in great delight walked away and informed Phû-î-tsze of it, who said to him, 'Do you (only) now know it?' He of the line of Yü was not equal to him of the line of Thâi. He of Yü still kept in himself (the idea of) benevolence by which to constrain (the submission of) men; and he did win men, but he had not begun to proceed by what did not belong to him as a man. He of the line of Thâi would sleep tranquilly, and awake in contented simplicity. He would consider himself now (merely) as a horse, and now (merely) as an ox. His knowledge was real and untroubled by doubts; and his virtue was very true:-- he had not begun to proceed by what belonged to him as a man.

2. Kien Wû went to see the mad (recluse), Khieh-yü, who said to him, 'What did Zah-kung Shih tell you?' The reply was, 'He told me that when rulers gave forth their regulations according to their own views and enacted righteous measures, no one would venture not to obey them, and all would be transformed.' Khieh-yü said, 'That is but the hypocrisy of virtue. For the right ordering of the world it would be like trying to wade through the sea and dig through the Ho, or employing a musquito to carry a mountain on its back. And when a sage is governing, does he govern men's outward actions? He is (himself) correct, and so (his government) goes on;-- this is the simple and certain way by which he secures the success of his affairs. Think of the bird which flies high, to avoid being hurt by the dart on the string of the archer, and the little mouse which makes its hole deep under Shan-khiû to avoid the danger of being smoked or dug out;-- are (rulers) less knowing than these two little creatures?'

3. Thien Kan, rambling on the south of (mount) Yin, came to the neighbourhood of the Liâo-water. Happening there to meet with the man whose name is not known, he put a question to him, saying, 'I beg to ask what should be done in order to (carry on) the government of the world.' The nameless man said, 'Go away; you are a rude borderer. Why do you put to me a question for which you are unprepared? I would simply play the part of the Maker of (all) things. When wearied, I would mount on the bird of the light and empty air, proceed beyond the six cardinal points, and wander in the region of nonentity, to dwell in the wilderness of desert space. What method have you, moreover, for the government

of the world that you (thus) agitate my mind?' (Thien Kan), however, again asked the question, and the nameless man said, 'Let your mind find its enjoyment in pure simplicity; blend yourself with (the primary) ether in idle indifference; allow all things to take their natural course; and admit no personal or selfish consideration:-- do this and the world will be governed.'

4. Yang Tsze-kü, having an interview with Lâo Tan, said to him, 'Here is a man, alert and vigorous in responding to all matters, clearsighted and widely intelligent, and an unwearied student of the Tâo;-- can he be compared to one of the intelligent kings?' The reply was, 'Such a man is to one of the intelligent kings but as the bustling underling of a court who toils his body and distresses his mind with his various contrivances. And moreover, it is the beauty of the skins of the tiger and leopard which makes men hunt them; the agility of the monkey, or (the sagacity of) the dog that catches the yak, which make men lead them in strings; but can one similarly endowed be compared to the intelligent kings?'

Yang Tsze-kü looked discomposed and said, 'I venture to ask you what the government of the intelligent kings is.' Lâo Tan replied, 'In the governing of the intelligent kings, their services overspread all under the sky, but they did not seem to consider it as proceeding from themselves; their transforming influence reached to all things, but the people did not refer it to them with hope. No one could tell the name of their agency, but they made men and things be joyful in themselves. Where they took their stand could not be fathomed, and they found their enjoyment in (the realm of) nonentity.'

5. In Kang there was a mysterious wizard called Ki-hsien. He knew all about the deaths and births of men, their preservation and ruin, their misery and happiness, and whether their lives would be long or short, foretelling the year, the month, the decade and the day like a spirit. When the people of Kang saw him, they all ran out of his way. Lieh-tsze went to see him, and was fascinated by him. Returning, he told Hû- tsze of his interview, and said, 'I considered your doctrine, my master, to be perfect, but I have found another which is superior to it.' Hû-tsze replied, 'I have communicated to you but the outward letter of my doctrine, and have not communicated its reality and spirit; and do you think that you are in possession of it? However many hens there be, if there be not the cock among them, how should they lay (real) eggs? When you confront the world with your doctrine, you are sure to show in your countenance (all that is in your mind), and so enable (this) man to succeed in interpreting your physiognomy. Try and come to me with him, that I may show myself to him.'

On the morrow, accordingly, Lieh-tsze came with the man and saw Hû-tsze. When they went out, the wizard said, 'Alas! your master is a dead man. He will not live;-- not for ten days more! I saw something strange about him;-- I saw the ashes (of his life) all slaked with water!' When Lieh-tsze reentered, he wept till the front of his jacket was wet with his tears, and told Hû-tsze what the man had said. Hû-tsze said, 'I showed myself to him with the forms of (vegetation beneath) the earth. There were the sprouts indeed, but without (any appearance of) growth or regularity:-- he seemed to see me with the springs of my (vital) power closed up. Try and come to me with him again.'

Next day, accordingly, Lieh-tsze brought the man again and saw Hû-tsze. When they went out, the man said, 'It is a fortunate thing for your master that he met with me. He will get better; he has all the signs of living! I saw the balance (of the springs of life) that had been stopped (inclining in his favour).' Lieh-tsze went in, and reported these words to his master, who said, 'I showed myself to him after the pattern of the earth (beneath the) sky. Neither semblance nor reality entered (into my exhibition), but the springs (of life) were issuing from beneath my feet;-- he seemed to see me with the springs of vigorous action in full play. Try and come with him again.'

Next day Lieh-tsze came with the man again, and again saw Hû-tsze with him. When they went out, the wizard said, 'Your master is never the same. I cannot understand his physiognomy. Let him try to steady himself, and I will again view him.' Lieh-tsze went in and reported this to Hû-tsze, who said, 'This time I showed myself to him after the pattern of the grand harmony (of the two elemental forces), with the superiority inclining to neither. He seemed to see me with the springs of (vital) power in equal balance. Where the water wheels about from (the movements of) a dugong, there is an abyss; where it does so from the arresting (of its course), there is an abyss; where it does so, and the water keeps flowing on, there is an abyss. There are nine abysses with their several names, and I have only exhibited three of them. Try and come with him again.'

Next day they came, and they again saw Hû-tsze. But before he had settled himself in his position, the wizard lost himself and ran away. 'Pursue him,' said Hû-tsze, and Lieh-tsze did so, but could not come up with him. He returned, and told Hû-tsze, saying, 'There is an end of him; he is lost; I could not find him.' Hû-tsze rejoined, 'I was showing him myself after the pattern of what was before I began to come from my author. I confronted him with pure vacancy, and an easy indifference. He did not know what I meant to represent. Now he thought it was the idea of exhausted strength, and now that of an onward flow, and therefore he ran away.'

After this, Lieh-tsze considered that he had not yet begun to learn (his master's doctrine). He returned to his house, and for three years did not go out. He did the cooking for his wife. He fed the pigs as if he were feeding men. He took no part or interest in occurring affairs. He put away the carving and sculpture about him, and returned to pure simplicity. Like a clod of earth he stood there in his bodily presence. Amid all distractions he was (silent) and shut up in himself. And in this way he continued to the end of his life.

6. Non-action (makes its exemplifier) the lord of all fame; non-action (serves him as) the treasury of all plans; non-action (fits him for) the burden of all offices; non-action (makes him) the lord of all wisdom. The range of his action is inexhaustible, but there is nowhere any trace of his presence. He fulfils all that he has received from Heaven, but he does not see that he was the recipient of anything. A pure vacancy (of all purpose) is what characterises him. When the perfect man employs his mind, it is a mirror. It conducts nothing and anticipates nothing; it responds to (what is before it), but does not retain it. Thus he is able to deal successfully with all things, and injures none.

7. The Ruler of the Southern Ocean was Shû, the Ruler of the Northern Ocean was Hû, and the Ruler of the Centre was Chaos. Shû and Hû were continually meeting in the land of Chaos, who treated them very well. They consulted together how they might repay his kindness, and said, 'Men all have seven orifices for the purpose of seeing, hearing, eating, and breathing, while this (poor) Ruler alone has not one. Let us try and make them for him.' Accordingly they dug one orifice in him every day; and at the end of seven days Chaos died.

Phien Mâu, or 'Webbed Toes.'

1. A ligament uniting the big toe with the other toes and an extra finger may be natural growths, but they are more than is good for use. Excrescences on the person and hanging tumours are growths from the body, but they are unnatural additions to it. There are many arts of benevolence and righteousness, and the exercise of them is distributed among the five viscera; but this is not the correct method according to the characteristics of the Tâo. Thus it is that the addition to the foot is but the attachment to it of so much useless flesh, and the addition to the hand is but the planting on it of a useless finger. (So it is that) the connecting (the virtues) with the five viscera renders, by excess or restraint, the action of benevolence and righteousness bad, and leads to many arts as in the employment of (great) powers of hearing or of vision.

2. Therefore an extraordinary power of vision leads to the confusion of the five colours and an excessive use of ornament. (Its possessor), in the resplendence of his green and yellow, white and black, black and green, will not stop till he has become a Lî Kû. An extraordinary power of hearing leads to a confusion of the five notes, and an excessive use of the six musical accords. (Its possessor), in bringing out the tones from the instruments of metal, stone, silk, and bamboo, aided by the Hwang-kung and Tâ-lü (tubes), will not stop till he has become a Shih Khwang. (So), excessive benevolence eagerly brings out virtues and restrains its (proper) nature, that (its possessor) may acquire a famous reputation, and cause all the organs and drums in the world to celebrate an unattainable condition; and he will not stop till he has become a Tsang (Shan) or a Shih (Tshiû). An extraordinary faculty in debating leads to the piling up of arguments like a builder with his bricks, or a netmaker with his string. (Its possessor) cunningly contrives his sentences and enjoys himself in discussing what hardness is and what whiteness is, where views agree and where they differ, and pressing on, though weary, with short steps, with (a multitude of) useless words to make good his opinion; nor will he stop till he has become a Yang (Kû) or Mo (Tî). But in all these cases the parties, with their redundant and divergent methods, do not proceed by that which is the correct path for all under the sky. That which is the perfectly correct path is not to lose the real character of the nature with which we are endowed. Hence the union (of parts) should not be considered redundance, nor their divergence superfluity; what is long should not be considered too long, nor what is short too short. A duck's legs, for instance, are short, but if we try to lengthen them, it occasions pain; and a crane's legs are long, but if we try to cut off a portion of them, it produces

grief. Where a part is by nature long, we are not to amputate, or where it is by nature short, we are not to lengthen it. There is no occasion to try to remove any trouble that it may cause.

3. The presumption is that benevolence and righteousness are not constituents of humanity; for to how much anxiety does the exercise of them give rise! Moreover when another toe is united to the great toe, to divide the membrane makes you weep; and when there is an extra finger, to gnaw it off makes you cry out. In the one case there is a member too many, and in the other a member too few; but the anxiety and pain which they cause is the same. The benevolent men of the present age look at the evils of the world, as with eyes full of dust, and are filled with sorrow by them, while those who are not benevolent, having violently altered the character of their proper nature, greedily pursue after riches and honours. The presumption therefore is that benevolence and righteousness are contrary to the nature of man:-- how full of trouble and contention has the world been ever since the three dynasties began!

And moreover, in employing the hook and line, the compass and square, to give things their correct form you must cut away portions of what naturally belongs to them; in employing strings and fastenings, glue and varnish to make things firm, you must violently interfere with their qualities. The bendings and stoppings in ceremonies and music, and the factitious expression in the countenance of benevolence and righteous-ness, in order to comfort the minds of men:-- these all show a failure in observing the regular principles (of the human constitution). All men are furnished with such regular principles; and according to them what is bent is not made so by the hook, nor what is straight by the line, nor what is round by the compass, nor what is square by the carpenter's square. Nor is adhesion effected by the use of glue and varnish, nor are things bound together by means of strings and bands. Thus it is that all in the world are produced what they are by a certain guidance, while they do not know how they are produced so; and they equally attain their several ends while they do not know how it is that they do so. Anciently it was so, and it is so now; and this constitution of things should not be made of none effect. Why then should benevolence and righteousness be employed as connecting (links), or as glue and varnish, strings and bands, and the enjoyment arising from the Tâo and its characteristics be attributed to them?-- it is a deception practised upon the world. Where the deception is small, there will be a change in the direction (of the objects pursued); where it is great, there will be a change of the nature itself. How do I know that it is so? Since he of the line of Yü called in his benevolence and righteousness to distort and vex the world, the world has not ceased to hurry about to execute their commands;-- has not this been by means of benevolence and righteousness to change (men's views) of their nature?

4. I will therefore try and discuss this matter. From the commencement of the three dynasties downwards, nowhere has there been a man who has not under (the influence of external) things altered (the course of) his nature. Small men for the sake of gain have sacrificed their persons; scholars for the sake of fame have done so; great officers, for the sake of their families; and sagely men, for the sake of the kingdom. These several classes, with different occupations, and different reputations, have agreed in doing injury to their nature and sacrificing their persons. Take the case of a male and female slave;-- they have to feed the sheep together, but they both lose their sheep. Ask the one what he was doing, and you will find that he was holding his bamboo tablets and reading. Ask the other, and you will find that she was amusing herself with some game. They were differently occupied, but they equally lose their sheep. (So), Po-î died at the foot of Shâu-yang to maintain his fame, and the robber Kih died on the top of Tung-ling in his eagerness for gain. Their deaths were occasioned by different causes, but they equally shortened their lives and did violence to their nature;-- why must we approve of Po-î, and condemn the robber Kih? In cases of such sacrifice all over the world, when one makes it for the sake of benevolence and righteousness, the common people style him 'a superior man,' but when another does it for the sake of goods and riches, they style him 'a small man.' The action of sacrificing is the same, and yet we have 'the superior man' and 'the small man!' In the matter of destroying his life, and doing injury to his nature, the robber Kih simply did the same as Po-î;-- why must we make the distinction of 'superior man' and 'small man' between them?

5. Moreover, those who devote their nature to (the pursuit) of benevolence and righteousness, though they should attain to be like Tsang (Shan) and Shih (Tshiû), I do not pronounce to be good; those who devote it to (the study of) the five flavours, though they attain to be like Shû-r, I do not pronounce to be good; those who devote it to the (discrimination of the) five notes, though they attain to be like Shih Khwang, I do not pronounce to be quick of hearing; those who devote it to the (appreciation of the) five colours, though they attain to be like Lî Kû, I do not pronounce to be clear of vision. When I pronounce men to be good, I am not speaking of their benevolence and righteousness;-- the goodness is simply (their possession of) the qualities (of the Tâo). When I pronounce them to be good, I am not speaking of what are called benevolence and righteousness; but simply of their allowing the nature with which they are endowed to have its free course. When I pronounce men to be quick of hearing, I do not mean that they hearken to anything else, but that they hearken to themselves; when I pronounce them to be clear of vision, I do not mean

that they look to anything else, but that they look to themselves. Now those who do not see themselves but see other things, who do not get possession of themselves but get possession of other things, get possession of what belongs to others, and not of what is their own; and they reach forth to what attracts others, and not to that in themselves which should attract them. But thus reaching forth to what attracts others and not to what should attract them in themselves, be they like the robber Kih or like Po-î, they equally err in the way of excess or of perversity. What I am ashamed of is erring in the characteristics of the Tâo, and therefore, in the higher sphere, I do not dare to insist on the practice of benevolence and righteousness, and, in the lower, I do not dare to allow myself either in the exercise of excess or perversity.

Mâ Thî, or 'Horses's Hoofs.'

1. Horses can with their hoofs tread on the hoarfrost and snow, and with their hair withstand the wind and cold; they feed on the grass and drink water; they prance with their legs and leap:-- this is the true nature of horses. Though there were made for them grand towers and large dormitories, they would prefer not to use them. But when Po-lâo (arose and) said, 'I know well how to manage horses,' (men proceeded) to singe and mark them, to clip their hair, to pare their hoofs, to halter their heads, to bridle them and hobble them, and to confine them in stables and corrals. (When subjected to this treatment), two or three in every ten of them died. (Men proceeded further) to subject them to hunger and thirst, to gallop them and race them, and to make them go together in regular order. In front were the evils of the bit and ornamented breastbands, and behind were the terrors of the whip and switch. (When so treated), more than half of them died.

The (first) potter said, 'I know well how to deal with clay;' and (men proceeded) to mould it into circles as exact as if made by the compass, and into squares as exact as if formed by the measuring square. The (first) carpenter said, 'I know well how to deal with wood;' and (men proceeded) to make it bent as if by the application of the hook, and straight as if by the application of the plumb-line. But is it the nature of clay and wood to require the application of the compass and square, of the hook and line? And yet age after age men have praised Po-lâo, saying, 'He knew well how to manage horses,' and also the (first) potter and carpenter, saying, 'They knew well how to deal with clay and wood.' This is just the error committed by the governors of the world.

2. According to my idea, those who knew well to govern mankind would not act so. The people had their regular and constant nature:-- they wove and made themselves clothes; they tilled the ground and got food. This was their common faculty. They were all one in this, and did not form themselves into separate classes; so were they constituted and left to their natural tendencies. Therefore in the age of perfect virtue men walked along with slow and grave step, and with their looks steadily directed forwards. At that time, on the hills there were no foot-paths, nor excavated passages; on the lakes there were no boats nor dams; all creatures lived in companies; and the places of their settlement were made close to one another. Birds and beasts multiplied to flocks and herds; the grass and trees grew luxuriant and long. In this condition the birds and beasts might be led about without feeling the constraint; the nest of the magpie might be climbed to, and peeped into. Yes, in the age of perfect

virtue, men lived in common with birds and beasts, and were on terms of equality with all creatures, as forming one family;-- how could they know among themselves the distinctions of superior men and small men? Equally without knowledge, they did not leave (the path of) their natural virtue; equally free from desires, they were in the state of pure simplicity. In that state of pure simplicity, the nature of the people was what it ought to be. But when the sagely men appeared, limping and wheeling about in (the exercise of) benevolence, pressing along and standing on tiptoe in the doing of righteousness, then men universally began to be perplexed. (Those sages also) went to excess in their performances of music, and in their gesticulations in the practice of ceremonies, and then men began to be separated from one another. If the raw materials had not been cut and hacked, who could have made a sacrificial vase from them? If the natural jade had not been broken and injured, who could have made the handles for the libation-cups from it? If the attributes of the Tâo had not been disallowed, how should they have preferred benevolence and righteousness? If the instincts of the nature had not been departed from, how should ceremonies and music have come into use? If the five colours had not been confused, how should the ornamental figures have been formed? If the five notes had not been confused, how should they have supplemented them by the musical accords? The cutting and hacking of the raw materials to form vessels was the crime of the skilful workman; the injury done to the characteristics of the Tâo in order to the practice of benevolence and righteousness was the error of the sagely men.

3. Horses, when living in the open country, eat the grass, and drink water; when pleased, they intertwine their necks and rub one another; when enraged, they turn back to back and kick one another;-- this is all that they know to do. But if we put the yoke on their necks, with the moon-like frontlet displayed on all their foreheads, then they know to look slily askance, to curve their necks, to rush viciously, trying to get the bit out of their mouths, and to filch the reins (from their driver); this knowledge of the horse and its ability thus to act the part of a thief is the crime of Po-lâo. In the time of (the Ti) Ho-hsü, the people occupied their dwellings without knowing what they were doing, and walked out without knowing where they were going. They filled their mouths with food and were glad; they slapped their stomachs to express their satisfaction. This was all the ability which they possessed. But when the sagely men appeared, with their bendings and stoppings in ceremonies and music to adjust the persons of all, and hanging up their benevolence and righteousness to excite the endeavours of all to reach them, in order to comfort their minds, then the people began to stump and limp about in their love of knowledge, and strove with one another in their pursuit of gain, so that there was no stopping them:-- this was the error of those sagely men.

Khü Khieh, or 'Cutting Open Satchels.'

1. In taking precautions against thieves who cut open satchels, search bags, and break open boxes, people are sure to cord and fasten them well, and to employ strong bonds and clasps; and in this they are ordinarily said to show their wisdom. When a great thief comes, however, he shoulders the box, lifts up the satchel, carries off the bag, and runs away with them, afraid only that the cords, bonds, and clasps may not be secure; and in this case what was called the wisdom (of the owners) proves to be nothing but a collecting of the things for the great thief. Let me try and set this matter forth. Do not those who are vulgarly called wise prove to be collectors for the great thieves? And do not those who are called sages prove to be but guardians in the interest of the great thieves?

How do I know that the case is so? Formerly, in the state of Khî, the neighbouring towns could see one another; their cocks and dogs never ceased to answer the crowing and barking of other cocks and dogs (between them). The nets were set (in the water and on the land); and the ploughs and hoes were employed over more than a space of two thousand lî square. All within its four boundaries, the establishment of the ancestral temples and of the altars of the land and grain, and the ordering of the hamlets and houses, and of every corner in the districts, large, medium, and small, were in all particulars according to the rules of the sages. So it was; but yet one morning, Thien Khang-tsze killed the ruler of Khî, and stole his state. And was it only the state that he stole? Along with it he stole also the regulations of the sages and wise men (observed in it). And so, though he got the name of being a thief and a robber, yet he himself continued to live as securely as Yâo and Shun had done. Small states did not dare to find fault with him; great states did not dare to take him off; for twelve generations (his descendants) have possessed the state of Khî. Thus do we not have a case in which not only did (the party) steal the state of Khî, but at the same time the regulations of its sages and wise men, which thereby served to guard the person of him, thief and robber as he was?

2. Let me try to set forth this subject (still further). Have not there been among those vulgarly styled the wisest, such as have collected (their wealth) for the great chief? and among those styled the most sage such as have guarded it for him? How do I know that it has been so? Formerly, Lung-fang was beheaded; Pî-kan had his heart torn out; Khang Hung was ripped open; and Tsze-hsü was reduced to pulp (in the Khang). Worthy as those four men were, they did not escape such dreadful deaths. The followers of the robber Kih asked him, saying, 'Has the robber also any

method or principle (in his proceedings)?' He replied, 'What profession is there which has not its principles? That the robber in his recklessness comes to the conclusion that there are valuable deposits in an apartment shows his sageness; that he is the first to enter it shows his bravery; that he is the last to quit it shows his righteousness; that he knows whether (the robbery) may be attempted or not shows his wisdom; and that he makes an equal division of the plunder shows his benevolence. Without all these five qualities no one in the world has ever attained to become a great robber.' Looking at the subject in this way, we see that good men do not arise without having the principles of the sages, and that Kih could not have pursued his course without the same principles. But the good men in the world are few, and those who are not good are many;-- it follows that the sages benefit the world in a few instances and injure it in many. Hence it is that we have the sayings,

'When the lips are gone the teeth are cold;' 'The poor wine of Lû gave occasion to the siege of Han-tan;'

'When sages are born great robbers arise.' When the stream is dried, the valley is empty; when the mound is levelled, the deep pool (beside it) is filled up. When the sages have died, the great robbers will not arise; the world would be at peace, and there would be no more troubles. While the sagely men have not died, great robbers will not cease to appear. The more right that is attached to (the views of) the sagely men for the government of the world, the more advantage will accrue to (such men as) the robber Kih. If we make for men pecks and bushels to measure (their wares), even by means of those pecks and bushels should we be teaching them to steal; if we make for them weights and steelyards to weigh (their wares), even by means of those weights and steelyards shall we be teaching them to steal. If we make for them tallies and seals to secure their good faith, even by means of those tallies and seals shall we be teaching them to steal. If we make for them benevolence and righteousness to make their doings correct, even by means of benevolence and righteousness shall we be teaching them to steal. How do I know that it is so? Here is one who steals a hook (for his girdle);-- he is put to death for it: here is another who steals a state;-- he becomes its prince. But it is at the gates of the princes that we find benevolence and righteousness (most strongly) professed;-- is not this stealing benevolence and righteousness, sageness and wisdom? Thus they hasten to become great robbers, carry off princedoms, and steal benevolence and righteousness, with all the gains springing from the use of pecks and bushels, weights and steelyards, tallies and seals:-- even the rewards of carriages and coronets have no power to influence (to a different course), and the terrors of the axe have no power to restrain in such cases. The giving of so great gain to robbers (like) Kih, and making it impossible to restrain them;-- this is the error committed by the sages.

3. In accordance with this it is said, 'Fish should not be taken from (the protection of) the deep waters; the agencies for the profit of a state should not be shown to men.' But those sages (and their teachings) are the agencies for the profit of the world, and should not be exhibited to it. Therefore if an end were put to sageness and wisdom put away, the great robbers would cease to arise. If jade were put away and pearls broken to bits, the small thieves would not appear. If tallies were burned and seals broken in pieces, the people would become simple and unsophisticated. If pecks were destroyed and steelyards snapped in two, the people would have no wrangling. If the rules of the sages were entirely set aside in the world, a beginning might be made of reasoning with the people. If the six musical accords were reduced to a state of utter confusion, organs and lutes all burned, and the ears of the (musicians like the) blind Khwang stopped up, all men would begin to possess and employ their (natural) power of hearing. If elegant ornaments were abolished, the five embellishing colours disused and the eyes of (men like) Lî Kû glued up, all men would begin to possess and employ their (natural) power of vision. If the hook and line were destroyed, the compass and square thrown away, and the fingers of men (like) the artful Khui smashed, all men would begin to possess and employ their (natural) skill;-- as it is said, 'The greatest art is like stupidity.' If conduct such as that of Tsang (Shan) and Shih (Khiû) were discarded, the mouths of Yang (Kû) and Mo (Tî) gagged, and benevolence and righteousness seized and thrown aside, the virtue of all men would begin to display its mysterious excellence. When men possessed and employed their (natural) power of vision, there would be no distortion in the world. When they possessed and employed their (natural) power of hearing, there would be no distractions in the world. When they possessed and employed their (natural) faculty of knowledge, there would be no delusions in the world. When they possessed and employed their (natural) virtue, there would be no depravity in the world. Men like Tsang (Shan), Shih (Khiû), Yang (Kû), Mo (Tî), Shih Khwang (the musician), the artist Khui, and Lî Kû, all display their qualities outwardly, and set the world in a blaze (of admiration) and confound it;-- a method which is of no use!

4. Are you, Sir, unacquainted with the age of perfect virtue? Anciently there were Yung-khang, Tâ-thing, Po-hwang, Kang-yang, Lî-Lû, Lî-khû, Hsien-yüan, Ho-hsü, Tsun-lû, Kû-yung, Fû-hsî, and Shan-nang. In their times the people made knots on cords in carrying on their affairs. They thought their (simple) food pleasant, and their (plain) clothing beautiful. They were happy in their (simple) manners, and felt at rest in their (poor) dwellings. (The people of) neighbouring states might be able to descry one another; the voices of their cocks and dogs might be heard (all the way) from one to the other; they might not die till they were old; and yet

all their life they would have no communication together. In those times perfect good order prevailed.

Now-a-days, however, such is the state of things that you shall see the people stretching out their necks, and standing on tiptoe, while they say, 'In such and such a place there is a wise and able man.' Then they carry with them whatever dry provisions they may have left, and hurry towards it, abandoning their parents in their homes, and neglecting the service of their rulers abroad. Their footsteps may be traced in lines from one state to another, and the ruts of their chariot-wheels also for more than a thousand lî. This is owing to the error of their superiors in their (inordinate) fondness for knowledge. When those superiors do really love knowledge, but do not follow the (proper) course, the whole world is thrown into great confusion.

How do I know that the case is so? The knowledge shown in the (making of) bows, cross-bows, band-nets, stringed arrows, and contrivances with springs is great, but the birds are troubled by them above; the knowledge shown in the hooks, baits, various kinds of nets, and bamboo traps is great, but the fishes are disturbed by them in the waters; the knowledge shown in the arrangements for setting nets, and the nets and snares themselves, is great, but the animals are disturbed by them in the marshy grounds. (So), the versatility shown in artful deceptions becoming more and more pernicious, in ingenious discussions as to what is hard and what is white, and in attempts to disperse the dust and reconcile different views, is great, but the common people are perplexed by all the sophistry. Hence there is great disorder continually in the world, and the guilt of it is due to that fondness for knowledge. Thus it is that all men know to seek for the knowledge that they have not attained to; and do not know to seek for that which they already have (in themselves); and that they know to condemn what they do not approve (in others), and do not know to condemn what they have allowed in themselves;-- it is this which occasions the great confusion and disorder. It is just as if, above, the brightness of the sun and moon were darkened; as if, beneath, the productive vigour of the hills and streams were dried up; and as if, between, the operation of the four seasons were brought to an end:-- in which case there would not be a single weak and wriggling insect, nor any plant that grows up, which would not lose its proper nature. Great indeed is the disorder produced in the world by the love of knowledge. From the time of the three dynasties downwards it has been so. The plain and honest-minded people are neglected, and the plausible representations of restless spirits received with pleasure; the quiet and unexciting method of non-action is put away, and pleasure taken in ideas garrulously expressed. It is this garrulity of speech which puts the world in disorder.

Tsâi Yû, or 'Letting Be, and Exercising Forbearance.'

1. I have heard of letting the world be, and exercising forbearance; I have not heard of governing the world. Letting be is from the fear that men, (when interfered with), will carry their nature beyond its normal condition; exercising forbearance is from the fear that men, (when not so dealt with), will alter the characteristics of their nature. When all men do not carry their nature beyond its normal condition, nor alter its characteristics, the good government of the world is secured.

Formerly, Yâo's government of the world made men look joyful; but when they have this joy in their nature, there is a want of its (proper) placidity. The government of the world by Kieh, (on the contrary), made men look distressed; but when their nature shows the symptoms of distress, there is a want of its (proper) contentment. The want of placidity and the want of contentment are contrary to the character (of the nature); and where this obtains, it is impossible that any man or state should anywhere abide long. Are men exceedingly joyful?-- the Yang or element of expansion in them is too much developed. Are they exceedingly irritated?-- the Yin or opposite element is too much developed. When those elements thus predominate in men, (it is as if) the four seasons were not to come (at their proper times), and the harmony of cold and heat were not to be maintained;-- would there not result injury to the bodies of men? Men's joy and dissatisfaction are made to arise where they ought not to do so; their movements are all uncertain; they lose the mastery of their thoughts; they stop short midway, and do not finish what they have begun. In this state of things the world begins to have lofty aims, and jealous dislikes, ambitious courses, and fierce animosities, and then we have actions like those of the robber Kih, or of Tsang (Shan) and Shih (Tshiû). If now the whole world were taken to reward the good it would not suffice, nor would it be possible with it to punish the bad. Thus the world, great as it is, not sufficing for rewards and punishments, from the time of the three dynasties downwards, there has been nothing but bustle and excitement. Always occupied with rewards and punishments, what leisure have men had to rest in the instincts of the nature with which they are endowed?

2. Moreover, delight in the power of vision leads to excess in the pursuit of (ornamental) colours; delight in the power of hearing, to excess in seeking (the pleasures of) sound; delight in benevolence tends to disorder that virtue (as proper to the nature); delight in righteousness

sets the man in opposition to what is right in reason; delight in (the practice of) ceremonies is helpful to artful forms; delight in music leads to voluptuous airs; delight in sageness is helpful to ingenious contrivances; delight in knowledge contributes to fault-finding. If all men were to rest in the instincts of their nature, to keep or to extinguish these eight delights might be a matter of indifference; but if they will not rest in those instincts, then those eight delights begin to be imperfectly and unevenly developed or violently suppressed, and the world is thrown into disorder. But when men begin to honour them, and to long for them, how great is the deception practised on the world! And not only, when (a performance of them) is once over, do they not have done with them, but they prepare themselves (as) with fasting to describe them, they seem to kneel reverentially when they bring them forward, and they go through them with the excitements of music and singing; and then what can be done (to remedy the evil of them)? Therefore the superior man, who feels himself constrained to engage in the administration of the world will find it his best way to do nothing. In (that policy of) doing nothing, he can rest in the instincts of the nature with which he is endowed. Hence he who will administer (the government of) the world honouring it as he honours his own person, may have that government committed to him, and he who will administer it loving it as he loves his own person, may have it entrusted to him. Therefore, if the superior man will keep (the faculties lodged in) his five viscera unemployed, and not display his powers of seeing and hearing, while he is motionless as a representative of the dead, his dragon-like presence will be seen; while he is profoundly silent, the thunder (of his words) will resound; while his movements are (unseen) like those of a spirit, all heavenly influences will follow them; while he is (thus) unconcerned and does nothing, his genial influence will attract and gather all things round him:-- what leisure has he to do anything more for the government of the world?

3. Tshui Khü asked Lâo Tan, saying, 'If you do not govern the world, how can you make men's minds good?' The reply was, 'Take care how you meddle with and disturb men's minds. The mind, if pushed about, gets depressed; if helped forward, it gets exalted. Now exalted, now depressed, here it appears as a prisoner, and there as a wrathful fury. (At one time) it becomes pliable and soft, yielding to what is hard and strong; (at another), it is sharp as the sharpest corner, fit to carve or chisel (stone or jade). Now it is hot as a scorching fire, and anon it is cold as ice. It is so swift that while one is bending down and lifting up his head, it shall twice have put forth a soothing hand beyond the four seas. Resting, it is still as a deep abyss; moving, it is like one of the bodies in the sky; in its resolute haughtiness, it refuses to be bound;-- such is the mind of man!'

Anciently, Hwang-Tî was the first to meddle with and disturb the mind of man with his benevolence and righteousness. After him, Yâo and Shun wore their thighs bare and the hair off the calves of their legs, in their labours to nourish the bodies of the people. They toiled painfully with all the powers in their five viscera at the practice of their benevolence and righteousness; they tasked their blood and breath to make out a code of laws;-- and after all they were unsuccessful. On this Yâo sent away Hwan Tâu to Khung hill, and (the Chiefs of) the Three Miâo to San-wei, and banished the Minister of Works to the Dark Capital; so unequal had they been to cope with the world. Then we are carried on to the kings of the

Three (dynasties), when the world was in a state of great distraction. Of the lowest type of character there were Kieh and Kih; of a higher type there were Tsang (Shan) and Shih (Tshiû). At the same time there arose the classes of the Literati and the Mohists. Hereupon, complacency in, and hatred of, one another produced mutual suspicions; the stupid and the wise imposed on one another; the good and the bad condemned one another; the boastful and the sincere interchanged their recriminations;-- and the world fell into decay. Views as to what was greatly virtuous did not agree, and the nature with its endowments became as if shrivelled by fire or carried away by a flood. All were eager for knowledge, and the people were exhausted with their searchings (after what was good). On this the axe and the saw were brought into play; guilt was determined as by the plumb-line and death inflicted; the hammer and gouge did their work. The world fell into great disorder, and presented the appearance of a jagged mountain ridge. The crime to which all was due was the meddling with and disturbing men's minds. The effect was that men of ability and worth lay concealed at the foot of the crags of mount Thâi, and princes of ten thousand chariots were anxious and terrified in their ancestral temples. In the present age those who have been put to death in various ways lie thick as if pillowed on each other; those who are wearing the cangue press on each other (on the roads); those who are suffering the bastinado can see each other (all over the land). And now the Literati and the Mohists begin to stand, on tiptoe and with bare arms, among the fettered and manacled crowd! Ah! extreme is their shamelessness, and their failure to see the disgrace! Strange that we should be slow to recognise their sageness and wisdom in the bars of the cangue, and their benevolence and righteousness in the rivets of the fetters and handcuffs! How do we know that Tsang and Shih are not the whizzing arrows of Kieh and Kih? Therefore it is said, 'Abolish sageness and cast away knowledge, and the world will be brought to a state of great order.'

4. Hwang-Tî had been on the throne for nineteen years, and his ordinances were in operation all through the kingdom, when he heard that Kwang Khang-tsze was living on the summit of Khung-thung, and

went to see him. 'I have heard,' he said, 'that you, Sir, are well acquainted with the perfect Tâo. I venture to ask you what is the essential thing in it. I wish to take the subtlest influences of heaven and earth, and assist with them the (growth of the) five cereals for the (better) nourishment of the people. I also wish to direct the (operation of the) Yin and Yang, so as to secure the comfort of all living beings. How shall I proceed to accomplish those objects?' Kwang Khang-tsze replied, 'What you wish to ask about is the original substance of all things; what you wish to have the direction of is that substance as it was shattered and divided. According to your government of the world, the vapours of the clouds, before they were collected, would descend in rain; the herbs and trees would shed their leaves before they became yellow; and the light of the sun and moon would hasten to extinction. Your mind is that of a flatterer with his plausible words;-- it is not fit that I should tell you the perfect Tâo.'

Hwang-Tî withdrew, gave up (his government of) the kingdom, built himself a solitary apartment, spread in it a mat of the white mâo grass, dwelt in it unoccupied for three months, and then went again to seek an interview with (the recluse). Kwang Khang-tsze was then lying down with his head to the south. Hwang-Tî, with an air of deferential submission, went forward on his knees, twice bowed low with his face to the ground, and asked him, saying, 'I have heard that you, Sir, are well acquainted with the perfect Tâo;-- I venture to ask how I should rule my body, in order that it may continue for a long time.' Kwang Khang-tsze hastily rose, and said, 'A good question! Come and I will tell you the perfect Tâo. Its essence is (surrounded with) the deepest obscurity; its highest reach is in darkness and silence. There is nothing to be seen; nothing to be heard. When it holds the spirit in its arms in stillness, then the bodily form of itself will become correct. You must be still; you must be pure; not subjecting your body to toil, not agitating your vital force;-- then you may live for long. When your eyes see nothing, your ears hear nothing, and your mind knows nothing, your spirit will keep your body, and the body will live long. Watch over what is within you, shut up the avenues that connect you with what is external;-- much knowledge is pernicious. I (will) proceed with you to the summit of the Grand Brilliance, where we come to the source of the bright and expanding (element); I will enter with you the gate of the Deepest Obscurity, where we come to the source of the dark and repressing (element). There heaven and earth have their controllers; there the Yin and Yang have their Repositories. Watch over and keep your body, and all things will of themselves give it vigour. I maintain the (original) unity (of these elements), and dwell in the harmony of them. In this way I have cultivated myself for one thousand and two hundred years, and my bodily form has undergone no decay.'

Hwang-Tî twice bowed low with his head to the ground, and said, 'In Kwang Khang-tsze we have an example of what is called Heaven.' The other said, 'Come, and I will tell you:-- (The perfect Tâo) is something inexhaustible, and yet men all think it has an end; it is something unfathomable, and yet men all think its extreme limit can be reached. He who attains to my Tâo, if he be in a high position, will be one of the August ones, and in a low position, will be a king. He who fails in attaining it, in his highest attainment will see the light, but will descend and be of the Earth. At present all things are produced from the Earth and return to the Earth. Therefore I will leave you, and enter the gate of the Unending, to enjoy myself in the fields of the Illimitable. I will blend my light with that of the sun and moon, and will endure while heaven and earth endure. If men agree with my views, I will be unconscious of it; if they keep far apart from them, I will be unconscious of it; they may all die, and I will abide alone!'

5. Yün Kiang, rambling to the east, having been borne along on a gentle breeze, suddenly encountered Hung Mung, who was rambling about, slapping his buttocks and hopping like a bird. Amazed at the sight, Yün Kiang stood reverentially, and said to the other, 'Venerable Sir, who are you? and why are you doing this ?' Hung Mung went on slapping his buttocks and hopping like a bird, but replied, 'I am enjoying myself.' Yün Kiang said, 'I wish to ask you a question.' Hung Mung lifted up his head, looked at the stranger, and said, 'Pooh!' Yün Kiang, however, continued, 'The breath of heaven is out of harmony; the breath of earth is bound up; the six elemental influences do not act in concord; the four seasons do not observe their proper times. Now I wish to blend together the essential qualities of those six influences in order to nourish all living things;-- how shall I go about it?' Hung Mung slapped his buttocks, hopped about, and shook his head, saying, 'I do not know; I do not know!'

Yün Kiang could not pursue his question; but three years afterwards, when (again) rambling in the east, as he was passing by the wild of Sung, he happened to meet Hung Mung. Delighted with the rencontre, he hastened to him, and said, 'Have you forgotten me, 0 Heaven? Have you forgotten me, 0 Heaven?' At the same time, he bowed twice with his head to the ground, wishing to receive his instructions. Hung Mung said, 'Wandering listlessly about, I know not what I seek; carried on by a wild impulse, I know not where I am going. I wander about in the strange manner (which you have seen), and see that nothing proceeds without method and order;-- what more should I know?' Yün Kiang replied, 'I also seem carried on by an aimless influence, and yet the people follow me wherever I go. I cannot help their doing so. But now as they thus imitate me, I wish to hear a word from you (in the case).' The other said,

'What disturbs the regular method of Heaven, comes into collision with the nature of things, prevents the accomplishment of the mysterious (operation of) Heaven, scatters the herds of animals, makes the birds all sing at night, is calamitous to vegetation, and disastrous to all insects;-- all this is owing, I conceive, to the error of governing men.' 'What then,' said Yün Kiang, 'shall I do?' 'Ah,' said the other, 'you will only injure them! I will leave you in my dancing way, and return to my place.' Yün Kiang rejoined, 'It has been a difficult thing to get this meeting with you, 0 Heaven! I should like to hear from you a word (more).' Hung Mung said,

'Ah! your mind (needs to be) nourished. Do you only take the position of doing nothing, and things will of themselves become transformed. Neglect your body; cast out from you your power of hearing and sight; forget what you have in common with things; cultivate a grand similarity with the chaos of the plastic ether; unloose your mind; set your spirit free; be still as if you had no soul. Of all the multitude of things every one returns to its root. Every one returns to its root, and does not know (that it is doing so). They all are as in the state of chaos, and during all their existence they do not leave it. If they knew (that they were returning to their root), they would be (consciously) leaving it. They do not ask its name; they do not seek to spy out their nature; and thus it is that things come to life of themselves.'

Yün Kiang said, 'Heaven, you have conferred on me (the knowledge of) your operation, and revealed to me the mystery of it. All my life I had been seeking for it, and now I have obtained it.' He then bowed twice, with his head to the ground, arose, took his leave, and walked away.

6. The ordinary men of the world all rejoice in men's agreeing with themselves, and dislike men's being different from themselves. This rejoicing and this dislike arise from their being bent on making themselves distinguished above all others. But have they who have this object at heart so risen out above all others? They depend on them to rest quietly (in the position which they desire), and their knowledge is not equal to the multitude of the arts of all those others! When they wish again to administer a state for its ruler, they proceed to employ all the methods which the kings of the three dynasties considered profitable without seeing the evils of such a course. This is to make the state depend on the peradventure of their luck. But how seldom it is that that peradventure does not issue in the ruin of the state! Not once in ten thousand instances will such men preserve a state. Not once will they succeed, and in more than ten thousand cases will they ruin it. Alas that the possessors of territory,-- (the rulers of states),-- should not know the danger (of employing such men)! Now the possessors of territory possess the greatest of (all) things. Possessing the greatest of all things,-- (possessing, that is, men),-- they should not

try to deal with them as (simply) things. And it is he who is not a thing (himself) that is therefore able to deal with (all) things as they severally require. When (a ruler) clearly understands that he who should so deal with all things is not a thing himself, will he only rule the kingdom? He will go out and in throughout the universe (at his pleasure); he will roam over the nine regions, alone in going, alone in coming. Him we call the sole possessor (of this ability); and the sole possessor (of this ability) is what is called the noblest of all.

The teaching of (this) great man goes forth as the shadow from the substance, as the echo responds to the sound. When questioned, he responds, exhausting (from his own stores) all that is in the (enquirer's) mind, as if front to front with all under heaven. His resting-place gives forth no sound; his sphere of activity has no restriction of place, He conducts every one to his proper goal, proceeding to it and bringing him back to it as by his own movement. His movements have no trace; his going forth and his re-enterings have no deviation; his course is like that of the sun without beginning (or ending).

If you would praise or discourse about his personality, he is united with the great community of existences. He belongs to that great community, and has no individual self. Having no individual self, how should he have anything that can be called his? If you look at those who have what they call their own, they are the superior men of former times; if you look at him who has nothing of the kind, he is the friend of heaven and earth.

7. Mean, and yet demanding to be allowed their free course;-- such are Things. Low, and yet requiring to be relied on;-- such are the People. Hidden (as to their issues), and yet requiring to be done;-- such are Affairs. Coarse, and yet necessary to be set forth;-- such are Laws. Remote, and yet necessary to have dwelling (in one's self);-- such is Righteousness. Near, and yet necessary to be widely extended;-- such is Benevolence. Restrictive, and yet necessary to be multiplied;-- such are Ceremonies. Lodged in the centre, and yet requiring to be exalted;-- such is Virtue. Always One, and yet requiring to be modified;-- such is the Tâo. Spirit like, and yet requiring to be exercised;-- such is Heaven.

Therefore the sages contemplated Heaven, but did not assist It. They tried to perfect their virtue, but did not allow it to embarrass them. They proceeded according to the Tâo, but did not lay any plans. They associated benevolence (with all their doings), but did not rely on it. They pursued righteousness extensively, but did not try to accumulate it. They responded to ceremonies, but did not conceal (their opinion as to the troublesomeness of them). They engaged in affairs as they occurred, and did not decline them. They strove to render their laws uniform, but (feared that confusion) might arise from them. They relied upon the people, and did not set light by them. They depended on things as their instruments, and did not discard them.

They did not think things equal to what they employed them for, but yet they did not see that they could do without employing them. Those who do not understand Heaven are not pure in their virtue. Those who do not comprehend the Tâo have no course which they can pursue successfully. Alas for them who do not clearly understand the Tâo!

What is it that we call the Tâo? There is the Tâo, or Way of Heaven; and there is the Tâo, or Way of Man. Doing nothing and yet attracting all honour is the Way of Heaven; Doing and being embarrassed thereby is the Way of Man. It is the Way of Heaven that plays the part of the Lord; it is the Way of Man that plays the part of the Servant. The Way of Heaven and the Way of Man are far apart. They should be clearly distinguished from each other.

Thien Tî, or 'Heaven and Earth.'

1. Notwithstanding the greatness of heaven and earth, their transforming power proceeds from one lathe; notwithstanding the number of the myriad things, the government of them is one and the same; notwithstanding the multitude of mankind, the lord of them is their (one) ruler. The ruler's (course) should proceed from the qualities (of the Tâo) and be perfected by Heaven, when it is so, it is called 'Mysterious and Sublime.' The ancients ruled the world by doing nothing;-- simply by this attribute of Heaven.

If we look at their words in the light of the Tâo, (we see that) the appellation for the ruler of the world was correctly assigned; if we look in the same light at the distinctions which they instituted, (we see that) the separation of ruler and ministers was right; if we look at the abilities which they called forth in the same light, (we see that the duties of) all the offices were well performed; and if we look generally in the same way at all things, (we see that) their response (to this rule) was complete. Therefore that which pervades (the action of) Heaven and Earth is (this one) attribute; that which operates in all things is (this one) course; that by which their superiors govern the people is the business (of the various departments); and that by which aptitude is given to ability is skill. The skill was manifested in all the (departments of) business; those departments were all administered in righteousness; the righteousness was (the outflow of) the natural virtue; the virtue was manifested according to the Tâo; and the Tâo was according to (the pattern of) Heaven.

Hence it is said, 'The ancients who had the nourishment of the world wished for nothing and the world had enough; they did nothing and all things were transformed; their stillness was abysmal, and the people were all composed.' The Record says, 'When the one (Tâo) pervades it, all business is completed. When the mind gets to be free from all aim, even the Spirits submit.'

2. The Master said, 'It is the Tâo that overspreads and sustains all things. How great It is in Its overflowing influence! The Superior man ought by all means to remove from his mind (all that is contrary to It).

Acting without action is what is called Heaven(-like). Speech coming forth of itself is what is called (a mark of) the (true) Virtue. Loving men and benefiting things is what is called Benevolence. Seeing wherein things that are different yet agree is what is called being Great. Conduct free from the ambition of being distinguished above others is what is called being

Generous. The possession in himself of a myriad points of difference is what is called being Rich. Therefore to hold fast the natural attributes is what is called the Guiding Line (of government); the perfecting of those attributes is what is called its

Establishment; accordance with the Tâo is what is called being Complete; and not allowing anything external to affect the will is what is called being Perfect. When the Superior man understands these ten things, he keeps all matters as it were sheathed in himself, showing the greatness of his mind; and through the outflow of his doings, all things move (and come to him). Being such, he lets the gold lie hid in the hill, and the pearls in the deep; he considers not property or money to be any gain; he keeps aloof from riches and honours; he rejoices not in long life, and grieves not for early death; he does not account prosperity a glory, nor is ashamed of indigence; he would not grasp at the gain of the whole world to be held as his own private portion; he would not desire to rule over the whole world as his own private distinction. His distinction is in understanding that all things belong to the one treasury, and that death and life should be viewed in the same way.

3. The Master said, 'How still and deep is the place where the Tâo resides! How limpid is its purity! Metal and stone without It would give forth no sound. They have indeed the (power of) sound (in them), but if they be not struck, they do not emit it. Who can determine (the qualities that are in) all things?

'The man of kingly qualities holds on his way unoccupied, and is ashamed to busy himself with (the conduct of) affairs. He establishes himself in (what is) the root and source (of his capacity), and his wisdom grows to be spirit-like. In this way his attributes become more and more great, and when his mind goes forth, whatever things come in his way, it lays hold of them (and deals with them). Thus, if there were not the Tâo, the bodily form would not have life, and its life, without the attributes (of the Tâo), would not be manifested. Is not he who preserves the body and gives the fullest development to the life, who establishes the attributes of the Tâo and clearly displays It, possessed of kingly qualities? How majestic is he in his sudden issuings forth, and in his unexpected movements, when all things follow him!-- This we call the man whose qualities fit him to rule.'

He sees where there is the deepest obscurity; he hears where there is no sound. In the midst of the deepest obscurity, he alone sees and can distinguish (various objects); in the midst of a soundless (abyss), he alone can hear a harmony (of notes). Therefore where one deep is succeeded by a greater, he can people all with things; where one mysterious range is followed by another that is more so, he can lay hold of the subtlest character of each. In this way in his intercourse with all things, while he is farthest from having anything, he can yet give to them what they seek; while he is always hurrying forth, he yet returns to his resting-place; now large, now small; now long, now short; now distant, now near.'

4. Hwang-Tî, enjoying himself on the north of the Red-water, ascended to the height of the Khwan-lun (mountain), and having looked towards the south, was returning home, when he lost his dark-coloured pearl. He employed Wisdom to search for it, but he could not find it. He employed (the clear-sighted) Lî Kû to search for it, but he could not find it. He employed (the vehement debater) Khieh Khâu to search for it, but he could not find it. He then employed Purposeless, who found it; on which Hwang-Tî said, 'How strange that it was Purposeless who was able to find it!'

5. The teacher of Yâo was Hsü Yû; of Hsü Yû, Nieh Khüeh; of Nieh Khüeh, Wang Î; of Wang Î, Pheî-î. Yâo asked Hsü Yû, saying, 'Is Nieh Khüeh fit to be the correlate of Heaven? (If you think he is), I will avail myself of the services of Wang Î to constrain him (to take my place).' Hsü Yû replied, 'Such a measure would be hazardous, and full of peril to the kingdom! The character of Nieh Khüeh is this;-- he is acute, perspicacious, shrewd and knowing, ready in reply, sharp in retort, and hasty; his natural (endowments) surpass those of other men, but by his human qualities he seeks to obtain the Heavenly gift; he exercises his discrimination in suppressing his errors, but he does not know what is the source from which his errors arise. Make him the correlate of Heaven! He would employ the human qualities, so that no regard would be paid to the Heavenly gift. Moreover, he would assign different functions to the different parts of the one person. Moreover, honour would be given to knowledge, and he would have his plans take effect with the speed of fire. Moreover, he would be the slave of everything he initiated. Moreover, he would be embarrassed by things. Moreover, he would be looking all round for the response of things (to his measures). Moreover, he would be responding to the opinion of the multitude as to what was right. Moreover, he would be changing as things changed, and would not begin to have any principle of constancy. How can such a man be fit to be the correlate of Heaven? Nevertheless, as there are the smaller branches of a family and the common ancestor of all its branches, he might be the father of a branch, but not the father of the fathers of all the branches. Such government (as he would conduct) would lead to disorder. It would be calamity in one in the position of a minister, and ruin if he were in the position of the sovereign.'

6. Yâo was looking about him at Hwâ, the border-warden of which

said, 'Ha! the sage! Let me ask blessings on the sage! May he live long!' Yâo said, 'Hush!' but the other went on, 'May the sage become rich!' Yâo (again) said, 'Hush!' but (the warden) continued, 'May the sage have many sons!' When Yâo repeated his 'Hush,' the warden said, 'Long life, riches, and many sons are what men wish for;-- how is it that you alone do not wish for them?' Yâo replied, 'Many sons bring many fears; riches bring many troubles; and long life gives rise to many obloquies. These three things do not help to nourish virtue; and therefore I wish to decline them.' The warden rejoined, 'At first I considered you to be a sage; now I see in you only a Superior man. Heaven, in producing the myriads of the people, is sure to have appointed for them their several offices. If you had many sons, and gave them (all their) offices, what would you have to fear? If you had riches, and made other men share them with you, what trouble would you have? The sage finds his dwelling like the quail (without any choice of its own), and is fed like the fledgling; he is like the bird which passes on (through the air), and leaves no trace (of its flight). When good order prevails in the world, he shares in the general prosperity. When there is no such order, he cultivates his virtue, and seeks to be unoccupied. After a thousand years, tired of the world, he leaves it, and ascends among the immortals. He mounts on the white clouds, and arrives at the place of God. The three forms of evil do not reach him, his person is always free from misfortune;-- what obloquy has he to incur?'

With this the border-warden left him. Yâo followed him, saying, 'I beg to ask-- ;' but the other said, 'Begone!'

7. When Yâo was ruling the world, Po-khang Tsze-kâo was appointed by him prince of one of the states. From Yâo (afterwards) the throne passed to Shun, and from Shun (again) to Yü; and (then) Po-khang Tsze-kâo resigned his principality and began to cultivate the ground. Yü went to see him, and found him ploughing in the open country. Hurrying to him, and bowing low in acknowledgment of his superiority, Yü then stood up, and asked him, saying, 'Formerly, when Yâo was ruling the world, you, Sir, were appointed prince of a state. He gave his sovereignty to Shun, and Shun gave his to me, when you, Sir, resigned your dignity, and are (now) ploughing (here);-- I venture to ask the reason of your conduct.'

Tsze-kâo said, 'When Yâo ruled the world, the people stimulated one another (to what was right) without his offering them rewards, and stood in awe (of doing wrong) without his threatening them with punishments. Now you employ both rewards and punishments, and the people notwithstanding are not good. Their virtue will from this time decay; punishments will from this time prevail; the disorder of future ages will from this time begin. Why do you, my master, not go away, and not interrupt my work?' With this he resumed his ploughing with his head bent down, and did not (again) look round.

8. In the Grand Beginning (of all things) there was nothing in all
the vacancy of space; there was nothing that could be named. It was in
this state that there arose the first existence;-- the first existence, but still
without bodily shape. From this things could then be produced, (receiving) what we call their proper character. That which had no bodily shape
was divided; and then without intermission there was what we call the
process of conferring. (The two processes) continuing in operation,
things were produced. As things were completed, there were produced
the distinguishing lines of each, which we call the bodily shape. That
shape was the body preserving in it the spirit, and each had its peculiar
manifestation, which we call its Nature. When the Nature has been cultivated, it returns to its proper character; and when that has been fully
reached, there is the same condition as at the Beginning. That sameness
is pure vacancy, and the vacancy is great. It is like the closing of the beak
and silencing the singing (of a bird). That closing and silencing is like
the union of heaven and earth (at the beginning). The union, effected, as
it is, might seem to indicate stupidity or darkness, but it is what we call
the 'mysterious quality' (existing at the beginning); it is the same as the
Grand Submission (to the Natural Course).

9. The Master asked Lâo Tan, saying, 'Some men regulate the Tâo
(as by a law), which they have only to follow;-- (a thing, they say,) is
admissible or it is inadmissible; it is so, or it is not so. (They are like) the
sophists who say that they can distinguish what is hard and what is white
as clearly as if the objects were houses suspended in the sky. Can such
men be said to be sages?' The reply was, 'They are like the busy under-
lings of a court, who toil their bodies and distress their minds with their
various artifices;-- dogs, (employed) to their sorrow to catch the yak, or
monkeys that are brought from their forests (for their tricksiness). Khiû,
I tell you this;-- it is what you cannot hear, and what you cannot speak
of:-- Of those who have their heads and feet, and yet have neither minds
nor ears, there are multitudes; while of those who have their bodies, and
at the same time preserve that which has no bodily form or shape, there
are really none. It is not in their movements or stoppages, their dying or
living, their falling and rising again, that this is to be found. The regulation of the course lies in (their dealing with) the human element in them.
When they have forgotten external things, and have also forgotten the
heavenly element in them, they may be named men who have forgotten
themselves. The man who has forgotten himself is he of whom it is said
that he has become identified with Heaven.'

10. At an interview with Kî Khêh, Kiang-lü Mien said to him, 'Our
ruler of Lû asked to receive my instructions. I declined, on the ground that

I had not received any message for him. Afterwards, however, I told him
(my thoughts). I do not know whether (what I said) was right or not, and
I beg to repeat it to you. I said to him, "You must strive to be courteous
and to exercise self-restraint; you must distinguish the public-spirited
and loyal, and repress the cringing and selfish;-- who among the people
will in that case dare not to be in harmony with you?"' Kî Khêh laughed
quietly and said, 'Your words, my master, as a description of the right
course for a Tî or King, were like the threatening movement of its arms
by a mantis which would thereby stop the advance of a carriage;-- inad-
equate to accomplish your object. And moreover, if he guided himself
by your directions, it would be as if he were to increase the dangerous
height of his towers and add to the number of his valuables collected in
them;-- the multitudes (of the people) would leave their (old) ways, and
bend their steps in the same direction.'

Kiang-lü Mien was awe-struck, and said in his fright, 'I am startled
by your words, Master, nevertheless, I should like to hear you describe
the influence (which a ruler should exert).' The other said, 'If a great sage
ruled the kingdom, he would stimulate the minds of the people, and cause
them to carry out his instructions fully, and change their manners; he
would take their minds which had become evil and violent and extinguish
them, carrying them all forward to act in accordance with the (good) will
belonging to them as individuals, as if they did it of themselves from their
nature, while they knew not what it was that made them do so. Would
such an one be willing to lookup to Yâo and Shun in their instruction
of the people as his elder brothers? He would treat them as his juniors,
belonging himself to the period of the original plastic ether. His wish
would be that all should agree with the virtue (of that early period), and
quietly rest in it.'

11. Tsze-kung had been rambling in the south in Khû, and was
returning to Tsin. As he passed (a place) on the north of the Han, he saw
an old man who was going to work on his vegetable garden. He had dug
his channels, gone to the well, and was bringing from it in his arms a jar
of water to pour into them. Toiling away, he expended a great deal of
strength, but the result which he accomplished was very small. Tsze-kung
said to him, 'There is a contrivance here, by means of which a hundred
plots of ground may be irrigated in one day. With the expenditure of a
very little strength, the result accomplished is great. Would you, Master,
not like (to try it)?' The gardener looked up at him, and said, 'How does it
work?' Tsze-kung said, 'It is a lever made of wood, heavy behind, and light
in front. It raises the water as quickly as you could do with your hand, or
as it bubbles over from a boiler. Its name is a shadoof.' The gardener put
on an angry look, laughed, and said, 'I have heard from my teacher that,

where there are ingenious contrivances, there are sure to be subtle doings; and that, where there are subtle doings, there is sure to be a scheming mind. But, when there is a scheming mind in the breast, its pure simplicity is impaired. When this pure simplicity is impaired, the spirit becomes unsettled, and the unsettled spirit is not the proper residence of the Tâo. It is not that I do not know (the contrivance which you mention), but I should be ashamed to use it.'

(At these words) Tsze-kung looked blank and ashamed; he hung down his head, and made no reply. After an interval, the gardener said to him, 'Who are you, Sir?' 'A disciple of Khung Khiû,' was the reply. The other continued, 'Are you not the scholar whose great learning makes you comparable to a sage, who make it your boast that you surpass all others, who sing melancholy ditties all by yourself, thus purchasing a famous reputation throughout the kingdom? If you would (only) forget the energy of your spirit, and neglect the care of your body, you might approximate (to the Tâo). But while you cannot regulate yourself, what leisure have you to be regulating the world? Go on your way, Sir, and do not interrupt my work.'

Tsze-kung shrunk back abashed, and turned pale. He was perturbed, and lost his self-possession, nor did he recover it, till he had walked a distance of thirty lî. His disciples then said, 'Who was that man? Why, Master, when you saw him, did you change your bearing, and become pale, so that you have been all day without returning to yourself?' He replied to them, 'Formerly I thought that there was but one man in the world, and did not know that there was this man. I have heard the Master say that to seek for the means of conducting his undertakings so that his success in carrying them out may be complete, and how by the employment of a little strength great results may be obtained, is the way of the sage. Now (I perceive that) it is not so at all. They who hold fast and cleave to the Tâo are complete in the qualities belonging to it. Complete in those qualities, they are complete in their bodies. Complete in their bodies, they are complete in their spirits. To be complete in spirit is the way of the sage. (Such men) live in the world in closest union with the people, going along with them, but they do not know where they are going. Vast and complete is their simplicity! Success, gain, and ingenious contrivances, and artful cleverness, indicate (in their opinion) a forgetfulness of the (proper) mind of man. These men will not go where their mind does not carry them, and will do nothing of which their mind does not approve. Though all the world should praise them, they would (only) get what they think should be loftily disregarded; and though all the world should blame them, they would but lose (what they think) fortuitous and not to be received;-- the world's blame and praise can do them neither benefit nor injury. Such men may be described as possessing all the attributes (of the Tâo), while I can only be called one of those who are like the waves carried about by the wind.' When he returned to Lû, (Tsze-kung) reported the interview and conversation to Confucius, who said, 'The man makes a pretence of cultivating the arts of the Embryonic Age. He knows the first thing, but not the sequel to it. He regulates what is internal in himself, but not what is external to himself. If he had intelligence enough to be entirely unsophisticated, and by doing nothing to seek to return to the normal simplicity, embodying (the instincts of) his nature, and keeping his spirit (as it were) in his arms, so enjoying himself in the common ways, you might then indeed be afraid of him! But what should you and I find in the arts of the embryonic time, worth our knowing?'

12. Kun Mâng, on his way to the ocean, met with Yüan Fung on the shore of the eastern sea, and was asked by him where he was going. 'I am going,' he replied, 'to the ocean;' and the other again asked, 'What for?' Kun Mâng said, 'Such is the nature of the ocean that the waters which flow into it can never fill it, nor those which flow from it exhaust it. I will enjoy myself, rambling by it.' Yüan Fung replied, 'Have you no thoughts about mankind? I should like to hear from you about sagely government.' Kun Mâng said, 'Under the government of sages, all offices are distributed according to the fitness of their nature; all appointments are made according to the ability of the men; whatever is done is after a complete survey of all circumstances; actions and words proceed from the inner impulse, and the whole world is transformed. Wherever their hands are pointed and their looks directed, from all quarters the people are all sure to come (to do what they desire):-- this is what is called government by sages.'

'I should like to hear about (the government of) the kindly, virtuous men,' (continued Yüan Fung). The reply was, 'Under the government of the virtuous, when quietly occupying (their place), they have no thought, and, when they act, they have no anxiety; they do not keep stored (in their minds) what is right and what is wrong, what is good and what is bad. They share their benefits among all within the four seas, and this produces what is called (the state of) satisfaction; they dispense their gifts to all, and this produces what is called (the state of) rest. (The people) grieve (on their death) like babies who have lost their mothers, and are perplexed like travellers who have lost their way. They have a superabundance of wealth and all necessaries, and they know not whence it comes; they have a sufficiency of food and drink, and they know not from whom they get it:-- such are the appearances (under the government) of the kindly and virtuous.'

'I should like to hear about (the government of) the spirit-like men,' (continued Yüan Fung once more). The reply was, 'Men of the highest spirit-like qualities mount up on the light, and (the limitations of) the body vanish. This we call being bright and ethereal. They carry out to the utmost the powers with which they are endowed, and have not a single attribute unexhausted. Their joy is that of heaven and earth, and all embarrassments of affairs melt away and disappear; all things return to their proper nature:-- and this is what is called (the state of) chaotic obscurity.'

13. Man Wû-kwei and Khih-kang Man-khî had been looking at the army of king Wû, when the latter said, 'It is because he was not born in the time of the Lord of Yü, that therefore he is involved in this trouble (of war).' Man Wû-kwei replied, 'Was it when the kingdom was in good order, that the Lord of Yu governed it? or was it after it had become disordered that he governed it?' The other said, 'That the kingdom be in a condition of good order, is what (all) desire, and (in that case) what necessity would there be to say anything about the Lord of Yü? He had medicine for sores; false hair for the bald; and healing for those who were ill:-- he was like the filial son carrying in the medicine to cure his kind father, with every sign of distress in his countenance. A sage would be ashamed (of such a thing).

'In the age of perfect virtue they attached no value to wisdom, nor employed men of ability. Superiors were (but) as the higher branches of a tree; and the people were like the deer of the wild. They were upright and correct, without knowing that to be so was Righteousness; they loved one another, without knowing that to do so was Benevolence; they were honest and leal-hearted, without knowing that it was Loyalty; they fulfilled their engagements, without knowing that to do so was Good Faith; in their simple movements they employed the services of one another, without thinking that they were conferring or receiving any gift. Therefore their actions left no trace, and there was no record of their affairs.'

14. The filial son who does not flatter his father, and the loyal minister who does not fawn on his ruler, are the highest examples of a minister and a son. When a son assents to all that his father says, and approves of all that his father does, common opinion pronounces him an unworthy son; when a minister assents to all that his ruler says, and approves of all that his ruler does, common opinion pronounces him an unworthy minister. Nor does any one reflect that this view is necessarily correct. But when common opinion (itself) affirms anything and men therefore assent to it, or counts anything good and men also approve of it, then it is not said that they are mere consenters and flatterers;-- is common opinion then more authoritative than a father, or more to be honoured than a ruler? Tell a man that he is merely following (the opinions) of another, or that he is a flatterer of others, and at once he flushes with anger. And yet all

his life he is merely following others, and flattering them. His illustrations are made to agree with theirs; his phrases are glossed:-- to win the approbation of the multitudes. From first to last, from beginning to end, he finds no fault with their views. He will let his robes hang down, display the colours on them, and arrange his movements and bearing, so as to win the favour of his age, and yet not call himself a flatterer. He is but a follower of those others, approving and disapproving as they do, and yet he will not say that he is one of them. This is the height of stupidity.

He who knows his stupidity is not very stupid; he who knows that he is under a delusion is not greatly deluded. He who is greatly deluded will never shake the delusion off; he who is very stupid will all his life not become intelligent. If three men be walking together, and (only) one of them be under a delusion (as to their way), they may yet reach their goal, the deluded being the fewer; but if two of them be under the delusion, they will not do so, the deluded being the majority. At the present time, when the whole world is under a delusion, though I pray men to go in the right direction, I cannot make them do so;-- is it not a sad case?

Grand music does not penetrate the ears of villagers; but if they hear 'The Breaking of the Willow,' or 'The Bright Flowers,' they will roar with laughter. So it is that lofty words do not remain in the minds of the multitude, and that perfect words are not heard, because the vulgar words predominate. By two earthenware instruments the (music of) a bell will be confused, and the pleasure that it would afford cannot be obtained. At the present time the whole world is under a delusion, and though I wish to go in a certain direction, how can I succeed in doing so? Knowing that I cannot do so, if I were to try to force my way, that would be another delusion. Therefore my best course is to let my purpose go, and no more pursue it. If I do not pursue it, whom shall I have to share in my sorrow?

If an ugly man have a son born to him at midnight, he hastens with a light to look at it. Very eagerly he does so, only afraid that it may be like himself.

15. From a tree a hundred years old a portion shall be cut and fashioned into a sacrificial vase, with the bull figured on it, which is ornamented further with green and yellow, while the rest (of that portion) is cut away and thrown into a ditch. If now we compare the sacrificial vase with what was thrown into the ditch, there will be a difference between them as respects their beauty and ugliness; but they both agree in having lost the (proper) nature of the wood. So in respect of their practice of righteousness there is a difference between (the robber) Kih on the one hand, and Tsang (Sh~in) or Shih (Tshiü) on the other; but they all agree

in having lost (the proper qualities of) their nature.

Now there are five things which produce (in men) the loss of their (proper) nature. The first is (their fondness for) the five colours which disorder the eye, and take from it its (proper) clearness of vision; the second is (their fondness for) the five notes (of music), which disorder the ear and take from it its (proper) power of hearing; the third is (their fondness for) the five odours which penetrate the nostrils, and produce a feeling of distress all over the forehead; the fourth is (their fondness for) the five flavours, which deaden the mouth, and pervert its sense of taste; the fifth is their preferences and dislikes, which unsettle the mind, and cause the nature to go flying about. These five things are all injurious to the life; and now Yang and Mo begin to stretch forward from their different standpoints, each thinking that he has hit on (the proper course for men).

But the courses they have hit on are not what I call the proper course. What they have hit on (only) leads to distress;-- can they have hit on what is the right thing? If they have, we may say that the dove in a cage has found the right thing for it. Moreover, those preferences and dislikes, that (fondness for) music and colours, serve but to pile up fuel (in their breasts); while their caps of leather, the bonnet with kingfishers' plumes, the memorandum tablets which they carry, and their long girdles, serve but as restraints on their persons. Thus inwardly stuffed full as a hole for fuel, and outwardly fast bound with cords, when they look quietly round from out of their bondage, and think they have got all they could desire, they are no better than criminals whose arms are tied together, and their fingers subjected to the screw, or than tigers and leopards in sacks or cages, and yet thinking that they have got (all they could wish).

Thien Tâo, or 'The Way of Heaven.'

1. The Way of Heaven operates (unceasingly), and leaves no accumulation (of its influence) in any particular place, so that all things are brought to perfection by it; so does the Way of the Tîs operate, and all under the sky turn to them (as their directors); so also does the Way of the Sages operate, and all within the seas submit to them. Those who clearly understand (the Way of) Heaven, who are in sympathy with (that of) the sages, and familiar through the universe and in the four quarters (of the earth) with the work of the Tîs and the kings, yet act spontaneously from themselves:-- with the appearance of being ignorant they are yet entirely still.

The stillness of the sages does not belong to them as a consequence of their skilful ability; all things are not able to disturb their minds;-- it is on this account that they are still. When water is still, its clearness shows the beard and eyebrows (of him who looks into it). It is a perfect Level, and the greatest artificer takes his rule from it. Such is the clearness of still water, and how much greater is that of the human Spirit! The still mind of the sage is the mirror of heaven and earth, the glass of all things.

Vacancy, stillness, placidity, tastelessness, quietude, silence, and non-action;-- this is the Level of heaven and earth, and the perfection of the Tâo and its characteristics. Therefore the Tîs, Kings, and Sages found in this their resting-place. Resting here, they were vacant; from their vacancy came fullness; from their fullness came the nice distinctions (of things). From their vacancy came stillness; that stillness was followed by movement; their movements were successful. From their stillness came their non-action. Doing-nothing, they devolved the cares of office on their employés, Doing-nothing was accompanied by the feeling of satisfaction. Where there is that feeling of satisfaction, anxieties and troubles find no place; and the years of life are many.

Vacancy, stillness, placidity, tastelessness, quietude, silence, and doing-nothing are the root of all things. When this is understood, we find such a ruler on the throne as Yâo, and such a minister as Shun. When with this a high position is occupied, we find the attributes of the Tîs and kings,-- the sons of Heaven; with this in a low position, we find the mysterious sages, the uncrowned kings, with their ways. With this retiring (from public life), and enjoying themselves at leisure, we find the scholars who dwell by the rivers and seas, among the hills and forests, all submissive to it; with this coming forward to active life and comforting their age, their merit is great, and their fame is distinguished;-- and all the world becomes united in one.

2. (Such men) by their stillness become sages; and by their movement, kings. Doing-nothing, they are honoured; in their plain simplicity, no one in the world can strive with them (for the palm of) excellence. The clear understanding of the virtue of Heaven and Earth is what is called 'The Great Root,' and 'The Great Origin;'-- they who have it are in harmony with Heaven, and so they produce all equable arrangements in the world;-- they are those who are in harmony with men. Being in harmony with men is called the joy of men; being in harmony with Heaven is called the joy of Heaven. Kwang-tsze said, 'My Master! my Master! He shall hash and blend all things in mass without being cruel; he shall dispense his favours to all ages without being benevolent. He is older than the highest antiquity, and yet is not old. He overspreads the heavens and sustains the earth; from him is the carving of all forms without any artful skill! This is what is called the Joy of Heaven. Hence it is said, "Those who know the joy of Heaven during their life, act like Heaven, and at death undergo transformation like (other) things; in their stillness they possess the quality of the Yin, and in their movement they flow abroad as the Yang. Therefore he who knows the Joy of Heaven has no murmuring against Heaven, nor any fault-finding with men; and suffers no embarrassment from things, nor any reproof from ghosts. Hence it is said, 'His movements are those of Heaven; his stillness is that of Earth; his whole mind is fixed, and he rules over the world. The spirits of his dead do not come to scare him; he is not worn out by their souls. His words proceeding from his vacancy and stillness, yet reach to heaven and earth, and show a communication with all things:-- this is what is called the Joy of Heaven. This Joy of Heaven forms the mind of the sage whereby he nurtures all under the sky."'"

3. It was the Way of the Tîs and Kings to regard Heaven and Earth as their Author, the Tâo and its characteristics as their Lord, and Doing-nothing as their constant rule. Doing-nothing, they could use the whole world in their service and might have done more; acting, they were not sufficient for the service required of them by the world. Hence the men of old held non-inaction in honour. When superiors do nothing and their inferiors also do nothing, inferiors and superiors possess the same virtue; and when inferiors and superiors possess the same virtue, there are none to act as ministers. When inferiors act, and their superiors also act, then superiors and inferiors possess the same Tâo; and when superiors and inferiors possess the same Tâo, there is none to preside as Lord. But that the superiors do nothing and yet thereby use the world in their service, and that the inferiors, while acting, be employed in the

service of the world, is an unchangeable principle. Therefore the ancient kings who presided over the world, though their knowledge embraced (all the operations of) Heaven and Earth, took no thought of their own about them; though their nice discrimination appreciated the fine fashioning of all things, they said not a word about it; though their power comprehended all within the seas, they did nothing themselves. Heaven produces nothing, yet all things experience their transformations; Earth effects no growth, yet all things receive their nurture; the Tîs and Kings did nothing, yet all the world testified their effective services. Hence it is said, 'There is nothing more spiritlike than Heaven; there is nothing richer than Earth; there are none greater than the Tîs and Kings.' Hence it is said (further), 'The attributes of the Tîs and kings corresponded to those of Heaven and Earth.' It was thus that they availed themselves of (the operations of) Heaven and Earth, carried all things on unceasingly (in their courses), and employed the various classes of men in their service.

4. Originating belongs to those in the higher position; details (of work) to those who are in the lower. The compendious decision belongs to the lord; the minutiae of execution, to his ministers. The direction of the three hosts and their men with the five weapons is but a trifling quality; rewards and penalties with their advantages and sufferings, and the inflictions of the five punishments are but trivial elements of instruction; ceremonies, laws, measures, and numbers, with all the minutiae of jurisprudence, are small matters in government; the notes of bells and drums, and the display of plumes and flags are the slightest things in music, and the various grades of the mourning garments are the most unimportant manifestations of grief. These five unimportant adjuncts required the operation of the excited spirit and the employment of the arts of the mind, to bring them into use. The men of old had them indeed, but they did not give them the first place.

The ruler precedes, and the minister follows; the father precedes, and the son follows; the elder brother precedes, and the younger follows; the senior precedes, and the junior follows; the male precedes, and the female follows; the husband precedes, and the wife follows.

This precedence of the more honourable and sequence of the meaner is seen in the (relative) action of heaven and earth, and hence the sages took them as their pattern. The more honourable position of heaven and the lower one of earth are equivalent to a designation of their spirit-like and intelligent qualities. The precedence of spring and summer and the sequence of autumn and winter mark the order of the four seasons. In the transformations and growth of all things, every bud and feature has its proper form; and in this we have their gradual maturing and decay, the constant flow of transformation and change. Thus since Heaven and Earth, which are most spirit-like, are distinguished as more honourable and less, and by precedence and sequence, how much more must we look for this in the ways of men! In the ancestral temple it is to kinship that honour is given; in court, to rank; in the neighbourhoods and districts, to age; in the conduct of affairs, to wisdom; such is the order in those great ways. If we speak of the course (to be pursued in them), and do not observe their order, we violate their course. If we speak of the course, and do not observe it, why do we apply that name to it?

5. Therefore the ancients who clearly understood the great Tâo first sought to apprehend what was meant by Heaven, and the Tâo and its characteristics came next. When this was apprehended, then came Benevolence and Righteousness. When these were apprehended, then came the Distinction of duties and the observance of them. This accomplished, there came objects and their names. After objects and their names, came the employment of men according to their qualities: on this there followed the examination of the men and of their work. This led to the approval or disapproval of them, which again was succeeded by the apportioning of rewards and penalties. After this the stupid and the intelligent understood what was required of them, and the honourable and the mean occupied their several positions. The good and the able, and those inferior to them, sincerely did their best. Their ability was distributed; the duties implied in their official names were fulfilled. In this way did they serve their superiors, nourish their inferiors, regulate things, and cultivate their persons. They did not call their knowledge and schemes into requisition; they were required to fall back upon (the method of) Heaven:-- this was what is called the Perfection of the Rule of Great Peace. Hence it is said in the Book, 'There are objects and there are their names.' Objects and their names the ancients had; but they did not put them in the foremost place.

When the ancients spoke of the Great Tâo, it was only after four other steps that they gave a place to 'Objects and their Names,' and after eight steps that they gave a place to 'Rewards and Penalties.' If they had all at once spoken of 'Objects and their Names,' they would have shown an ignorance of what is the Root (of government); if they had all at once spoken of 'Rewards and Penalties,' they would have shown an ignorance of the first steps of it. Those whose words are thus an inversion of the (proper) course, or in opposition to it, are (only fit to be) ruled by others;-- how can they rule others? To speak all at once of 'Objects and their Names,' and of 'Rewards and Penalties,' only shows that the speaker knows the instruments of government, but does not know the method of it, is fit to be used as an instrument in the world, but not fit to use others as his instruments:-- he is what we call a mere sophist, a man of one small idea. Ceremonies, laws, numbers, measures, with all the minutiae of jurisprudence, the ancients had; but it is by these that inferiors serve their superiors; it is not by them that those superiors nourish the world.

6. Anciently, Shun asked Yâo, saying, 'In what way does your Majesty by the Grace of Heaven exercise your mind?' The reply was, 'I simply show no arrogance towards the helpless; I do not neglect the poor people; I grieve for those who die; I love their infant children; and I compassionate their widows.' Shun rejoined, 'Admirable, as far as it goes; but it is not what is Great.' 'How then,' asked Yâo, 'do you think I should do?' Shun replied, 'When (a sovereign) possesses the virtue of Heaven, then when he shows himself in action, it is in stillness. The sun and moon (simply) shine, and the four seasons pursue their courses. So it is with the regular phenomena of day and night, and with the movement of the clouds by which the rain is distributed.' Yâo said, 'Then I have only been persistently troubling myself! What you wish is to be in harmony with Heaven, while I wish to be in harmony with men.' Now (the Way of) Heaven and Earth was much thought of of old, and Hwang-Tî, Yâo, and Shun united in admiring it. Hence the kings of the world of old did nothing, but tried to imitate that Way.

7. Confucius went to the west to deposit (some) writings in the library of Kâu, when Tsze-lû counselled him, saying, 'I have heard that the officer in charge of this Kang Repository of Kâu was one Lâo Tan, who has given up his office, and is living in his own house. As you, Master, wish to deposit these writings here, why not go to him, and obtain his help (to accomplish your object).' Confucius said, 'Good;' and he went and saw Lâo Tan, who refused his assistance. On this he proceeded to give an abstract of the Twelve Classics to bring the other over to his views. Lâo Tan, however, interrupted him while he was speaking, and said, 'This is too vague; let me hear the substance of them in brief.' Confucius said, 'The substance of them is occupied with Benevolence and Righteousness.' The other said, 'Let me ask whether you consider Benevolence and Righteousness to constitute the nature of man?' 'I do,' was the answer. 'If the superior man be not benevolent, he will not fulfil his character; if he be not righteous, he might as well not have been born. Benevolence and Righteousness are truly the nature of man.' Lâo Tan continued, 'Let me ask you what you mean by Benevolence and Righteousness.' Confucius said, 'To be in one's inmost heart in kindly sympathy with all things; to love all men; and to allow no selfish thoughts;-- this is the nature of Benevolence and Righteousness.' Lâo Tan exclaimed, 'Ah! you almost show your inferiority by such words! "To love all men!" is not that vague and extravagant? "To be seeking to allow no selfish thoughts!"-- that is selfishness! If you,

Master, wish men not to be without their (proper) shepherding, think of Heaven and Earth, which certainly pursue their invariable course; think of the sun and moon, which surely maintain their brightness; think of the stars in the zodiac, which preserve their order and courses; think of birds and beasts, which do not fail to collect together in their flocks and herds; and think of the trees, which do not fail to stand up (in their places). Do you, Master, imitate this way and carry it into practice; hurry on, following this course, and you will reach your end. Why must you further be vehement in putting forward your Benevolence and Righteousness, as if you were beating a drum, and seeking a fugitive son, (only making him run away the more)? Ah! Master, you are introducing disorder into the nature of man!'

8. Shih-khang Khî, having an interview with Lâo-tsze, asked him, saying, 'I heard, Master, that you were a sage, and I came here, wishing to see you, without grudging the length of the journey. During the stages of the hundred days, the soles of my feet became quite callous, but I did not dare to stop and rest. Now I perceive that you are not a sage. Because there was some rice left about the holes of the rats, you sent away your younger sister, which was unkind; when your food, whether raw or cooked, remains before you not all consumed, you keep on hoarding it up to any extent.' Lâ-tsze looked indifferent, and gave him no answer.

Next day Khî again saw Lâo-tsze, and said, 'Yesterday I taunted you; but to-day I have gone back to a better mood of mind. What is the cause (of the change)?' Lâo-tsze replied, 'I consider that I have freed myself from the trammels of claiming to be artfully knowing, spirit-like, and sage. Yesterday if you had called me an ox, you might have done so; or if you had called me a horse, you might have done so. If there be a reality (corresponding to men's ideas), and men give it a name, which another will not receive, he will in the sequel suffer the more. My manner was what I constantly observe;-- I did not put it on for the occasion.'

Shih-khang Khî sidled away out of Lâo's shadow; then he retraced his steps, advanced forward, and asked how he should cultivate himself. The reply was, 'Your demeanour is repelling; you stare with your eyes; your forehead is broad and yet tapering; you bark and growl with your mouth; your appearance is severe and pretentious; you are like a horse held by its tether, you would move, but are restrained, and (if let go) would start off like an arrow from a bow; you examine all the minutiae of a thing; your wisdom is artful, and yet you try to look at ease. All these are to be considered proofs of your want of sincerity. If on the borders one were to be found with them, he would be named a Thief.'

9. The Master said, 'The Tâo does not exhaust itself in what is greatest, nor is it ever absent from what is least; and therefore it is to be found complete and diffused in all things. How wide is its universal comprehension! How deep is its unfathomableness! The embodiment of its attributes in benevolence and righteousness is but a small result of its spirit-like (working); but it is only the perfect man who can determine this. The perfect man has (the charge of) the world;-- is not the charge great? and yet it is not sufficient to embarrass him. He wields the handle of power over the whole world, and yet it is nothing to him. His discrimination detects everything false, and no consideration of gain moves him. He penetrates to the truth of things, and can guard that which is fundamental. So it is that heaven and earth are external to him, and he views all things with indifference, and his spirit is never straitened by them. He has comprehended the Tâo, and is in harmony with its characteristics; he pushes back benevolence and righteousness (into their proper place), and deals with ceremonies and music as (simply) guests:-- yes, the mind of the perfect man determines all things aright.'

10. What the world thinks the most valuable exhibition of the Tâo is to be found in books. But books are only a collection of words. Words have what is valuable in them;-- what is valuable in words is the ideas they convey. But those ideas are a sequence of something else;-- and what that something else is cannot be conveyed by words. When the world, because of the value which it attaches to words, commits them to books, that for which it so values them may not deserve to be valued;-- because that which it values is not what is really valuable.

Thus it is that what we look at and can see is (only) the outward form and colour, and what we listen to and can hear is (only) names and sounds. Alas! that men of the world should think that form and colour, name and sound, should be sufficient to give them the real nature of the Tâ. The form and colour, the name and sound, are certainly not sufficient to convey its real nature; and so it is that 'the wise do not speak and those who do speak are not wise.' How should the world know that real nature?

Duke Hwan, seated above in his hall, was (once) reading a book, and the wheelwright Phien was making a wheel below it. Laying aside his hammer and chisel, Phien went up the steps, and said, 'I venture to ask your Grace what words you are reading?' The duke said, 'The words of the sages.' 'Are those sages alive?' Phien continued. 'They are dead,' was the reply. 'Then,' said the other, 'what you, my Ruler, are reading are only the dregs and sediments of those old men.' The duke said, 'How should you, a wheelwright, have anything to say about the book which I am reading? If you can explain yourself, very well; if you cannot, you shall, die!' The wheelwright said, 'Your servant will look at the thing from the point of view of his own art. In making a wheel, if I proceed gently, that is pleasant enough, but the workmanship is not strong; if I proceed violently, that is toilsome and the joinings do not fit. If the movements of my hand are neither (too) gentle nor (too) violent, the idea in my mind is realised. But I cannot tell (how to do this) by word of mouth; there is a knack in it. I cannot teach the knack to my son, nor can my son learn it from me. Thus it is that I am in my seventieth year, and am (still) making wheels in my old age. But these ancients, and what it was not possible for them to convey, are dead and gone:-- so then what you, my Ruler, are reading is but their dregs and sediments!'

Thien Yün, or 'The Revolution of Heaven.'

1. How (ceaselessly) heaven revolves! How (constantly) earth abides at rest! And do the sun and moon contend about their (respective) places? Who presides over and directs these (things)? Who binds and connects them together? Who is it that, without trouble or exertion on his part, causes and maintains them? Is it, perhaps, that there is some secret spring, in consequence of which they cannot be but as they are? Or is it, perhaps, that they move and turn as they do, and cannot stop of themselves? (Then) how the clouds become rain! And how the rain again forms the clouds! Who diffuses them so abundantly? Who is it that, without trouble or exertion on his part, produces this elemental enjoyment, and seems to stimulate it?

The winds rise in the north; one blows to the west, and another to the east; while some rise upwards, uncertain in their direction. By whose breathing are they produced? Who is it that, without any trouble and exertion of his own, effects all their undulations? I venture to ask their cause.

Wû-hsien Thiâo said, 'Come, and I will tell you. To heaven there belong the six Extreme Points, and the five Elements. When the Tîs and Kings acted in accordance with them, there was good government; when they acted contrary to them, there was evil. Observing the things (described) in the nine divisions (of the writing) of Lo, their government was perfected and their virtue was complete. They inspected and enlightened the kingdom beneath them, and all under the sky acknowledged and sustained them. Such was the condition under the august (sovereigns) and those before them.'

2. Tang, the chief administrator of Shang, asked Kwang-tsze about Benevolence, and the answer was, 'Wolves and tigers are benevolent.' 'What do you mean?' said Tang. Kwang-tsze replied, 'Father and son (among them) are affectionate to one another. Why should they be considered as not benevolent?' 'Allow me to ask about perfect benevolence,' pursued the other. Kwang-tsze said, 'Perfect benevolence does not admit (the feeling) of affection.' The minister said, 'I have heard that, without (the feeling of) affection there is no love, and without love there is not filial duty;-- is it permissible to say that the perfectly benevolent are not filial?' Kwang-tsze rejoined, 'That is not the way to put the case. Perfect Benevolence is the very highest thing;-- filial duty is by no means sufficient to describe it. The saying which you quote is not to the effect that (such benevolence) transcends filial duty;-- it does not refer to such duty at all.

One, travelling to the south, comes (at last) to Ying, and there, standing with his face to the north, he does not see mount Ming. Why does he not see it? Because he is so far from it. Hence it is said, "Filial duty as a part of reverence is easy, but filial duty as a part of love is difficult. If it be easy as a part of love, yet it is difficult to forget one's parents. It may be easy for me to forget my parents, but it is difficult to make my parents forget me. If it were easy to make my parents forget me, it is difficult for me to forget all men in the world. If it were easy to forget all men in the world, it is difficult to make them all forget me."

'This virtue might make one think light of Yâo and Shun, and not wish to be they. The profit and beneficial influences of it extend to a myriad ages, and no one in the world knows whence they come. How can you simply heave a great sigh, and speak (as you do) of benevolence and filial duty? Filial duty, fraternal respect, benevolence, righteousness, loyalty, sincerity, firmness, and purity;-- all these may be pressed into the service of this virtue, but they are far from sufficient to come up to it. Therefore it is said, "To him who has what is most noble, all the dignities of a state are as nothing; to him who has what is the greatest riches, all the wealth of a state is as nothing; to him who has all that he could wish, fame and praise are as nothing." It is thus that the Tâo admits of no substitute.'

3. Pei-min Khang asked Hwang-Tî, saying, 'You were celebrating, O Tî, a performance of the music of the Hsien-khih, in the open country near the Thung-thing lake. When I heard the first part of it, I was afraid; the next made me weary; and the last perplexed me. I became agitated and unable to speak, and lost my self-possession.' The Tî said, 'It was likely that it should so affect you! It was performed with (the instruments of) men, and all attuned according to (the influences of) Heaven. It proceeded according to (the principles of) propriety and righteousness, and was pervaded by (the idea of) the Grand Purity.

'The Perfect Music first had its response in the affairs of men, and was conformed to the principles of Heaven; it indicated the action of the five virtues, and corresponded to the spontaneity (apparent in nature). After this it showed the blended distinctions of the four seasons, and the grand harmony of all things;-- the succession of those seasons one after another, and the production of things in their proper order. Now it swelled, and now it died away, its peaceful and military strains clearly distinguished and given forth. Now it was clear, and now rough, as if the contracting and expanding of the elemental processes blended harmoniously (in its notes). Those notes then flowed away in waves of light, till, as when the hibernating insects first begin to move, I commanded the terrifying crash of thunder. Its end was marked by no formal conclusion, and it began again without any prelude. It seemed to die away, and then it burst into life; it came to a close, and then it rose again. So it went on regularly and inexhaustibly, and without the intervention of any pause:-- it was this which made you afraid.

'In the second part (of the performance), I made it describe the harmony of the Yin and Yang, and threw round it the brilliance of the sun and moon. Its notes were now short and now long, now soft and now hard. Their changes, however, were marked by an unbroken unity, though not dominated by a fixed regularity. They filled every valley and ravine; you might shut up every crevice, and guard your spirit (against their entrance), yet there was nothing but gave admission to them. Yea, those notes resounded slowly, and might have been pronounced high and clear. Hence the shades of the dead kept in their obscurity; the sun and moon, and all the stars of the zodiac, pursued their several courses. I made (my instruments) leave off, when (the performance) came to an end, and their (echoes) flowed on without stopping. You thought anxiously about it, and were not able to understand it; you looked for it, and were not able to see it; you pursued it, and were not able to reach it. All-amazed, you stood in the way all open around you, and then you leant against an old rotten dryandra-tree and hummed. The power of your eyes was exhausted by what you wished to see; your strength failed in your desire to pursue it, while I myself could not reach it. Your body was but so much empty vacancy while you endeavoured to retain your self-possession:-- it was that endeavour which made you weary.

'In the last part (of the performance), I employed notes which did not have that wearying effect. I blended them together as at the command of spontaneity. Hence they came as if following one another in confusion, like a clump of plants springing from one root, or like the music of a forest produced by no visible form. They spread themselves all around without leaving a trace (of their cause); and seemed to issue from deep obscurity where there was no sound. Their movements came from nowhere; their home was in the deep darkness;-- conditions which some would call death, and some life; some, the fruit, and some, (merely) the flower. Those notes, moving and flowing on, separating and shifting, and not following any regular sounds, the world might well have doubts about them, and refer them to the judgment of a sage, for the sages understand the nature of this music, and judge in accordance with the prescribed (spontaneity). While the spring of that spontaneity has not been touched, and yet the regulators of the five notes are all prepared;-- this is what is called the music of Heaven, delighting the mind without the use of words. Hence it is said in the eulogy of the Lord of Piâo, "You listen for it, and do not hear its sound; you look for it, and do not perceive its form; it fills heaven and earth; it envelopes all within the universe." You wished to hear it, but could not take it in; and therefore you were perplexed.

'I performed first the music calculated to awe; and you were frightened as if by a ghostly visitation. I followed it with that calculated to weary; and in your weariness you would have withdrawn. I concluded with that calculated to perplex; and in your perplexity you felt your stupidity. But that stupidity is akin to the Tâo; you may with it convey the Tâo in your person, and have it (ever) with you.'

4. When Confucius was travelling in the west in Wei, Yen Yüan asked the music-master Kin, saying, 'How is it, do you think, with the course of the Master?' The music-master replied, 'Alas! it is all over with your Master!' 'How so?' asked Yen Yüan; and the other said, 'Before the grass-dogs are set forth (at the sacrifice), they are deposited in a box or basket, and wrapt up with elegantly embroidered cloths, while the representative of the dead and the officer of prayer prepare themselves by fasting to present them. After they have been set forth, however, passers-by trample on their heads and backs, and the grass- cutters take and burn them in cooking. That is all they are good for. If one should again take them, replace them in the box or basket, wrap them up with embroidered cloths, and then in rambling, or abiding at the spot, should go to sleep under them, if he do not get (evil) dreams, he is sure to be often troubled with the nightmare. Now here is your Master in the same way taking the grass-dogs, presented by the ancient kings, and leading his disciples to wander or abide and sleep under them. Owing to this, the tree (beneath which they were practising ceremonies) in Sung was cut down; he was obliged to leave Wei; he was reduced to extremities in Shang and Kâu:-- were not those experiences like having (evil) dreams? He was kept in a state of siege between Khan and Tshâi, so that for seven days he had no cooked food to eat, and was in a situation between life and death:-- were not those experiences like the nightmare ?

'If you are travelling by water, your best plan is to use a boat; if by land, a carriage. Take a boat, which will go (easily) along on the water, and try to push it along on the land, and all your lifetime it will not go so much as a fathom or two:-- are not ancient time and the present time like the water and the dry land? and are not Kâu and Lû like the boat and the carriage? To seek now to practise (the old ways of) Kâu in Lû is like pushing along a boat on the dry land. It is only a toilsome labour, and has no success; he who does so is sure to meet with calamity. He has not learned that in handing down the arts (of one time) he is sure to be reduced to extremity in endeavouring to adapt them to the conditions (of another).

'And have you not seen the working of a shadoof? When (the rope of) it is pulled, it bends down; and when it is let go, it rises up. It is pulled by a man, and does not pull the man; and so, whether it bends down or rises up, it commits no offence against the man. In the same way the rules of propriety, righteousness, laws, and measures of the three Hwangs and five Tîs derived their excellence, not from their being the same as those of the present day, but from their (aptitude for) government. We may compare them to haws, pears, oranges, and pummeloes, which are different in flavour, but all suitable to be eaten. Just so it is that the rules of propriety, righteousness, laws, and measures, change according to the time.

'If now you take a monkey, and dress it in the robes of the duke of Kâu, it will bite and tear them, and will not be satisfied till it has got rid of them altogether. And if you look at the difference between antiquity and the present time it is as great as that between the monkey and the duke of Kâu. In the same way, when Hsî Shih was troubled in mind, she would knit her brows and frown on all in her neighbourhood. An ugly woman of the neighbourhood, seeing and admiring her beauty, went home, and also laying her hands on her heart proceeded to stare and frown on all around her. When the rich people of the village saw her, they shut fast their doors and would not go out; when the poor people saw her, they took their wives and children and ran away from her. The woman knew how to admire the frowning beauty, but she did not know how it was that she, though frowning, was beautiful. Alas! it is indeed all over with your Master!'

5. When Confucius was in his fifty-first year, he had not heard of the Tâo, and went south to Phei to see Lâo Tan, who said to him, 'You have come, Sir; have you? I have heard that you are the wisest man of the North; have you also got the Tâo?' 'Not yet,' was the reply; and the other went on, 'How have you sought it?' Confucius said, 'I sought it in measures and numbers, and after five years I had not got it.' 'And how then did you seek it?' 'I sought it in the Yin and Yang, and after twelve years I have not found it.' Lâo-tsze said, 'Just so! If the Tâo could be presented (to another), men would all present it to their rulers; if it could be served up (to others), men would all serve it up to their parents; if it could be told (to others), men would all tell it to their brothers; if it could be given to others, men would all give it to their sons and grandsons. The reason why it cannot be transmitted is no other but this,-- that if, within, there be not the presiding principle, it will not remain there, and if, outwardly, there be not the correct obedience, it will not be carried out. When that which is given out from the mind (in possession of it) is not received by the mind without, the sage will not give it out; and when, entering in from

without, there is no power in the receiving mind to entertain it, the sage will not permit it to lie hid there. Fame is a possession common to all; we should not seek to have much of it. Benevolence and righteousness were as the lodging-houses of the former kings; we should only rest in them for a night, and not occupy them for long. If men see us doing so, they will have much to say against us.

'The perfect men of old trod the path of benevolence as a path which they borrowed for the occasion, and dwelt in Righteousness as in a lodging which they used for a night. Thus they rambled in the vacancy of Untroubled Ease, found their food in the fields of Indifference, and stood in the gardens which they had not borrowed. Untroubled Ease requires the doing of nothing; Indifference is easily supplied with nourishment; not borrowing needs no outlay. The ancients called this the Enjoyment that Collects the True.

'Those who think that wealth is the proper thing for them cannot give up their revenues; those who seek distinction cannot give up the thought of fame; those who cleave to power cannot give the handle of it to others. While they hold their grasp of those things, they are afraid (of losing them). When they let them go, they are grieved; and they will not look at a single example, from which they might perceive the (folly) of their restless pursuits:-- such men are under the doom of Heaven.

'Hatred and kindness; taking and giving; reproof and instruction; death and life:-- these eight things are instruments of rectification, but only those are able to use them who do not obstinately refuse to comply with their great changes. Hence it is said, "Correction is Rectification." When the minds of some do not acknowledge this, it is because the gate of Heaven (in them) has not been opened.'

6. At an interview with Lâo Tan, Confucius spoke to him of benevolence and righteousness. Lâo Tan said, 'If you winnow chaff, and the dust gets into your eyes, then the places of heaven and earth and of the four cardinal points are all changed to you. If musquitoes or gadflies puncture your skin, it will keep you all the night from sleeping. But this painful iteration of benevolence and righteousness excites my mind and produces in it the greatest confusion. If you, Sir, would cause men not to lose their natural simplicity, and if you would also imitate the wind in its (unconstrained) movements, and stand forth in all the natural attributes belonging to you!-- why must you use so much energy, and carry a great drum to seek for the son whom you have lost? The snow-goose does not bathe every day to make itself white, nor the crow blacken itself every day to make itself black. The natural simplicity of their black and white does

not afford any ground for controversy; and the fame and praise which men like to contemplate do not make them greater than they naturally are. When the springs (supplying the pools) are dried up, the fishes huddle together on the dry land. Than that they should moisten one another there by their gasping, and keep one another wet by their milt, it would be better for them to forget one another in the rivers and lakes.'

From this interview with Lâo Tan, Confucius returned home, and for three days did not speak. His disciples (then) asked him, saying, 'Master, you have seen Lâo Tan; in what way might you admonish and correct him?' Confucius said, 'In him (I may say) that I have now seen the dragon. The dragon coils itself up, and there is its body; it unfolds itself and becomes the dragon complete. It rides on the cloudy air, and is nourished by the Yin and Yang. I kept my mouth open, and was unable to shut it;-- how could I admonish and correct Lâo Tan?'

7. Tsze-kung said, 'So then, can (this) man indeed sit still as a representative of the dead, and then appear as the dragon? Can his voice resound as thunder, when he is profoundly still? Can he exhibit himself in his movements like heaven and earth? May I, Tshze, also get to see him?' Accordingly with a message from Confucius he went to see Lâo Tan.

Lâ Tan was then about to answer (his salutation) haughtily in the hall, but he said in a low voice, 'My years have rolled on and are passing away, what do you, Sir, wish to admonish me about?' Tsze-kung replied, 'The Three Kings and Five Tîs ruled the world not in the same way, but the fame that has accrued to them is the same. How is it that you alone consider that they were not sages?' 'Come forward a little, my son. Why do you say that (their government) was not the same?' 'Yâo,' was the reply, 'gave the kingdom to Shun, and Shun gave it to Yü. Yü had recourse to his strength, and Thang to the force of arms. King Wan was obedient to Kâu (-hsin), and did not dare to rebel; king Wû rebelled against Kâu, and would not submit to him. And I say that their methods were not the same.' Lâo Tan said, 'Come a little more forward, my son, and I will tell you how the Three Hwangs and the Five Tîs ruled the world. Hwang- Tî ruled it, so as to make the minds of the people all conformed to the One (simplicity). If the parents of one of them died, and he did not wail, no one blamed him. Yâo ruled it so as to cause the hearts of the people to cherish relative affection. If any, however, made the observances on the death of other members of their kindred less than those for their parents, no one blamed them. Shun ruled it, so as to produce a feeling of rivalry in the minds of the people. Their wives gave birth to their children in the tenth month of their pregnancy, but those children could speak at five months; and before they were three years old, they began to call people by their surnames and names. Then it was that men began to die prematurely. Yû ruled it, so as to cause the minds of the people to become changed. Men's minds became scheming, and they used their weapons as if they might legitimately do so, (saying that they were) killing thieves and not killing other men. The people formed themselves into different combinations;-- so it was throughout the kingdom. Everywhere there was great consternation, and then arose the Literati and (the followers of) Mo (Tî). From them came first the doctrine of the relationships (of society); and what can be said of the now prevailing customs (in the marrying of) wives and daughters? I tell you that the rule of the Three Kings and Five Tîs may be called by that name, but nothing can be greater than the disorder which it produced. The wisdom of the Three Kings was opposed to the brightness of the sun and moon above, contrary to the exquisite purity of the hills and streams below, and subversive of the beneficent gifts of the four seasons between. Their wisdom has been more fatal than the sting of a scorpion or the bite of a dangerous beast. Unable to rest in the true attributes of their nature and constitution, they still regarded themselves as sages: was it not a thing to be ashamed of? But they were shameless.' Tsze-kung stood quite disconcerted and ill at ease.

8. Confucius said to Lâo Tan, 'I have occupied myself with the Shih, the Shû, the Lî, the Yo, the Yî, and the Khun Khiû, those six Books, for what I myself consider a long time, and am thoroughly acquainted with their contents. With seventy-two rulers, all offenders against the right, I have discoursed about the ways of the former kings, and set forth the examples of (the dukes of) Kâu and Shâo; and not one of them has adopted (my views) and put them in practice:-- how very difficult it is to prevail on such men, and to make clear the path to be pursued!'

Lâo-tsze replied, 'It is fortunate that you have not met with a ruler fitted to rule the age. Those six writings are a description of the vestiges left by the former kings, but do not tell how they made such vestiges; and what you, Sir, speak about are still only the vestiges. But vestiges are the prints left by the shoes;-- are they the shoes that produced them? A pair of white herons look at each other with pupils that do not move, and impregnation takes place; the male insect emits its buzzing sound in the air above, and the female responds from the air below, and impregnation takes place; the creatures called lêi are both male and female, and each individual breeds of itself. The nature cannot be altered; the conferred constitution cannot be changed; the march of the seasons cannot be arrested; the Tâo cannot be stopped. If you get the Tâo, there is no effect that cannot be produced; if you miss it, there is no effect that can.'

Confucius (after this) did not go out, till at the end of three months he went again to see Lâo Tan, and said,

'I have got it. Ravens produce their young by hatching; fishes by the communication of their milt; the small-waisted wasp by transformation; when a younger brother comes, the elder weeps. Long is it that I have not played my part in harmony with these processes of transformation. But as I did not play my part in harmony with such transformation, how could I transform men?' Lâo-tsze said, 'You will do. Khiû, you have found the Tâo.'

Kho Î, or 'Ingrained Ideas.'

1. Ingrained ideas and a high estimate of their own conduct; leaving the world, and pursuing uncommon ways; talking loftily and in resentful disparagement of others;-- all this is simply symptomatic of arrogance. This is what scholars who betake themselves to the hills and valleys, who are always blaming the world, and who stand aloof like withered trees, or throw themselves into deep pools, are fond of.

Discoursing of benevolence, righteousness, loyalty, and good faith; being humble and frugal, self-forgetful and courteous;-- all this is simply symptomatic of (self-)cultivation. This is what scholars who wish to tranquillise the world, teachers and instructors, men who pursue their studies at home and abroad, are fond of.

Discoursing of their great merit and making a great name for themselves; insisting on the ceremonies between ruler and minister; and rectifying the relations between high and low;-- all this shows their one object to be the promotion of government. This is what officers of the court, men who honour their lord and would strengthen the state and who would do their utmost to incorporate other states with their own, are fond of.

Resorting to marshes and lakes; dwelling in solitary places; occupying themselves with angling and living at ease;-- all this shows their one object to be to do nothing. This is what gentlemen of the rivers and seas, men who avoid the society of the world and desire to live at leisure, are fond of.

Blowing and breathing with open mouth; inhaling and exhaling the breath; expelling the old breath and taking in new; passing their time like the (dormant) bear, and stretching and twisting (the neck) like a bird;-- all this simply shows the desire for longevity. This is what the scholars who manipulate their breath, and the men who nourish the body and wish to live as long as Pang Tsû, are fond of.

As to those who have a lofty character without any ingrained ideas; who pursue the path of self- cultivation without benevolence and righteousness; who succeed in government without great services or fame; who enjoy their ease without resorting to the rivers and seas; who attain to longevity without the management (of the breath); who forget all things and yet possess all things; whose placidity is unlimited, while all things to be valued attend them:-- such men pursue the way of heaven and earth, and display the characteristics of the sages. Hence it is said, 'Placidity,

indifference, silence, quietude, absolute vacancy, and non-action:-- these
are the qualities which maintain the level of heaven and earth and are the
substance of the Tâo and its characteristics.'

2. In accordance with this it is said, 'The sage is entirely restful, and
so (his mind) is evenly balanced and at ease. This even balance and ease
appears in his placidity and indifference. In this state of even balance and
ease, of placidity and indifference, anxieties and evils do not find access
to him, no depraving influence can take him by surprise; his virtue is
complete, and his spirit continues unimpaired.'

Therefore it is (also) said, 'The life of the sage is (like) the action of
Heaven; and his death is the transformation common to (all) things. In
his stillness his virtue is the same as that of the Yin, and in movement his
diffusiveness is like that of the Yang. He does not take the initiative in producing either happiness or calamity. He responds to the influence acting
on him, and moves as he feels the pressure. He rises to act only when he
is obliged to do so. He discards wisdom and the memories of the past; he
follows the lines of his Heaven (-given nature); and therefore he suffers
no calamity from Heaven, no involvement from things, no blame from
men, and no reproof from the spirits of the dead. His life seems to float
along; his death seems to be a resting. He does not indulge any anxious
doubts; he does not lay plans beforehand. His light is without display; his
good faith is without previous arrangement. His sleep is untroubled by
dreams; his waking is followed by no sorrows. His spirit is guileless and
pure; his soul is not subject to weariness. Vacant and without self-assertion, placid and indifferent, he agrees with the virtue of Heaven.'

Therefore it is said (further), 'Sadness and pleasure show a depraving-
ing element in the virtue (of those who feel them); joy and anger show
some error in their course; love and hatred show a failure of their virtue.
Hence for the mind to be free from sorrow and pleasure is the perfection of virtue; to be of one mind that does not change is the perfection of
quietude; to be conscious of no opposition is the perfection of vacancy;
to have no intercourse with (external) things is the perfection of indifference; and to have no rebellious dissatisfactions is the perfection of purity.'

3. Therefore it is said (still further), 'If the body be toiled, and does
not rest, it becomes worn out; if the spirit be used without cessation, it
becomes toiled; and when toiled, it becomes exhausted. It is the nature of
water, when free from admixture, to be clear, and, when not agitated, to
be level; while if obstructed and not allowed to flow, it cannot preserve its
clearness;-- being an image of the virtue of Heaven.' Hence it is said (once
again), 'To be guileless and pure, and free from all admixture; to be still

and uniform, without undergoing any change; to be indifferent and do nothing; to move and yet to act like Heaven:-- this is the way to nourish the spirit. Now he who possesses a sword made at Kan-yüeh preserves it carefully in a box, and does not dare to use it;-- it is considered the perfection of valuable swords. But the human spirit goes forth in all directions, flowing on without limit, reaching to heaven above, and wreathing round the earth beneath. It transforms and nourishes all things, and cannot be represented by any form. Its name is "the Divinity (in man)." It is only the path of pure simplicity which guards and preserves the Spirit. When this path is preserved and not lost, it becomes one with the Spirit; and in this ethereal amalgamation, it acts in harmony with the orderly operation of Heaven.'

There is the vulgar saying, 'The multitude of men consider gain to be the most important thing; pure scholars, fame; those who are wise and able value their ambition; the sage prizes essential purity.' Therefore simplicity is the denomination of that in which there is no admixture; purity of that in which the spirit is not impaired. It is he who can embody simplicity and purity whom we call the True Man.

Shan Hsing, or 'Correcting the Nature.'

1. Those who would correct their nature by means of the vulgar learning, seeking to restore it to its original condition, and those who would regulate their desires, by the vulgar ways of thinking, seeking thereby to carry their intelligence to perfection, must be pronounced to be deluded and ignorant people. The ancients who regulated the Tâo nourished their faculty of knowledge by their placidity, and all through life abstained from employing that faculty in action;-- they must be pronounced to have (thus also) nourished their placidity by their knowledge.

When the faculty of knowledge and the placidity (thus) blend together, and they nourish each other, then from the nature there come forth harmony and orderly method. The attributes (of the Tâo) constitute the harmony; the Tâo (itself) secures the orderly method. When the attributes appear in a universal practice of forbearance, we have Benevolence; when the path is all marked by orderly method, we have Righteousness; when the righteousness is clearly manifested, and (all) things are regarded with affection, we have Leal-heartedness; when the (heart's) core is thus (pure) and real, and carried back to its (proper) qualities, we have Music; when this sincerity appears in all the range of the capacity, and its demonstrations are in accordance with what is elegant, we have Ceremony. If ceremonies and Music are carried out in an imperfect and one-sided manner, the world is thrown into confusion. When men would rectify others, and their own virtue is beclouded, it is not sufficient to extend itself to them. If an attempt be made so to extend it, they also will lose their (proper) nature.

2. The men of old, while the chaotic condition was yet undeveloped, shared the placid tranquillity which belonged to the whole world. At that time the Yin and Yang were harmonious and still; their resting and movement proceeded without any disturbance; the four seasons had their definite times; not a single thing received any injury, and no living being came to a premature end. Men might be possessed of (the faculty of) knowledge, but they had no occasion for its use. This was what is called the state of Perfect Unity. At this time, there was no action on the part of any one, but a constant manifestation of spontaneity.

This condition (of excellence) deteriorated and decayed, till Sui-zan and Fû-hsî arose and commenced their administration of the world; on which came a compliance (with their methods), but the state of unity was lost. The condition going on to deteriorate and decay, Shan Nang and

Hwang-Tî arose, and took the administration of the world, on which (the people) rested (in their methods), but did not themselves comply with them. Still the deterioration and decay continued till the lords of Thang and Yü began to administer the world. These introduced the method of governing by transformation, resorting to the stream (instead of to the spring), thus vitiating the purity and destroying the simplicity (of the nature). They left the Tào, and substituted the Good for it, and pursued the course of Haphazard Virtue. After this they forsook their nature and followed (the promptings of) their minds. One mind and another associated their knowledge, but were unable to give rest to the world. Then they added to this knowledge (external and) elegant forms, and went on to make these more and more numerous. The forms extinguished the (primal) simplicity, till the mind was drowned by their multiplicity. After this the people began to be perplexed and disordered, and had no way by which they might return to their true nature, and bring back their original condition.

3. Looking at the subject from this point of view, we see how the world lost the (proper) course, and how the course (which it took) only led it further astray. The world and the Way, when they came together, being (thus) lost to each other, how could the men of the Way make themselves conspicuous in the world? and how could the world rise to an appreciation of the Way? Since the Way had no means to make itself conspicuous in the world, and the world had no means of rising to an appreciation of the Way, though sagely men might not keep among the hills and forests, their virtue was hidden;-- hidden, but not because they themselves sought to hide it.

Those whom the ancients called 'Retired Scholars' did not conceal their persons, and not allow themselves to be seen; they did not shut up their words, and refuse to give utterance to them; they did not hide away their knowledge, and refuse to bring it forth. The conditions laid on them by the times were very much awry. If the conditions of the times had allowed them to act in the world on a great scale, they would have brought back the state of unity without any trace being perceived (of how they did so), When those conditions shut them up entirely from such action, they struck their roots deeper (in themselves), were perfectly still and waited. It was thus that they preserved (the Way in) their own persons.

4. The ancients who preserved (the Way in) their own persons did not try by sophistical reasonings to gloss over their knowledge; they did not seek to embrace (everything in) the world in their knowledge, nor to comprehend all the virtues in it. Solitary and trembling they remained where they were, and sought the restoration of their nature. What had

they to do with any further action? The Way indeed is not to be pursued, nor (all) its characteristics to be known on a small scale. A little knowledge is injurious to those characteristics; small doings are injurious to the Way;-- hence it is said, 'They simply rectified themselves.' Complete enjoyment is what is meant by 'the Attainment of the Aim.'

What was anciently called 'the Attainment of the Aim' did not mean the getting of carriages and coronets; it simply meant that nothing more was needed for their enjoyment. Now-a-days what is called 'the Attainment of the Aim' means the getting of carriages and coronets. But carriages and coronets belong to the body; they do not affect the nature as it is constituted. When such things happen to come, it is but for a time; being but for a time, their coming cannot be obstructed and their going cannot be stopped. Therefore we should not because of carriages and coronets indulge our aims, nor because of distress and straitness resort to the vulgar (learning and thinking); the one of these conditions and the other may equally conduce to our enjoyment, which is simply to be free from anxiety. If now the departure of what is transient takes away one's enjoyment, this view shows that what enjoyment it had given was worthless. Hence it is said, 'They who lose themselves in their pursuit of things, and lose their nature in their study of what is vulgar, must be pronounced people who turn things upside down.'

Khiû Shui, or 'The Floods of Autumn.'

1. The time of the autumnal floods was come, and the hundred streams were all discharging themselves into the Ho. Its current was greatly swollen, so that across its channel from bank to bank one could not distinguish an ox from a horse. On this the (Spirit-) earl of the Ho laughed with delight, thinking that all the beauty of the world was to be found in his charge. Along the course of the river he walked east till he came to the North Sea, over which he looked, with his face to the east, without being able to see where its waters began. Then he began to turn his face round, looked across the expanse, (as if he were) confronting Zo, and said with a sigh, 'What the vulgar saying expresses about him who has learned a hundred points (of the Tâo), and thinks that there is no one equal to himself, was surely spoken of me.

And moreover, I have heard parties making little of the knowledge of Kung-nî and the righteousness of Po-î, and at first I did not believe them. Now I behold the all-but-boundless extent (of your realms). If I had not come to your gate, I should have been in danger (of continuing in my ignorance), and been laughed at for long in the schools of our great System.'

Zo, (the Spirit-lord) of the Northern Sea, said, 'A frog in a well cannot be talked with about the sea;-- he is confined to the limits of his hole. An insect of the summer cannot be talked with about ice;-- it knows nothing beyond its own season. A scholar of limited views cannot be talked with about the Tâo;-- he is bound by the teaching (which he has received). Now you have come forth from between your banks, and beheld the great sea. You have come to know your own ignorance and inferiority, and are in the way of being fitted to be talked with about great principles. Of all the waters under heaven there are none so great as the sea. A myriad streams flow into it without ceasing, and yet it is not filled; and afterwards it discharges them (also) without ceasing, and yet it is not emptied. In spring and in autumn it undergoes no change; it takes no notice of floods or of drought. Its superiority over such streams even as the Kiang and the Ho cannot be told by measures or numbers; and that I have never, notwithstanding this, made much of myself, is because I compare my own bodily form with (the greatness of) heaven and earth, and (remember that) I have received my breath from the Yin and Yang. Between heaven and earth I am but as a small stone or a small tree on a great hill. So long as I see myself to be thus small, how should I make much of myself? I estimate all within the four seas, compared with the space between heaven and earth, to be not so large as that occupied by a pile of stones in a large marsh! I estimate our Middle States, compared with the space between the four seas, to be smaller than a single little grain of rice in a great granary! When we would set forth the number of things (in existence), we speak of them as myriads; and man is only one of them. Men occupy all the nine provinces; but of all whose life is maintained by grain- food, wherever boats and carriages reach, men form only one portion. Thus compared with the myriads of things, they are not equal to a single fine hair on the body of a horse. Within this range are comprehended all (the territories) which the five Tîs received in succession from one another; all which the royal founders of the three dynasties contended for; all which excited the anxiety of Benevolent men; and all which men in office have toiled for. Po-î was accounted famous for declining (to share in its government), and Kung-nî was accounted great because of the lessons which he addressed to it. They acted as they did, making much of themselves;-- therein like you who a little time ago did so of yourself because of your (volume of) water!'

2. The earl of the Ho said, 'Well then, may I consider heaven and earth as (the ideal of) what is great, and the point of a hair as that of what is small?' Zo of the Northern Sea replied, 'No. The (different) capacities of things are illimitable; time never stops, (but is always moving on); man's lot is ever changing; the end and the beginning of things never occur (twice) in the same way. Therefore men of great wisdom, looking at things far off or near at hand, do not think them insignificant for being small, nor much of them for being great:-- knowing how capacities differ illimitably. They appeal with intelligence to things of ancient and recent occurrence, without being troubled by the remoteness of the former, or standing on tiptoe to lay hold of the latter:-- knowing that time never stops in its course. They examine with discrimination (cases of) fulness and of want, not overjoyed by success, nor disheartened by failure:-- knowing the inconstancy of man's lot. They know the plain and quiet path (in which things proceed), therefore they are not overjoyed to live, nor count it a calamity to die:-- the end and the beginning of things never occurring (twice) in the same way.

'We must reckon that what men know is not so much as what they do not know, and that the time since they were born is not so long as that which elapsed before they were born. When they take that which is most small and try to fill with it the dimensions of what is most great, this leads to error and confusion, and they cannot attain their end. Looking at the subject in this way, how can you know that the point of a hair is sufficient to determine the minuteness of what is most small, or that heaven and earth are sufficient to complete the dimensions of what is most large?'

3. The earl of the Ho said, 'The disputers of the world all say, "That which is most minute has no bodily form; and that which is most great cannot be encompassed;"-- is this really the truth?' Zo of the Northern Sea replied, 'When from the standpoint of what is small we look at what is great, we do not take it all in; when from the standpoint of what is great we look at what is small, we do not see it clearly. Now the subtile essence is smallness in its extreme degree; and the vast mass is greatness in its largest form. Different as they are, each has its suitability,-- according to their several conditions. But the subtile and the gross both presuppose that they have a bodily form. Where there is no bodily form, there is no longer a possibility of numerical division; where it is not possible to encompass a mass, there is no longer a possibility of numerical estimate. What can be discoursed about in words is the grossness of things; what can be reached in idea is the subtilty of things. What cannot be discoursed about in words, and what cannot be reached by nice discrimination of thought, has nothing to do either with subtilty or grossness.

'Therefore while the actions of the Great Man are not directed to injure men, he does not plume himself on his benevolence and kindness; while his movements are not made with a view to gain, he does not consider the menials of a family as mean; while he does not strive after property and wealth, he does not plume himself on declining them; while he does not borrow the help of others to accomplish his affairs, he does not plume himself on supporting himself by his own strength, nor does he despise those who in their greed do what is mean; while he differs in his conduct from the vulgar, he does not plume himself on being so different from them; while it is his desire to follow the multitude, he does not despise the glib- tongued flatterers. The rank and emoluments of the world furnish no stimulus to him, nor does he reckon its punishments and shame to be a disgrace. He knows that the right and the wrong can (often) not be distinguished, and that what is small and what is great can (often) not be defined. I have heard it said, "The Man of Tâo does not become distinguished; the greatest virtue is unsuccessful; the Great Man has no thought of self;"-- to so great a degree may the lot be restricted.'

4. The earl of the Ho said, 'Whether the subject be what is external in things, or what is internal, how do we come to make a distinction between them as noble and mean, and as great or small?' Zo of the Northern Sea replied, 'When we look at them in the light of the Tâo, they are neither noble nor mean. Looking at them in themselves, each thinks itself noble, and despises others. Looking at them in the light of common opinion, their being noble or mean does not depend on themselves. Looking at them in their differences from one another, if we call those great which are greater than others, there is nothing that is not great, and in the same

way there is nothing that is not small. We shall (thus) know that heaven and earth is but (as) a grain of the smallest rice, and that the point of a hair is (as) a mound or a mountain;-- such is the view given of them by their relative size. Looking at them from the services they render, allowing to everything the service which it does, there is not one which is not serviceable; and, extending the consideration to what it does not do, there is not one which is not unserviceable. We know (for instance) that East and West are opposed to each other, and yet that the one cannot be without (suggesting the idea of) the other;-- (thus) their share of mutual service is determined. Looking at them with respect to their tendencies, if we approve of what they approve, then there is no one who may not be approved of; and, if we condemn what they condemn, there is no one who may not be condemned. There are the cases of Yâo and Kieh, each of whom approved of his own course, and condemned the other;--such is the view arising from the consideration of tendency and aim.

'Formerly Yâo and Shun resigned (their thrones), and yet each continued to be Tî; Kih-khwâi resigned (his marquisate) which led to his ruin. Thang and Wû contended (for the sovereignty), and each became king; the duke a contended (for Khû), which led to his extinction. Looking at the subject from these examples of striving by force and of resigning, and from the conduct of Yâo (on the one hand) and of Kieh (on the other), we see that there is a time for noble acting, and a time for mean;-- these characteristics are subject to no regular rule.

5. 'A battering ram may be used against the wall of a city, but it cannot be employed to stop up a hole;--the uses of implements are different. The (horses) Khih-kî and Hwâ-liû could in one day gallop 1000 lî, but for catching rats they were not equal to a wild dog or a weasel;-- the gifts of creatures are different. The white horned owl collects its fleas in the night-time, and can discern the point of a hair, but in bright day it stares with its eyes and cannot see a mound or a hill;-- the natures of creatures are different.

'Hence the sayings, "Shall we not follow and honour the right, and have nothing to do with the wrong? shall we not follow and honour those who secure good government, and have nothing to do with those who produce disorder?" show a want of acquaintance with the principles of Heaven and Earth, and with the different qualities of things. It is like following and honouring Heaven and taking no account of Earth; it is like following and honouring the Yin and taking no account of the Yang. It is clear that such a course cannot be pursued. Yet notwithstanding they go on talking so:-- if they are not stupid, they are visionaries. The Tî sovereigns resigned their thrones to others in one way, and the rulers of the three dynasties transmitted their thrones to their successors in another. He who acts differently from the requirements of his time and contrary to its custom is called an usurper; he who complies with the time and follows the common practice is said to be righteous. Hold your peace, 0 earl of the Ho. How should you know what constitutes being noble and being mean, or who are the small and who the great?'

6. The earl of the Ho said, 'Very well. But what am I to do? and what am I not to do? How am I to be guided after all in regard to what I accept or reject, and what I pursue or put away from me?' Zo of the Northern Sea replied, 'From the standpoint of the Tâo, what is noble? and what is mean? These expressions are but the different extremes of the average level. Do not keep pertinaciously to your own ideas, which put you in such opposition to the Tâo. What are few? and what are many? These are denominations which we employ in thanking (donors) and dispensing gifts. Do not study to be uniform in doing so;-- it only shows how different you are from the Tâo. Be severe and strict, like the ruler of a state who does not selfishly bestow his favours. Be scrupulous, yet gentle, like the tutelary spirit of the land, when sacrifice is offered to him who does not bestow his blessing selfishly. Be large-minded like space, whose four terminating points are illimitable, and form no particular enclosures. Hold all things in your love, favouring and supporting none specially. This is called being without any local or partial regard; all things are equally regarded; there is no long or short among them.

'There is no end or beginning to the Tâo. Things indeed die and are born, not reaching a perfect state which can be relied on. Now there is emptiness, and now fulness;-- they do not continue in one form. The years cannot be reproduced; time cannot be arrested. Decay and growth, fulness and emptiness, when they end, begin again. It is thus that we describe the method of great righteousness, and discourse about the principle pervading all things. The life of things is like the hurrying and galloping along of a horse. With every movement there is a change; with every moment there is an alteration. What should you be doing? what should you not be doing? You have only to be allowing this course of natural transformation to be going on.'

7. The earl of the Ho said, 'What then is there so valuable in the Tâo?' Zo of the Northern Sea replied, 'He who knows the Tâo is sure to be well acquainted with the principles (that appear in the procedures of things). Acquainted with (those) principles, he is sure to understand how to regulate his conduct in all varying circumstances. Having that understanding, he will not allow things to injure himself. Fire cannot burn him who is (so) perfect in virtue, nor water drown him; neither

cold nor heat can affect him injuriously; neither bird nor beast can hurt him. This does not mean that he is indifferent to these things; it means that he discriminates between where he may safely rest and where he will be in peril; that he is tranquil equally in calamity and happiness; that he is careful what he avoids and what he approaches;-- so that nothing can injure him. Hence it is said, "What is heavenly is internal; what is human is external." The virtue (of man) is in what is Heavenly. If you know the operation of what is Heavenly and what is Human, you will have your root in what is Heavenly and your position in Virtue. You will bend or stretch (only) after the (necessary) hesitation; you will have returned to the essential, and may be pronounced to have reached perfection.'

'What do you mean,' pursued the earl, 'by the Heavenly, and by the Human?' Zo replied, 'Oxen and horses have four feet;-- that is what I call their Heavenly (constitution). When horses' heads are haltered, and the noses of oxen are pierced, that is what I call (the doing of) Man. Hence it is said, "Do not by the Human (doing) extinguish the Heavenly (constitution); do not for your (Human) purpose extinguish the appointment (of Heaven); do not bury your (proper) fame in (such) a pursuit of it; carefully guard (the Way) and do not lose it:-- this is what I call reverting to your True (Nature)."'

8. The khwei desires to be like the millipede; the millipede to be like the serpent; the serpent like the wind; the wind to be like the eye; and the eye to be like the mind.

The khwei said to the millipede, 'With my one leg I hop about, and can hardly manage to go along. Now you have a myriad feet which you can employ; how is it that you are so abundantly furnished?' The millipede said, 'It is not so. Have you not seen one ejecting saliva? The largest portion of it is like a pearl, while the smaller portions fall down like a shower of mist in innumerable drops. Now I put in motion the springs set in me by Heaven, without knowing how I do so.'

The millipede said to the serpent, 'I go along by means of my multitude of feet; and yet how is it that I do not go so fast as you who have no feet at all?' The serpent replied, 'How can the method of moving by the springs set in us by Heaven be changed? How could I make use of feet?'

The serpent said to the wind, 'I get along by moving my backbone and ribs, thus appearing to have some (bodily) means of progression. But now you, Sir, rise with a blustering force in the North Sea, and go on in the same way to the South Sea;-- seemingly without any such means. How does it take place?' The wind said, 'Yes. With such a blustering force I rise in the North Sea and go on to the South Sea. But you can point to me, and therein are superior to me, as you are also in treading on me. Yet notwithstanding, it is only I who can break great trees, and blow down great houses. Therefore he whom all that are small cannot overcome is a great overcomer. But it is only he who is the sagely man that is the Great Conqueror (of all).'

9. When Confucius was travelling in Khwang, some people of Sung (once) surrounded him (with a hostile intention) several ranks deep; but he kept singing to his lute without stopping. Tsze-lû came in, and saw him, and said, 'How is it, Master, that you are so pleased?' Confucius said, 'Come here, and I will tell you. I have tried to avoid being reduced to such a strait for a long time; and that I have not escaped shows that it was so appointed for me. I have sought to find a ruler that would employ me for a long time, and that I have not found one, shows the character of the time. Under Yâo and Shun there was no one in the kingdom reduced to straits like mine; and it was not by their sagacity that men succeeded as they did.

Under Kieh and Kâu no (good and able man) in the kingdom found his way to employment; and it was not for (want of) sagacity that they failed to do so. It was simply owing to the times and their character.

'People that do business on the water do not shrink from meeting iguanodons and dragons;-- that is the courage of fishermen. Those who do business on land do not shrink from meeting rhinoceroses and tigers;-- that is the courage of hunters. When men see the sharp weapons crossed before them, and look on death as going home;-- that is the courage of the determined soldier. When he knows that his strait is determined for him, and that the employment of him by a ruler depends on the character of the time, and then meeting with great distress is yet not afraid;-- that is the courage of the sagely man. Wait, my good Yû, and you will see what there is determined for me in my lot.' A little afterwards, the leader of the armed men approached and took his leave, saying, 'We thought you were Yang Hû, and therefore surrounded ypu. Now we see our mistake.' (With this) he begged to take his leave, and withdrew.

10. Kung-sun Lung asked Mâu of Wei, saying, 'When I was young, I learned the teachings of the former kings; and when I was grown up, I became proficient in the practice of benevolence and righteousness. I brought together the views that agreed and disagreed; I considered the questions about hardness and whiteness; I set forth what was to be affirmed and what was not, and what was allowable and what was not; I studied painfully the various schools of thought, and made myself master of the reasonings of all their masters. I thought that I had reached a good understanding of every subject; but now that I have heard the words

of Kwang-tsze, they throw me into a flutter of surprise. I do not know whether it be that I do not come up to him in the power of discussion, or that my knowledge is not equal to his. But now I do not feel able to open my mouth, and venture to ask you what course I should pursue.' Kung-tsze Mâu leant forward on his stool, drew a long breath, looked up to heaven, smiled, and said, 'Have you not heard of the frog of the dilapidated well, and how it said to the turtle of the Eastern Sea, "How I enjoy myself? I leap upon the parapet of this well. I enter, and having by means of the projections formed by the fragments of the broken tiles of the lining proceeded to the water, I draw my legs together, keep my chin up, (and strike out). When I have got to the mud, I dive till my feet are lost in it. Then turning round, I see that of the shrimps, crabs, and tadpoles there is not one that can do like me. Moreover, when one has entire command of all the water in the gully, and hesitates to go forward, it is the greatest pleasure to enjoy one's self here in this dilapidated well;-- why do not you, Master, often come and enter, and see it for yourself?" The turtle of the Eastern Sea (was then proceeding to go forward), but before he had put in his left foot, he found his right knee caught and held fast. On this he hesitated, drew back, and told (the frog) all about the sea, saying, "A distance of a thousand lî is not sufficient to express its extent, nor would (a line of) eight thousand cubits be equal to sound its depth. In the time of Yü, for nine years out of ten the flooded land (all drained into it), and its water was not sensibly increased; and in the time of Thang for seven years out of eight there was a drought, but the rocks on the shore (saw) no diminution of the water because of it. Thus it is that no change is produced in its waters by any cause operating for a short time or a long, and that they do not advance nor recede for any addition or subtraction, whether great or small; and this is the great pleasure afforded by the Eastern Sea." When the frog of the dilapidated well heard this, he was amazed and terror-struck, and lost himself in surprise.

'And moreover, when you, who have not wisdom enough to know where the discussions about what is right and what is wrong should end, still desire to see through the words of Kwang-tsze, that is like employing a mosquito to carry a mountain on its back, or a millipede to gallop as fast as the Ho runs;-- tasks to which both the insects are sure to be unequal. Still further, when you, who have not wisdom enough to know the words employed in discussing very mysterious subjects, yet hasten to show your sharpness of speech on any occasion that may occur, is not this being like the frog of the dilapidated well?

'And that (Kwang-tsze) now plants his foot on the Yellow Springs (below the earth), and anon rises to the height of the Empyrean. Without any regard to south and north, with freedom he launches out in every direction, and is lost in the unfathomable. Without any regard to east and west, starting from what is abysmally obscure, he comes back to what is grandly intelligible. (All the while), you, Sir, in amazement, search for his views to examine them, and grope among them for matter for discussion;-- this is just like peeping at the heavens through a tube, or aiming at the earth with an awl; are not both the implements too small for the purpose? Go your ways, Sir.

'And have you not heard of the young learners of Sâau-ling, and how they did in Han-tan? Before they had acquired what they might have done in that capital, they had forgotten what they had learned to do in their old city, and were marched back to it on their hands and knees. If now you do not go away, you will forget your old acquirements, and fail in your profession.'

Kung-sun Lung gaped on the speaker, and could not shut his mouth, and his tongue clave to its roof. He slank away and ran off.

11. Kwang-tsze was (once) fishing in the river Phû, when the king of Khû sent two great officers to him, with the message, 'I wish to trouble you with the charge of all within my territories.' Kwang-tsze kept on holding his rod without looking round, and said, 'I have heard that in Khû there is a spirit-like tortoise- shell, the wearer of which died 3000 years ago, and which the king keeps, in his ancestral temple, in a hamper covered with a cloth. Was it better for the tortoise to die, and leave its shell to be thus honoured?

Or would it have been better for it to live, and keep on dragging its tail through the mud?' The two officers said, 'It would have been better for it to live, and draw its tail after it over the mud.' 'Go your ways. I will keep on drawing my tail after me through the mud.'

12. Hui-tsze being a minister of state in Liang, Kwang-tsze went to see him. Some one had told Hui-tsze that Kwang-tsze was come with a wish to supersede him in his office, on which he was afraid, and instituted a search for the stranger all over the kingdom for three days and three nights. (After this) Kwang-tsze went and saw him, and said, 'There is in the south a bird, called "the Young Phoenix;"-- do you know it? Starting from the South Sea, it flies to the Northern; never resting but on the bignonia, never eating but the fruit of the melia azederach, and never drinking but from the purest springs. An owl, which had got a putrid rat, (once), when a phoenix went passing overhead, looked up to it and gave an angry scream. Do you wish now, in your possession of the kingdom of Liang, to frighten me with a similar scream?'

13. Kwang-tsze and Hui-tsze were walking on the dam over the Hâo, when the former said, 'These thryssas come out, and play about at their ease;-- that is the enjoyment of fishes.' The other said, 'You are not a fish; how do you know what constitutes the enjoyment of fishes?' Kwang-tsze rejoined, 'You are not I. How do you know that I do not know what constitutes the enjoyment of fishes?' Hui-tsze said, 'I am not you; and though indeed I do not fully know you, you certainly are not a fish, and (the argument) is complete against your knowing what constitutes the happiness of fishes.' Kwang-tsze replied, 'Let us keep to your original question. You said to me, "How do you know what constitutes the enjoyment of fishes?" You knew that I knew it, and yet you put your question to me;-- well, I know it (from our enjoying ourselves together) over the Hâo.'

Kih Lo, or 'Perfect Enjoyment.'

1. Under the sky is perfect enjoyment to be found or not? Are there any who can preserve themselves alive or not? If there be, what do they do? What do they maintain? What do they avoid? What do they attend to? Where do they resort to? Where do they keep from? What do they delight in? What do they dislike?

What the world honours is riches, dignities, lonevity, and being deemed able. What it delights in is rest for the body, rich flavours, fine garments, beautiful colours, and pleasant music. What it looks down on are poverty and mean condition, short life and being deemed feeble. What men consider bitter experiences are that their bodies do not get rest and ease, that their mouths do not get food of rich flavour, that their persons are not finely clothed, that their eyes do not see beautiful colours, and that their ears do not listen to pleasant music. If they do not got these things, they are very sorrowful, and go on to be troubled with fears. Their thoughts are all about the body;-- are they not silly?

Now the rich embitter their lives by their incessant labours; they accumulate more wealth than they can use:-- while they act thus for the body, they make it external to themselves. Those who seek for honours carry their pursuit of them from the day into the night, full of anxiety about their methods whether they are skilful or not:-- while they act thus for the body they treat it as if it were indifferent to them. The birth of man is at the same time the birth of his sorrow; and if he live long he becomes more and more stupid, and the longer is his anxiety that he may not die; how great is his bitterness!-- while he thus acts for his body, it is for a distant result. Meritorious officers are regarded by the world as good; but (their goodness) is not sufficient to keep their persons alive. I do not know whether the goodness ascribed to them be really good or really not good. If indeed it be considered good, it is not sufficient to preserve their persons alive; if it be deemed not good, it is sufficient to preserve other men alive. Hence it is said, 'When faithful remonstrances are not listened to, (the remonstrant) should sit still, let (his ruler) take his course, and not strive with him.' Therefore when Tsze-hsü strove with (his ruler), he brought on himself the mutilation of his body. If he had not so striven, he would not have acquired his fame:-- was such (goodness) really good or was it not?

As to what the common people now do, and what they find their enjoyment in, I do not know whether the enjoyment be really enjoyment or really not. I see them in their pursuit of it following after all their aims

121

as if with the determination of death, and as if they could not stop in their course; but what they call enjoyment would not be so to me, while yet I do not say that there is no enjoyment in it. Is there indeed such enjoyment, or is there not? I consider doing nothing (to obtain it) to be the great enjoyment, while ordinarily people consider it to be a great evil. Hence it is said, 'Perfect enjoyment is to be without enjoyment; the highest praise is to be without praise.' The right and the wrong (on this point of enjoyment) cannot indeed be determined according to (the view of) the world; nevertheless, this doing nothing (to obtain it) may determine the right and the wrong. Since perfect enjoyment is (held to be) the keeping the body alive, it is only by this doing nothing that that end is likely to be secured. Allow me to try and explain this (more fully):-- Heaven does nothing, and thence comes its serenity; Earth does nothing, and thence comes its rest. By the union of these two inactivities, all things are produced. How vast and imperceptible is the process!-- they seem to come from nowhere! How imperceptible and vast!-- there is no visible image of it! All things in all their variety grow from this Inaction. Hence it is said, 'Heaven and Earth do nothing, and yet there is nothing that they do not do.' But what man is there that can attain to this inaction?

2. When Kwang-tsze's wife died, Hui-tsze went to condole with him, and, finding him squatted on the ground, drumming on the basin, and singing, said to him, 'When a wife has lived with her husband, and brought up children, and then dies in her old age, not to wail for her is enough. When you go on to drum on this basin and sing, is it not an excessive (and strange) demonstration?' Kwang-tsze replied, 'It is not so. When she first died, was it possible for me to be singular and not affected by the event? But I reflected on the commencement of her being. She had not yet been born to life; not only had she no life, but she had no bodily form; not only had she no bodily form, but she had no breath. During the intermingling of the waste and dark chaos, there ensued a change, and there was breath; another change, and there was the bodily form; another change, and there came birth and life. There is now a change again, and she is dead. The relation between these things is like the procession of the four seasons from spring to autumn, from winter to summer. There now she lies with her face up, sleeping in the Great Chamber; and if I were to fall sobbing and going on to wail for her, I should think that I did not understand what was appointed (for all). I therefore restrained myself!'

3. Mr. Deformed and Mr. One-foot were looking at the mound-graves of the departed in the wild of Khwan-lun, where Hwang-Tî had entered into his rest. Suddenly a tumour began to grow on their left wrists, which made them look distressed as if they disliked it. The former said to the other, 'Do you dread it?' 'No,' replied he, 'why should I dread it? Life is

a borrowed thing. The living frame thus borrowed is but so much dust. Life and death are like day and night. And you and I were looking at (the graves of) those who have undergone their change. If my change is coming to me, why should I dislike it?'

4. When Kwang-tsze went to Khû, he saw an empty skull, bleached indeed, but still retaining its shape. Tapping it with his horse-switch, he asked it, saying, 'Did you, Sir, in your greed of life, fail in the lessons of reason, and come to this? Or did you do so, in the service of a perishing state, by the punishment of the axe? Or was it through your evil conduct, reflecting disgrace on your parents and on your wife and children? Or was it through your hard endurances of cold and hunger? Or was it that you had completed your term of life?'

Having given expression to these questions, he took up the skull, and made a pillow of it when he went to sleep. At midnight the skull appeared to him in a dream, and said, 'What you said to me was after the fashion of an orator. All your words were about the entanglements of men in their lifetime. There are none of those things after death. Would you like to hear me, Sir, tell you about death?' 'I should,' said Kwang-tsze, and the skull resumed: 'In death there are not (the distinctions of) ruler above and minister below. There are none of the phenomena of the four seasons. Tranquil and at ease, our years are those of heaven and earth. No king in his court has greater enjoyment than we have.' Kwang-tsze did not believe it, and said, 'If I could get the Ruler of our Destiny to restore your body to life with its bones and flesh and skin, and to give you back your father and mother, your wife and children, and all your village acquaintances, would you wish me to do so?' The skull stared fixedly at him, knitted its brows, and said, 'How should I cast away the enjoyment of my royal court, and undertake again the toils of life among mankind?'

5. When Yen Yüan went eastwards to Khî, Confucius wore a look of sorrow. Tsze-kung left his mat, and asked him, saying, 'Your humble disciple ventures to ask how it is that the going eastwards of Hui to Khî has given you such a look of sadness.' Confucius said, 'Your question is good. Formerly Kwan-tsze used words of which I very much approve. He said, "A small bag cannot be made to contain what is large; a short rope cannot be used to draw water from a deep well." So it is, and man's appointed lot is definitely determined, and his body is adapted for definite ends, so that neither the one nor the other can be augmented or diminished. I am afraid that Hui will talk with the marquis of Khî about the ways of Hwang- Tî, Yâo, and Shun, and go on to relate the words of Sui-zan and Shan Nang. The marquis will seek (for the correspondence of what he is told) in himself; and, not finding it there, will suspect the speaker; and

that speaker, being suspected, will be put to death. And have you not heard this?-- Formerly a sea-bird alighted in the suburban country of Lû. The marquis went out to meet it, (brought it) to the ancestral temple, and prepared to banquet it there. The Kiû-shâo was performed to afford it music; an ox, a sheep, and a pig were killed to supply the food. The bird, however, looked at everything with dim eyes, and was very sad. It did not venture to eat a single bit of flesh, nor to drink a single cupful; and in three days it died.

'The marquis was trying to nourish the bird with what he used for himself, and not with the nourishment proper for a bird. They who would nourish birds as they ought to be nourished should let them perch in the deep forests, or roam over sandy plains; float on the rivers and lakes; feed on the eels and small fish; wing their flight in regular order and then stop; and be free and at ease in their resting-places. It was a distress to that bird to hear men speak; what did it care for all the noise and hubbub made about it? If the music of the Kiû-shâo or the Hsien-khih were per-formed in the wild of the Thung-thing lake, birds would fly away, and beasts would run off when they heard it, and fishes would dive down to the bottom of the water; while men, when they hear it, would come all round together, and look on. Fishes live and men die in the water. They are different in constitution, and therefore differ in their likes and dislikes. Hence it was that the ancient sages did not require (from all) the same ability, nor demand the same performances. They gave names accord-ing to the reality of what was done, and gave their approbation where it was specially suitable. This was what was called the method of universal adaptation and of sure success.'

6. Lieh-tsze (once) upon a journey took a meal by the road-side. There he saw a skull a hundred years old, and, pulling away the bush (under which it lay), he pointed to it and said, 'It is only you and I who know that you are not dead, and that (aforetime) you were not alive. Do you indeed really find (in death) the nourishment (which you like)? Do I really find (in life my proper) enjoyment? The seeds (of things) are multitudinous and minute. On the surface of the water they form a membranous tex-ture. When they reach to where the land and water join they become the (lichens which we call the) clothes of frogs and oysters. Coming to life on mounds and heights, they become the plantain; and, receiving manure, appear as crows' feet. The roots of the crow's foot become grubs, and its leaves, butterflies. This butterfly, known by the name of hsü, is changed into an insect, and comes to life under a furnace. Then it has the form of a moth, and is named the khü-to. The khü-to after a thousand days becomes a bird, called the kan-yü-kû. Its saliva becomes the stse-mî, and this again the shih-hsî (or pickle-eater). The î-lo is produced from the

pickle-eater; the hwang-kwang from the kiû-yû; the mâu-zui from the pû-khwan. The ying-hsî uniting with a bamboo, which has long ceased to put forth sprouts, produces the khing-ning; the khing-ning, the panther; the panther, the horse; and the horse, the man. Man then again enters into the great Machinery (of Evolution), from which all things come forth (at birth), and which they enter at death.

Tâ Shang, or 'The Full Understanding of Life.'

1. He who understands the conditions of Life does not strive after what is of no use to life; and he who understands the conditions of Destiny does not strive after what is beyond the reach of knowledge. In nourishing the body it is necessary to have beforehand the things (appropriate to its support); but there are cases where there is a superabundance of such things, and yet the body is not nourished. In order to have life it is necessary that it do not have left the body; but there are cases when the body has not been left by it, and yet the life has perished.

When life comes, it cannot be declined; when it goes, it cannot be detained. Alas! the men of the world think that to nourish the body is sufficient to preserve life; and when such nourishment is not sufficient to preserve the life, what can be done in the world that will be sufficient? Though (all that men can do) will be insufficient, yet there are things which they feel they ought to do, and they do not try to avoid doing them. For those who wish to avoid caring for the body, their best plan is to abandon the world. Abandoning the world, they are free from its entanglements. Free from its entanglements, their (minds) are correct and their (temperament) is equable. Thus correct and equable, they succeed in securing a renewal of life, as some have done. In securing a renewal of life, they are not far from the True (Secret of their being). But how is it sufficient to abandon worldly affairs? and how is it sufficient to forget the (business of) life? Through the renouncing of (worldly) affairs, the body has no more toil; through forgetting the (business of) life, the vital power suffers no diminution. When the body is completed and the vital power is restored (to its original vigour), the man is one with Heaven. Heaven and Earth are the father and mother of all things. It is by their union that the body is formed; it is by their separation that a (new) beginning is brought about. When the body and vital power suffer no diminution, we have what may be called the transference of power. From the vital force there comes another more vital, and man returns to be the assistant of Heaven.

2. My master Lieh-tsze asked Yin, (the warden) of the gate, saying, 'The perfect man walks under water without encountering any obstruction, treads on fire without being burned, and walks on high above all things without any fear; let me ask how he attains to do this?' The warden Yin replied, 'It is by his keeping of the pure breath (of life); it is not to be described as an achievement of his skill or daring. Sit down, and I will

explain it to you. Whatever has form, semblance, sound, and colour is a thing; how can one thing come to be different from another? But it is not competent for any of these things to reach to what preceded them all;-- they are but (form and) visibility. But (the perfect man) attains to be (as it were) without form, and beyond the capability of being transformed. Now when one attains to this and carries it out to the highest degree, how can other things come into his way to stop him? He will occupy the place assigned to him without going beyond it, and lie concealed in the clue which has no end. He will study with delight the process which gives their beginning and ending to all things. By gathering his nature into a unity, by nourishing his vital power, by concentrating his virtue, he will penetrate to the making of things. In this condition, with his heavenly constitution kept entire, and with no crevice in his spirit, how can things enter (and disturb his serenity)?

'Take the case of a drunken man falling from his carriage;-- though he may suffer injury, he will not die. His bones and joints are the same as those of other men, but the injury which he receives is different:--his spirit is entire. He knew nothing about his getting into the carriage, and knew nothing about his falling from it. The thought of death or life, or of any alarm or affright, does not enter his breast; and therefore he encounters danger without any shrinking from it. Completely under the influence of the liquor he has drunk, it is thus with him;-- how much more would it be so, if he were under the influence of his Heavenly constitution! The sagely man is kept hid in his Heavenly constitution, and therefore nothing can injure him.

'A man in the pursuit of vengeance would not break the (sword) Mo-yê or Yü-kiang (which had done the deed); nor would one, however easily made wrathful, wreak his resentment on the fallen brick. In this way all under heaven there would be peace, without the disorder of assaults and fighting, without the punishments of death and slaughter:-- such would be the issue of the course (which I have described). If the disposition that is of human origin be not developed, but that which is the gift of Heaven, the development of the latter will produce goodness, while that of the former would produce hurt. If the latter were not wearied of, and the former not slighted, the people would be brought nearly to their True nature.'

3. When Kung-nî was on his way to Khû, as he issued from a forest, he saw a hunchback receiving cicadas (on the point of a rod), as if he were picking them up with his hand. 'You are clever!' said he to the man. 'Is there any method in it?' The hunchback replied, 'There is. For five or six months, I practised with two pellets, till they never fell down, and

then I only failed with a small fraction of the cicadas (which I tried to catch). Having succeeded in the same way with three (pellets), I missed only one cicada in ten. Having succeeded with five, I caught the cicadas as if I were gathering them. My body is to me no more than the stump of a broken trunk, and my shoulder no more than the branch of a rotten tree. Great as heaven and earth are, and multitudinous as things are, I take no notice of them, but only of the wings of my cicadas; neither turning nor inclining to one side. I would not for them all exchange the wings of my cicadas;-- how should I not succeed in taking them?' Confucius looked round, and said to his disciples, '"Where the will is not diverted from its object, the spirit is concentrated;"-- this might have been spoken of this hunchback gentleman.'

4. Yen Yüan asked Kung-nî, saying, 'When I was crossing the gulf of Khang-shan, the ferryman handled the boat like a spirit. I asked him whether such management of a boat could be learned, and he replied, "It may. Good swimmers can learn it quickly; but as for divers, without having seen a boat, they can manage it at once." He did not directly tell me what I asked;-- I venture to ask you what he meant.' Kung-nî replied, 'Good swimmers acquire the ability quickly;-- they forget the water (and its dangers). As to those who are able to dive, and without having seen a boat are able to manage it at once, they look on the watery gulf as if it were a hill-side, and the upsetting of a boat as the going back of a carriage. Such upsettings and goings back have occurred before them multitudes of times, and have not seriously affected their minds. Wherever they go, they feel at ease on their occurrence.

'He who is contending for a piece of earthenware puts forth all his skill. If the prize be a buckle of brass, he shoots timorously; if it be for an article of gold, he shoots as if he were blind. The skill of the archer is the same in all the cases; but (in the two latter cases) he is under the influence of solicitude, and looks on the external prize as most important. All who attach importance to what is external show stupidity in themselves.'

5. Thien Khâi-kih was having an interview with duke Wei Of Kâ, who said to him, 'I have heard that (your master) Kû Hsin has studied the subject of Life. What have you, good Sir, heard from him about it in your intercourse with him?' Thien Khâi-kih replied, 'In my waiting on him in the courtyard with my broom, what should I have heard from my master?' Duke Wei said, 'Do not put the question off, Mr. Thien; I wish to hear what you have to say.' Khâi-kih then replied, 'I have heard my master say that they who skilfully nourish their life are like shepherds, who whip up the sheep that they see lagging behind.' 'What did he mean?' asked the duke. The reply was, 'In Lû there was a Shan Pâo, who lived among the

rocks, and drank only water. He would not share with the people in their toils and the benefits springing from them; and though he was now in his seventieth year, he had still the complexion of a child. Unfortunately he encountered a hungry tiger, which killed and ate him. There was also a Kang Î, who hung up a screen at his lofty door, and to whom all the people hurried (to pay their respects). In his fortieth year, he fell ill of a fever and died. (Of these two men), Pâo nourished his inner man, and a tiger ate his outer; while I nourished his outer man, and disease attacked his inner. Both of them neglected whipping up their lagging sheep.'

Kung-nî said, 'A man should not retire and hide himself; he should not push forward and display himself; he should be like the decayed tree which stands in the centre of the ground. Where these three conditions are fulfilled, the name will reach its greatest height. When people fear the dangers of a path, if one man in ten be killed, then fathers and sons, elder brothers and younger, warn one another that they must not go out on a journey without a large number of retainers;-- and is it not a mark of wisdom to do so? But there are dangers which men incur on the mats of their beds, and in eating and drinking; and when no warning is given against them;-- is it not a mark of error?'

6. The officer of Prayer in his dark and squarecut robes goes to the pig-pen, and thus counsels the pigs, 'Why should you shrink from dying? I will for three months feed you on grain. Then for ten days I will fast, and keep vigil for three days, after which I will put down the mats of white grass, and lay your shoulders and rumps on the carved stand; will not this suit you?' If he had spoken from the standpoint of the pigs, he would have said, 'The better plan will be to feed us with our bran and chaff, and leave us in our pen.' When consulting for himself, he preferred to enjoy, while he lived, his carriage and cap of office, and after death to be borne to the grave on the ornamented carriage, with the canopy over his coffin. Consulting for the pigs, he did not think of these things, but for himself he would have chosen them. Why did he think so differently (for himself and) for the pigs?

7. (Once), when duke Hwan was hunting by a marsh, with Kwan Kung driving the carriage, he saw a ghost. Laying his hand on that of Kwan Kung, he said to him, 'Do you see anything, Father Kung?' 'Your servant sees nothing,' was the reply. The duke then returned, talking incoherently and becoming ill, so that for several days he did not go out. Among the officers of Khî there was a Hwang-tsze Kâo-âo, who said to the duke, 'Your Grace is injuring yourself; how could a ghost injure you? When a paroxysm of irritation is dispersed, and the breath does not return (to the body), what remains in the body is not sufficient for its wants. When

it ascends and does not descend, the patient becomes accessible to gusts of anger. When it descends and does not ascend, he loses his memory of things. When it neither ascends nor descends, but remains about the heart in the centre of the body, it makes him ill.' The duke said, 'Yes, but are there ghostly sprites?' The officer replied, 'There are. About mountain tarns there is the Lî; about furnaces, the Khieh; about the dust-heaps inside the door, the Lei-thing. In low-lying places in the north-east, the Pei-a and Wa-lung leap about, and in similar places in the north-west there dwells the Yî-yang. About rivers there is the Wang-hsiang; about mounds, the Hsin; about hills, the Khwei; about wilds, the Fang-hwang; about marshes, the Wei-tho.' 'Let me ask what is the Wei-tho like?' asked the duke. Hwang-tsze said, 'It is the size of the nave of a chariot wheel, and the length of the shaft. It wears a purple robe and a red cap. It dislikes the rumbling noise of chariot wheels, and, when it hears it, it puts both its hands to its head and stands up. He who sees it is likely to become the leader of all the other princes.' Duke Hwan burst out laughing and said, 'This was what I saw.' On this he put his robes and cap to rights, and made Hwang-tsze sit with him. Before the day was done, his illness was quite gone, he knew not how.

8. Kî Hsing-tsze was rearing a fighting-cock for the king. Being asked after ten days if the bird were ready, he said, 'Not yet; he is still vain and quarrelsome, and relies on his own vigour.' Being asked the same after other ten days, he said, 'Not yet; he still responds to the crow and the appearance of another bird.' After ten days more, he replied, 'Not yet. He still looks angrily, and is full of spirit.' When a fourth ten days had passed, he replied to the question, 'Nearly so. Though another cock crows, it makes no change in him.

To look at him, you would say he was a cock of wood. His quality is complete. No other cock will dare to meet him, but will run from him.'

9. Confucius was looking at the cataract near the gorge of Lü, which fell a height of 240 cubits, and the spray of which floated a distance of forty lî, (producing a turbulence) in which no tortoise, gavial, fish, or turtle could play. He saw, however, an old man swimming about in it, as if he had sustained some great calamity, and wished to end his life. Confucius made his disciples hasten along the stream to rescue the man; and by the time they had gone several hundred paces, he was walking along singing, with his hair dishevelled, and enjoying himself at the foot of the embankment. Confucius followed and asked him, saying, 'I thought you were a sprite; but, when I look closely at you, I see that you are a man. Let me ask if you have any particular way of treading the water.' The man said, 'No, I have no particular way. I began (to learn the art) at the very earliest time; as I grew up, it became my nature to practise it; and my

success in it is now as sure as fate. I enter and go down with the water in the very centre of its whirl, and come up again with it when it whirls the other way. I follow the way of the water, and do nothing contrary to it of myself;-- this is how I tread it.' Confucius said, 'What do you mean by saying that you began to learn the art at the very earliest time; that as you grew up, it became your nature to practise it, and that your success in it now is as sure as fate?' The man replied, 'I was born among these hills and lived contented among them;-- that was why I say that I have trod this water from my earliest time. I grew up by it, and have been happy treading it;-- that is why I said that to tread it had become natural to me. I know not how I do it, and yet I do it;-- that is why I say that my success is as sure as fate.'

10. Khing, the Worker in Rottlera wood, carved a bell-stand, and when it was completed, all who saw it were astonished as if it were the work of spirits. The marquis of Lû went to see it, and asked by what art he had succeeded in producing it. 'Your subject is but a mechanic,' was the reply; 'what art should I be possessed of? Nevertheless, there is one thing (which I will mention). When your servant had undertaken to make the bell-stand, I did not venture to waste any of my power, and felt it necessary to fast in order to compose my mind. After fasting for three days, I did not presume to think of any congratulation, reward, rank, or emolument (which I might obtain by the execution of my task); after fasting five days, I did not presume to think of the condemnation or commendation (which it would produce), or of the skill or want of skill (which it might display). At the end of the seven days, I had forgotten all about myself;-- my four limbs and my whole person. By this time the thought of your Grace's court (for which I was to make the thing) had passed away; everything that could divert my mind from exclusive devotion to the exercise of my skill had disappeared. Then I went into the forest, and looked at the natural forms of the trees. When I saw one of a perfect form, then the figure of the bell-stand rose up to my view, and I applied my hand to the work. Had I not met with such a tree, I must have abandoned the object; but my Heaven-given faculty and the Heaven-given qualities of the wood were concentrated on it. So it was that my spirit was thus engaged in the production of the bell-stand.'

11. Tung-yê Kî was introduced to duke Kwang to exhibit his driving. His horses went forwards and backwards with the straightness of a line, and wheeled to the right and the left with the exactness of a circle. The duke thought that the lines and circles could not be surpassed if they were woven with silken strings, and told him to make a hundred circuits on the same lines. On the road Yen Ho met the equipage, and on entering (the palace), and seeing the duke, he said, 'Kî's horses will break down,'

but the duke was silent, and gave him no reply. After a little the horses did come back, having broken down; and the duke then said, 'How did you know that it would be so?' Yen Ho said, 'The horses were exhausted, and he was still urging them on. It was this which made me say that they would break down.'

12. The artisan Shui made things round (and square) more exactly than if he had used the circle and square. The operation of his fingers on (the forms of) things was like the transformations of them (in nature), and required no application of his mind; and so his Intelligence was entire and encountered no resistance.

13. To be unthought of by the foot that wears it is the fitness of a shoe; to be unthought of by the waist is the fitness of a girdle. When one's wisdom does not think of the right or the wrong (of a question under discussion), that shows the suitability of the mind (for the question); when one is conscious of no inward change, or outward attraction, that shows the mastery of affairs. He who perceives at once the fitness, and never loses the sense of it, has the fitness that forgets all about what is fitting.

14. There was a Sun Hsiû who went to the door of Tsze-pien Khing-tsze, and said to him in a strange perturbed way, 'When I lived in my village, no one took notice of me, but all said that I did not cultivate (my fields); in a time of trouble and attack, no one took notice of me, but all said that I had no courage. But that I did not cultivate my fields, was really because I never met with a good year; and that I did not do service for our ruler, was because I did not meet with the suitable opportunity to do so. I have been sent about my business by the villagers, and am driven away by the registrars of the district;-- what is my crime? 0 Heaven! how is it that I have met with such a fate?'

Pien-tsze said to him, 'Have you not heard how the perfect man deals with himself? He forgets that he has a liver and gall. He takes no thought of his ears and eyes. He seems lost and aimless beyond the dust and dirt of the world, and enjoys himself at ease in occupations untroubled by the affairs of business. He may be described as acting and yet not relying on what he does, as being superior and yet not using his superiority to exercise any control. But now you would make a display of your wisdom to astonish the ignorant; you would cultivate your person to make the inferiority of others more apparent; you seek to shine as if you were carrying the sun and moon in your hands. That you are complete in your bodily frame, and possess all its nine openings; that you have not met with any calamity in the middle of your course, such as deafness, blindness, or lameness, and can still take your place as a man among other men;-- in all this you are fortunate. What leisure have you to murmur against Heaven? Go away, Sir.'

Sun-tsze on this went out, and Pien-tsze went inside. Having sitten down, after a little time he looked up to heaven, and sighed. His disciples asked him why he sighed, and he said to them, 'Hsiû came to me a little while ago, and I told him the characteristics of the perfect man. I am afraid he will be frightened, and get into a state of perplexity.' His disciples said, 'Not so. If what he said was right, and what you said was wrong, the wrong will certainly not be able to perplex the right. If what he said was wrong, and what you said was right, it was just because he was perplexed that he came to you. What was your fault in dealing with him as you did?' Pien-tsze said, 'Not so. Formerly a bird came, and took up its seat in the suburbs of Lû. The ruler of Lû was pleased with it, and provided an ox, a sheep, and a pig to feast it, causing also the Kiû-shâo to be performed to delight it. But the bird began to be sad, looked dazed, and did not venture to eat or drink. This was what is called "Nourishing a bird, as you would nourish yourself." He who would nourish a bird as a bird should be nourished should let it perch in a deep forest, or let it float on a river or lake, or let it find its food naturally and undisturbed on the level dry ground. Now Hsiû (came to me), a man of slender intelligence, and slight information, and I told him of the characteristics of the perfect man, it was like using a carriage and horses to convey a mouse, or trying to delight a quail with the music of bells and drums;-- could the creatures help being frightened?'

Shan Mû, or 'The Tree on the Mountain.'

1. Kwang-tsze was walking on a mountain, when he saw a great tree with huge branches and luxuriant foliage. A wood-cutter was resting by its side, but he would not touch it, and, when asked the reason, said, that it was of no use for anything, Kwang-tsze then said to his disciples, 'This tree, because its wood is good for nothing, will succeed in living out its natural term of years.' Having left the mountain, the Master lodged in the house of an old friend, who was glad to see him, and ordered his waiting-lad to kill a goose and boil it. The lad said, 'One of our geese can cackle, and the other cannot;-- which of them shall I kill?' The host said, 'Kill the one that cannot cackle.'

Next day, his disciples asked Kwang-tsze, saying, 'Yesterday the tree on the mountain (you said) would live out its years because of the uselessness of its wood, and now our host's goose has died because of its want of power (to cackle);-- which of these conditions, Master, would you prefer to be in?' Kwang-tsze laughed and said, '(If I said that) I would prefer to be in a position between being fit to be useful and wanting that fitness, that would seem to be the right position, but it would not be so, for it would not put me beyond being involved in trouble; whereas one who takes his seat on the Tâo and its Attributes, and there finds his ease and enjoyment, is not exposed to such a contingency. He is above the reach both of praise and of detraction; now he (mounts aloft) like a dragon, now he (keeps beneath) like a snake; he is transformed with the (changing) character of the time, and is not willing to addict himself to any one thing; now in a high position and now in a low, he is in harmony with all his surroundings; he enjoys himself at ease with the Author of all things; he treats things as things, and is not a thing to them:-- where is his liability to be involved in trouble? This was the method of Shan Nang and Hwang-Tî. As to those who occupy themselves with the qualities of things, and with the teaching and practice of the human relations, it is not so with them. Union brings on separation; success, overthrow; sharp corners, the use of the file; honour, critical remarks; active exertion, failure; wisdom, scheming; inferiority, being despised:-- where is the possibility of unchangeableness in any of these conditions? Remember this, my disciples. Let your abode be here,-- in the Tâo and its Attributes.'

2. Î-liâo, an officer of Shih-nan, having an interview with the marquis of Lû, found him looking sad, and asked him why he was so. The marquis said, 'I have studied the ways of the former kings, and cultivated the inheritance left me by my predecessors. I reverence the spirits of the

departed and honour the men of worth, doing this with personal devotion, and without the slightest intermission. Notwithstanding, I do not
avoid meeting with calamity, and this it is which makes me sad.' The officer
said, 'The arts by which you try to remove calamity are shallow. Think of
the close-furred fox and of the elegantly-spotted leopard. They lodge in
the forests on the hills, and lurk in their holes among the rocks;-- keeping
still. At night they go about, and during day remain in their lairs;-- so
cautious are they. Even if they are suffering from hunger, thirst, and other
distresses, they still keep aloof from men, seeking their food about the
Kiang and the Ho;-- so resolute are they. Still they are not able to escape
the danger of the net or the trap; and what fault is it of theirs? It is their
skins which occasion them the calamity.

'And is not the state of Lû your lordship's skin? I wish your lordship
to rip your skin from your body, to cleanse your heart, to put away your
desires, and to enjoy yourself where you will be without the presence
of any one. In the southern state of Yüeh, there is a district called "the
State of Established Virtue." The people are ignorant and simple; their
object is to minimise the thought of self and make their desires few; they
labour but do not lay up their gains; they give but do not seek for any
return; they do not know what righteousness is required of them in any
particular case, nor by what ceremonies their performances should be
signalised; acting in a wild and eccentric way as if they were mad, they
yet keep to the grand rules of conduct. Their birth is an occasion for joy;
their death is followed by the rites of burial. I should wish your lordship
to leave your state; to give up your ordinary ways, and to proceed to that
country by the directest course.'

The ruler said, 'The way to it is distant and difficult; there are rivers
and hills; and as I have neither boat nor carriage, how am I to go?' The
officer from Shih-nan rejoined, 'If your lordship abjure your personal
state, and give up your wish to remain here, that will serve you for a carriage.' The ruler rejoined, 'The way to it is solitary and distant, and there
are no people on it;-- whom shall I have as my companions? I have no
provisions prepared, and how shall I get food?-- how shall I be able to get
(to the country)?' The officer said, 'Minimise your lordship's expenditure,
and make your wants few, and though you have no provisions prepared,
you will find you have enough. Wade through the rivers and float along
on the sea, where however you look, you see not the shore, and, the farther you go, you do not see where your journey is to end ;-- those who
escorted you to the shore will return, and after that you will feel yourself
far away. Thus it is that he who owns men (as their ruler) is involved in
troubles, and he who is owned by men (as their ruler) suffers from sadness; and hence Yâo would neither own men, nor be owned by them. I

wish to remove your trouble, and take away your sadness, and it is only (to be done by inducing you) to enjoy yourself with the Tâo in the land of Great Vacuity.

'If a man is crossing a river in a boat, and another empty vessel comes into collision with it, even though he be a man of a choleric temper, he will not be angry with it. If there be a person, however, in that boat, he will bawl out to him to haul out of the way. If his shout be not heard, he will repeat it; and if the other do not then hear, he will call out a third time, following up the shout with abusive terms. Formerly he was not angry, but now he is; formerly (he thought) the boat was empty, but now there is a person in it. If a man can empty himself of himself, during his time in the world, who can harm him?'

3. Pei-kung Shê was collecting taxes for duke Ling of Wei, to be employed in making (a peal of) bells. (In connexion with the work) he built an altar outside the gate of the suburban wall; and in three months the bells were completed, even to the suspending of the upper and lower (tiers). The king's son Khing-kî saw them, and asked what arts he had employed in the making of them. Shê replied, 'Besides my undivided attention to them, I did not venture to use any arts. I have heard the saying, "After all the carving and the chiselling, let the object be to return to simplicity." I was as a child who has no knowledge; I was extraordinarily slow and hesitating; they grew like the springing plants of themselves. In escorting those who went and meeting those who came, my object was neither to hinder the comers nor detain the goers. I suffered those who strongly opposed to take their way, and accepted those who did their best to come to terms. I allowed them all to do the utmost they could, and in this way morning and evening I collected the taxes. I did not have the slightest trouble, and how much more will this be the case with those who pursue the Great Way (on a grand scale)!'

4. Confucius was kept (by his enemies) in a state of siege between Khan and Tshâi, and for seven days had no food cooked with fire to eat. The Thâi-kung Zân went to condole with him, and said, 'You had nearly met with your death.' 'Yes,' was the reply. 'Do you dislike death?' 'I do.' Then Zan continued, 'Let me try and describe a way by which (such a) death may be avoided.-- In the eastern sea there are birds which go by the name of Î-îs; they fly low and slowly as if they were deficient in power. They fly as if they were leading and assisting one another, and they press on one another when they roost. No one ventures to take the lead in going forward, or to be the last in going backwards. In eating no one ventures to take the first mouthful, but prefers the fragments left by others. In this way (the breaks in) their line are not many, and men outside them cannot

harm them, so that they escape injury.

'The straight tree is the first to be cut down; the well of sweet water is the first to be exhausted. Your aim is to embellish your wisdom so as to startle the ignorant, and to cultivate your person to show the unsightliness of others. A light shines around you as if you were carrying with you the sun and moon, and thus it is that you do not escape such calamity. Formerly I heard a highly accomplished man say, "Those who boast have no merit. The merit which is deemed complete will begin to decay. The fame which is deemed complete will begin to wane." Who can rid himself of (the ideas of) merit and fame, and return and put himself on the level of the masses of men? The practice of the Tâo flows abroad, but its master does not care to dwell where it can be seen; his attainments in it hold their course, but he does not wish to appear in its display. Always simple and commonplace, he may seem to be bereft of reason. He obliterates the traces of his action, gives up position and power, and aims not at merit and fame.

Therefore he does not censure men, and men do not censure him. The perfect man does not seek to be heard of; how is it that you delight in doing so?'

Confucius said, 'Excellent;' and thereupon he took leave of his associates, forsook his disciples, retired to the neighbourhood of a great marsh, wore skins and hair cloth, and ate acorns and chestnuts. He went among animals without causing any confusion among their herds, and among birds without troubling their movements. Birds and beasts did not dislike him; how much less would men do so!

5. Confucius asked Tsze-sang Hû, saying, 'I was twice driven from Lû; the tree was felled over me in Sung; I was obliged to disappear from Wei; I was reduced to extreme distress in Shang and Kâu; and I was kept in a state of siege between Khan and Tshâi. I have encountered these various calamities; my intimate associates are removed from me more and more; my followers and friends are more and more dispersed;-- why have all these things befallen me?' Tsze-sang Hû replied, 'Have you not heard of the flight of Lin Hui of Kiâ;-- how he abandoned his round jade symbol of rank, worth a thousand pieces of silver, and hurried away with his infant son on his back? If it be asked, "Was it because of the market value of the child?" But that value was small (compared with the value of the jade token). If it be asked again, "Was it because of the troubles (of his office)?" But the child would occasion him much more trouble. Why was it then that, abandoning the jade token, worth a thousand pieces of silver, he hurried away with the child on his back? Lin Hui (himself) said, "The union between me and the token rested on the ground of gain;

that between me and the child was of Heaven's appointment." Where the bond of union is its profitableness, when the pressure of poverty, calamity, distress, and injury come, the parties abandon one another; when it is of Heaven's appointment, they hold in the same circumstances to one another. Now between abandoning one another, and holding to one another, the difference is great. Moreover, the intercourse of superior men is tasteless as water, while that of mean men is sweet as new wine. But the tastelessness of the superior men leads on to affection, and the sweetness of the mean men to aversion. The union which originates without any cause will end in separation without any cause.'

Confucius said, 'I have reverently received your instructions.' And hereupon, with a slow step and an assumed air of ease, he returned to his own house. There he made an end of studying and put away his books. His disciples came no more to make their bow to him (and be taught), but their affection for him increased the more.

Another day Sang Hû said further to him, 'When Shun was about to die, he charged Yü, saying, 'Be upon your guard. (The attraction of) the person is not like that of sympathy; the (power of) affection is not like the leading (of example). Where there is sympathy, there will not be separation; where there is (the leading of) example, there will be no toil. Where there is neither separation nor toil, you will not have to seek the decoration of forms to make the person attractive, and where there is no such need of those forms, there will certainly be none for external things.'

6. Kwang-tsze in a patched dress of coarse cloth, and having his shoes tied together with strings, was passing by the king of Wei, who said to him, 'How great, Master, is your distress?' Kwang-tsze replied, 'It is poverty, not distress! While a scholar possesses the Tâo and its Attributes, he cannot be going about in distress. Tattered clothes and shoes tied on the feet are the sign of poverty, and not of distress. This is what we call not meeting with the right time. Has your majesty not seen the climbing monkey? When he is among the plane trees, rottleras, oaks, and camphor trees, he grasps and twists their branches (into a screen), where he reigns quite at his ease, so that not even Î or Phang Mang could spy him out. When, however, he finds himself among the prickly mulberry and date trees, and other thorns, he goes cautiously, casts sidelong glances, and takes every trembling movement with apprehension;-- it is not that his sinews and bones are straitened, and have lost their suppleness, but the situation is unsuitable for him, and he cannot display his agility. And now when I dwell under a benighted ruler, and seditious ministers, how is it possible for me not to be in distress ? My case might afford an illustration of the cutting out the heart of Pî-kan!'

7. When Confucius was reduced to great distress between Khan and Khâi, and for seven days he had no cooked food to eat, he laid hold of a decayed tree with his left hand, and with his right hand tapped it with a decayed branch, singing all the while the ode of Piâo-shih. He had his instrument, but the notes were not marked on it. There was a noise, but no blended melody. The sound of the wood and the voice of the man came together like the noise of the plough through the ground, yet suitably to the feelings of the disciples around. Yen Hui, who was standing upright, with his hands crossed on his breast, rolled his eyes round to observe him. Kung-nî, fearing that Hui would go to excess in manifesting how he honoured himself, or be plunged in sorrow through his love for him, said to him, 'Hui, not to receive (as evils) the inflictions of Heaven is easy; not to receive (as benefits) the favours of men is difficult. There is no beginning which was not an end. The Human and the Heavenly may be one and the same. Who, for instance, is it that is now singing?' Hui said, 'I venture to ask how not to receive (as evils) the inflictions of Heaven is easy.' Kung-nî said, 'Hunger, thirst, cold, and heat, and having one's progress entirely blocked up;-- these are the doings of Heaven and Earth, necessary incidents in the revolutions of things. They are occurrences of which we say that we will pass on (composedly) along with them. The minister of another does not dare to refuse his commands; and if he who is discharging the duty of a minister feels it necessary to act thus, how much more should we wait with ease on the commands of Heaven!' 'What do you mean by saying that not to receive (as benefits) the favours of men is difficult?' Kung-nî said, 'As soon as one is employed in office, he gets forward in all directions; rank and emolument come to him together, and without end. But these advantages do not come from one's self;-- it is my appointed lot to have such external good. The superior man is not a robber; the man of worth is no filcher;-- if I prefer such things, what am I? Hence it is said, "There is no bird wiser than the swallow." Where its eye lights on a place that is not suitable for it, it does not give it a second glance. Though it may drop the food from its mouth, it abandons it, and hurries off. It is afraid of men, and yet it stealthily takes up its dwelling by his; finding its protection in the altars of the Land and Grain.'

'What do you mean by saying that there is no beginning which was not an end?' Kung-nî said, 'The change-- rise and dissolution-- of all things (continually) goes on, but we do not know who it is that maintains and continues the process. How do we know when any one begins? How do we know when he will end? We have simply to wait for it, and nothing more.'

'And what do you mean by saying that the Human and the Heavenly are one and the same?' Kung-nî said, 'Given man, and you have Heaven; given Heaven, and you still have Heaven (and nothing more). That man can not have Heaven is owing to the limitation of his nature. The sagely man quietly passes away with his body, and there is an end of it.'

8. As Kwang Kâu was rambling in the park of Tiâo-ling he saw a strange bird which came from the south. Its wings were seven cubits in width, and its eyes were large, an inch in circuit. It touched the forehead of Kâu as it passed him, and lighted in a grove of chestnut trees. 'What bird is this?' said he, 'with such great wings not to go on! and with such large eyes not to see me!' He lifted up his skirts, and hurried with his cross-bow, waiting for (an opportunity to shoot) it. (Meanwhile) he saw a cicada, which had just alighted in a beautiful shady spot, and forgot its (care for its) body. (Just then), a preying mantis raised its feelers, and pounced on the cicada, in its eagerness for its prey, (also) forgetting (its care for) its body; while the strange bird took advantage of its opportunity to secure them both, in view of that gain forgetting its true (instinct of preservation). Kwang Kâu with an emotion of pity, said, 'Ah! so it is that things bring evil on one another, each of these creatures invited its own calamity.' (With this) he put away his cross-bow, and was hurrying away back, when the forester pursued him with terms of reproach.

When he returned and went into his house, he did not appear in his courtyard for three months. (When he came out), Lan Tsü (his disciple) asked him, saying, 'Master, why have you for this some time avoided the courtyard so much?' Kwang-tsze replied, 'I was guarding my person, and forgot myself; I was looking at turbid water, till I mistook the clear pool. And moreover I have heard the Master say, "Going where certain customs prevail, you should follow those customs." I was walking about in the park of Tiâo-ling, and forgot myself. A strange bird brushed past my forehead, and went flying about in the grove of chestnuts, where it forgot the true (art of preserving itself). The forester of the chestnut grove thought that I was a fitting object for his reproach. These are the reasons why I have avoided the courtyard.'

9. Yang-tsze, having gone to Sung, passed the night in a lodging-house, the master of which had two concubines;-- one beautiful, the other ugly. The ugly one was honoured, however, and the beautiful one contemned. Yang-tsze asked the reason, and a little boy of the house replied, 'The beauty knows her beauty, and we do not recognise it. The ugly one knows her ugliness, and we do not recognise it.' Yang-tsze said, 'Remember it, my disciples. Act virtuously, and put away the practice of priding yourselves on your virtue. If you do this, where can you go to that you will not be loved?'

Thien Tsze-fang.

1. Thien Tsze-fang, sitting in attendance on the marquis Wan of Wei, often quoted (with approbation) the words of Khî Kung. The marquis said, 'Is Khî Kung your preceptor?' Tsze-fang replied, 'No. He only belongs to the same neighbourhood. In speaking about the Tâo, his views are often correct, and therefore I quote them as I do.' The marquis went on, 'Then have you no preceptor?' 'I have.' 'And who is he?' He is Tung-kwo Shun-tsze.' 'And why, my Master, have I never heard you quote his words?' Tsze-fang replied, 'He is a man who satisfies the true (ideal of humanity); a man in appearance, but (having the mind of) Heaven. Void of any thought of himself, he accommodates himself to others, and nourishes the true ideal that belongs to him. With all his purity, he is forbearing to others. Where they are without the Tâo, he rectifies his demeanour, so that they understand it, and in consequence their own ideas melt away and disappear. How should one like me be fit to quote his words?' When Tsze-fang went out, the marquis Wan continued in a state of dumb amazement all the day. He then called Lung Lî-khan, and said to him, 'How far removed from us is the superior man of complete virtue! Formerly I thought the words of the sages and wise men, and the practice of benevolence and righteousness, to be the utmost we could reach to. Since I have heard about the preceptor of Tsze-fang, my body is all unstrung, and I do not wish to move, and my mouth is closed up, and I do not wish to speak;-- what I have learned has been only a counterfeit of the truth. Yes, (the possession of Wei) has been an entanglement to me.'

2. Wan-po Hsüeh-tsze, on his way to Khî, stayed some time in Lû, where some persons of the state begged to have an interview with him. He refused them, saying, 'I have heard that the superior men of these Middle States understand the (subjects of) ceremony and righteousness, but are deplorably ignorant of the minds of men. I do not wish to see them.' He went on to Khî; and on his way back (to the south), he again stayed in Lû, when the same persons begged as before for an interview. He then said, 'Formerly they asked to see me, and now again they seek an interview. They will afford me some opportunity of bringing out my sentiments.' He went out accordingly and saw the visitors, and came in again with a sigh. Next day the same thing occurred, and his servant said to him, 'How is it that whenever you see those visitors, you are sure to come in again sighing?' ' I told you before,' was the reply, 'that the people of these Middle States understand (the subjects of) ceremony and righteousness, but are deplorably ignorant of the minds of men. Those men who have just seen me, as they came in and went out would describe, one a circle

and another a square, and in their easy carriage would be like, one a dragon and another a tiger. They remonstrated with me as sons (with their fathers), and laid down the way for me as fathers (for their sons). It was this which made me sigh.'

Kung-nî saw the man, but did not speak a word to him. Tsze-Lû said, 'You have wished, Sir, to see this Wan-po Hsüeh-tsze for a long time; what is the reason that when you have seen him, you have not spoken a word?' Kung-nî replied, 'As soon as my eyes lighted on that man, the Tâo in him was apparent. The situation did not admit of a word being spoken.'

3. Yen Yüan asked Kung-nî, saying, 'Master, when you pace quietly along, I also pace along; when you go more quickly, I also do the same; when you gallop, I also gallop; but when you race along and spurn the dust, then I can only stand and look, and keep behind you.' The Master said, 'Hui, what do you mean?' The reply was, 'In saying that "when you, Master, pace quietly along, I also pace along," I mean that when you speak, I also speak. By saying, "When you go more quickly, I also do the same," I mean that when you reason, I also reason. By saying, "When you gallop, I also gallop," I mean that when you speak of the Way, I also speak of the Way; but by saying, "When you race along and spurn the dust, then I can only stare, and keep behind you," I am thinking how though you do not speak, yet all men believe you; though you are no partisan, yet all parties approve your catholicity; and though you sound no instrument, yet people all move on harmoniously before you, while (all the while) I do not know how all this comes about; and this is all which my words are intended to express.'

Kung-nî said, 'But you must try and search the matter out. Of all causes for sorrow there is none so great as the death of the mind;-- the death of man's (body) is only next to it. The sun comes forth in the east, and sets in the extreme west;-- all things have their position determined by these two points. All that have eyes and feet wait for this (sun), and then proceed to do what they have to do. When this comes forth, they appear in their places; when it sets, they disappear. It is so with all things. They have that for which they wait, and (on its arrival) they die; they have that for which they wait, and then (again) they live. When once I receive my frame thus completed, I remain unchanged, awaiting the consummation of my course. I move as acted on by things, day and night without cessation, and I do not know when I will come to an end. Clearly I am here a completed frame, and even one who (fancies that he) knows what is appointed cannot determine it beforehand. I am in this way daily passing on, but all day long I am communicating my views to you; and now, as we are shoulder to shoulder you fail (to understand me);-- is it not matter for lamentation? You are able in a measure to set forth what I more clearly set forth; but that is passed away, and you look for it, as if it were still existing, just as if you were looking for a horse in the now empty place where it was formerly exhibited for sale. You have very much forgotten my service to you, and I have very much forgotten wherein I served you. But nevertheless why should you account this such an evil? What you forget is but my old self; that which cannot be forgotten remains with me.'

4. Confucius went to see Lâo Tan, and arrived just as he had completed the bathing of his head, and was letting his dishevelled hair get dry. There he was, motionless, and as if there were not another man in the world. Confucius waited quietly; and, when in a little time he was introduced, he said, 'Were my eyes dazed? Is it really you? Just now, your body, Sir, was like the stump of a rotten tree. You looked as if you had no thought of anything, as if you had left the society of men, and were standing in the solitude (of yourself).' Lâo Tan replied, 'I was enjoying myself in thinking about the commencement of things.' 'What do you mean?' 'My mind is so cramped, that I hardly know it; my tongue is so tied that I cannot tell it; but I will try to describe it to you as nearly as I can. When the state of Yin was perfect, all was cold and severe; when the state of Yang was perfect, all was turbulent and agitated. The coldness and severity came forth from Heaven; the turbulence and agitation issued from Earth. The two states communicating together, a harmony ensued and things were produced. Some one regulated and controlled this, but no one has seen his form. Decay and growth; fulness and emptiness; darkness and light; the changes of the sun and the transformations of the moon:-- these are brought about from day to day; but no one sees the process of production. Life has its origin from which it springs, and death has its place from which it returns. Beginning and ending go on in mutual contrariety without any determinable commencement, and no one knows how either comes to an end. If we disallow all this, who originates and presides over all these phenomena?'

Confucius said, 'I beg to ask about your enjoyment in these thoughts.' Lâo Tan replied, 'The comprehension of this is the most admirable and the most enjoyable (of all acquisitions). The getting of the most admirable and the exercise of the thoughts in what is the most enjoyable, constitutes what we call the Perfect man.' Confucius said, 'I should like to hear the method of attaining to it.' The reply was, 'Grass-eating animals do not dislike to change their pastures; creatures born in the water do not dislike to change their waters. They make a small change, but do not lose what is the great and regular requirement (of their nature); joy, anger, sadness, and delight do not enter into their breasts (in connexion with such events). Now the space under the sky is occupied by all things in their unity. When they possess that unity and equally share it, then the four limbs and hundred members of their body are but so much dust and dirt, while death and life, their ending and beginning, are but as the succession of day and night, which cannot disturb their enjoyment; and how much less will they be troubled by gains and losses, by calamity and happiness! Those who renounce the paraphernalia of rank do it as if they were casting away so much mud;-- they know that they are themselves more honourable than those paraphernalia. The honour belonging to one's self is not lost by any change (of condition). Moreover, a myriad transformations may take place before the end of them is reached. What is there in all this sufficient to trouble the mind? Those who have attained to the Tâo understand the subject.'

Confucius said, '0 Master, your virtue is equal to that of Heaven and Earth, and still I must borrow (some of your) perfect words (to aid me) in the cultivation of my mind. Who among the superior men of antiquity could give such expression to them?' Lâo Tan replied, 'Not so. Look at the spring, the water of which rises and overflows;-- it does nothing, but it naturally acts so. So with the perfect man and his virtue;-- he does not cultivate it, and nothing evades its influence. He is like heaven which is high of itself, like earth which is solid of itself, like the sun and moon which shine of themselves;-- what need is there to cultivate it?'

Confucius went out and reported the conversation to Yen Hui, saying, 'In the (knowledge of the) Tâo am I any better than an animalcule in vinegar? But for the Master's lifting the veil from me, I should not have known the grand perfection of Heaven and Earth.'

5. At an interview of Kwang-Tsze with duke Âi of Lû, the duke said, 'There are many of the Learned class in Lû; but few of them can be compared with you, Sir.' Kwang-Tsze replied, 'There are few Learned men in Lû.' 'Everywhere in Lû,' rejoined the duke, 'you see men wearing the dress of the Learned;-- how can you say that they are few?' 'I have heard,' said Kwang-Tsze, 'that those of them who wear round caps know the times of heaven; that those who wear square shoes know the contour of the ground; and that those who saunter about with semicircular stones at their girdle-pendents settle matters in dispute as they come before them. But superior men who are possessed of such knowledge will not be found wearing the dress, and it does not follow that those who wear the dress possess the knowledge. If your Grace think otherwise, why not issue a notification through the state, that it shall be a capital offence to wear the dress without possessing the knowledge.' On this the duke issued such a notification, and in five days, throughout all Lû, there was no one who dared to wear the dress of the Learned. There was only one old man who

came and stood in it at the duke's gate. The duke instantly called him in, and questioned him about the affairs of the state, when he talked about a thousand points and ten thousand divergences from them. Kwang-tsze said, 'When the state of Lû can thus produce but one man of the Learned class, can he be said to be many?'

6. The ideas of rank and emolument did not enter the mind of Pâi-lî Hsî, and so he became a cattle-feeder, and his cattle were all in fine condition. This made duke Mû of Khin forget the meanness of his position, and put the government (of his state) into his hands. Neither life nor death entered into the mind of (Shun), the Lord of Yü, and therefore he was able to influence others.

7. The ruler Yüan of Sung wishing to have a map drawn, the masters of the pencil all came (to undertake the task). Having received his instructions and made their bows, they stood, licking their pencils and preparing their ink. Half their number, however, remained outside. There was one who came late, with an air of indifference, and did not hurry forward. When he had received his instructions and made his bow, he did not keep standing, but proceeded to his shed. The duke sent a man to see him, and there he was, with his upper garment off, sitting cross-legged, and nearly naked. The ruler said, 'He is the man; he is a true draughtsman.'

8. King Wan was (once) looking about him at Tsang, when he saw an old man fishing. But his fishing was no fishing. It was not the fishing of one whose business is fishing. He was always fishing (as if he had no object in the occupation). The king wished to raise him to office, and put the government into his hands, but was afraid that such a step would give dissatisfaction to his great ministers, his uncles, and cousins. He then wished to dismiss the man altogether from his mind, but he could not bear the thought that his people should be without (such a) Heaven (as their Protector). On this, (next) morning, he called together his great officers, and said to them, 'Last night, I dreamt that I saw a good man, with a dark complexion and a beard, riding on a piebald horse, one half of whose hoofs were red, who commanded me, saying, "Lodge your government in the hands of the old man of Tsang; and perhaps the evils of your people will be cured."' The great officers said eagerly, 'It was the king, your father.' King Wan said, 'Let us then submit the proposal to the tortoise-shell.' They replied, 'It is the order of your father. Let not your majesty think of any other. Why divine about it?' (The king) then met the old man of Tsang, and committed the government to him.

The statutes and laws were not changed by him; not a one-sided order (of his own) was issued; but when the king made a survey of the kingdom after three years, he found that the officers had destroyed the plantations (which harboured banditti), and dispersed their occupiers, that the superintendents of the official departments did not plume themselves on their successes, and that no unusual grain measures were allowed within the different states. When the officers had destroyed the dangerous plantations and dispersed their occupants, the highest value was set on the common interests; when the chiefs of departments did not plume themselves on their successes, the highest value was set on the common business; when unusual grain measures did not enter the different states, the different princes had no jealousies. On this king Wan made the old man his Grand Preceptor, and asked him, with his own face to the north, whether his government might be extended to all the kingdom. The old man looked perplexed and gave no reply, but with aimless look took his leave. In the morning he had issued his orders, and at night he had gone his way; nor was he heard of again all his life. Yen Yüan questioned Confucius, saying, 'Was even king Wan unequal to determine his course? What had he to do with resorting to a dream?' Kung-nî replied, 'Be silent and do not say a word! King Wan was complete in everything. What have you to do with criticising him? He only had recourse (to the dream) to meet a moment's difficulty.'

9. Lieh Yü-khâu was exhibiting his archery to Po-hwan Wû-zan. Having drawn the bow to its full extent, with a cup of water placed on his elbow, he let fly. As the arrow was discharged, another was put in its place; and as that was sent off, a third was ready on the string. All the while he stood like a statue. Po- hwan Wû-zan said, 'That is the shooting of an archer, but not of one who shoots without thinking about his shooting. Let me go up with you to the top of a high mountain, treading with you among the tottering rocks, till we arrive at the brink of a precipice, 800 cubits deep, and (I will then see) if you can shoot.' On this they went up a high mountain, making their way among the tottering rocks, till they came to the brink of a precipice 800 cubits deep. Then Wû-zan turned round and walked backwards, till his feet were two-thirds of their length outside the edge, and beckoned Yü-khâu to come forward. He, however, had fallen prostrate on the ground, with the sweat pouring down to his heels. Then the other said, 'The Perfect man looks up to the azure sky above, or dives down to the yellow springs beneath, or soars away to the eight ends of the universe, without any change coming over his spirit or his breath. But now the trepidation of your mind appears in your dazed eyes; your inward feeling of peril is extreme!'

10. Kien Wû asked Sun-shû Âo, saying, 'You, Sir, were thrice chief minister, and did not feel elated; you were thrice dismissed from that position, without manifesting any sorrow. At first I was in doubt about

you, (but I am not now, since) I see how regularly and quietly the breath comes through your nostrils. How is it that you exercise your mind?' Sun-shû Âo replied, 'In what do I surpass other men? When the position came to me, I thought it should not be rejected; when it was taken away, I thought it could not be retained. I considered that the getting or losing it did not make me what I was, and was no occasion for any manifestation of sorrow;-- that was all. In what did I surpass other men? And moreover, I did not know whether the honour of it belonged to the dignity, or to myself. If it belonged to the dignity, it was nothing to me; if it belonged to me, it had nothing to do with the dignity. While occupied with these uncertainties, and looking round in all directions, what leisure had I to take knowledge of whether men honoured me or thought me mean?'

Kung-nî heard of all this, and said, 'The True men of old could not be fully described by the wisest, nor be led into excess by the most beautiful, nor be forced by the most violent robber. Neither Fû-hsî nor Hwang-Tî could compel them to be their friends. Death and life are indeed great considerations, but they could make no change in their (true) self; and how much less could rank and emolument do so? Being such, their spirits might pass over the Thâi mountain and find it no obstacle to them they might enter the greatest gulphs, and not be wet by them; they might occupy the lowest and smallest positions without being distressed by them. Theirs was the fulness of heaven and earth; the more that they gave to others, the more they had.'

The king of Khû and the ruler of Fan were sitting together. After a little while, the attendants of the king said, 'Fan has been destroyed three times.' The ruler of Fan rejoined, 'The destruction of Fan has not been sufficient to destroy what we had that was most deserving to be preserved.' Now, if the destruction of Fan had not been sufficient to destroy that which it had most deserving to be preserved, the preservation of Khû had not been sufficient to preserve that in it most deserving to be preserved. Looking at the matter from this point of view, Fan had not begun to be destroyed, and Khû had not begun to be preserved.

Kih Pei Yû, or 'Knowledge Rambling in the North.'

1. Knowledge had rambled northwards to the region of the Dark Water, where he ascended the height of Imperceptible Slope, when it happened that he met with Dumb Inaction. Knowledge addressed him, saying, 'I wish to ask you some questions:-- By what process of thought and anxious consideration do we get to know the Tâo? Where should we dwell and what should we do to find our rest in the Tâo? From what point should we start and what path should we pursue to make the Tâo our own?' He asked these three questions, but Dumb Inaction gave him no reply. Not only did he not answer, but he did not know how to answer.

Knowledge, disappointed by the fruitlessness of his questions, returned to the south of the Bright Water, and ascended the height of the End of Doubt, where he saw Heedless Blurter, to whom he put the same questions, and who replied, 'Ah! I know, and will tell you.' But while he was about to speak, he forgot what he wanted to say.

Knowledge, (again) receiving no answer to his questions, returned to the palace of the Tî, where he saw Hwang-Tî, and put the questions to him. Hwang-Tî said, 'To exercise no thought and no anxious consideration is the first step towards knowing the Tâo; to dwell nowhere and do nothing is the first step towards resting in the Tâo; to start from nowhere and pursue no path is the first step towards making the Tâo your own.'

Knowledge then asked Hwang-Tî, saying, 'I and you know this; those two did not know it; which of us is right?' The reply was, 'Dumb Inaction is truly right; Heedless Blurter has an appearance of being so; I and you are not near being so. (As it is said), "Those who know (the Tâo) do not speak of it; those who speak of it do not know it;" and "Hence the sage conveys his instructions without the use of speech." The Tâo cannot be made ours by constraint; its characteristics will not come to us (at our call). Benevolence may be practised; Righteousness may be partially attended to; by Ceremonies men impose on one another. Hence it is said, "When the Tâo was lost, its Characteristics appeared. When its Characteristics were lost, Benevolence appeared. When Benevolence was lost, Righteousness appeared. When Righteousness was lost, Ceremonies appeared. Ceremonies are but (the unsubstantial) flowers of the Tâo, and the commencement of disorder." Hence (also it is further said), "He who practises the Tâo, daily diminishes his doing. He diminishes it and again diminishes it, till he arrives at doing nothing. Having arrived at this non-inaction, there is nothing that he does not do." Here now there is something, a regularly fashioned utensil;-- if you wanted to make it return to the original condition of its materials, would it not be difficult to make it do so? Could any but the Great Man accomplish this easily?

'Life is the follower of death, and death is the predecessor of life; but who knows the Arranger (of this connexion between them)? The life is due to the collecting of the breath. When that is collected, there is life; when it is dispersed, there is death. Since death and life thus attend on each other, why should I account (either of) them an evil?

'Therefore all things go through one and the same experience. (Life) is accounted beautiful because it is spirit-like and wonderful, and death is accounted ugly because of its foetor and putridity. But the foetid and putrid is transformed again into the spirit-like and wonderful, and the spirit-like and wonderful is transformed again into the foetid and putrid. Hence it is said, "All under the sky there is one breath of life, and therefore the sages prized that unity."'

Knowledge said to Hwang-Tî, 'I asked Dumb Inaction, and he did not answer me. Not only did he not answer me, but he did not know how to answer me. I asked Heedless Blurter, and while he wanted to tell me, he yet did not do so. Not only did he not tell me, but while he wanted to tell me, he forgot all about my questions. Now I have asked you, and you knew (all about them);-- why (do you say that) you are not near doing so?' Hwang-Tî replied, 'Dumb Inaction was truly right, because he did not know the thing. Heedless Blurter was nearly right, because he forgot it. I and you are not nearly right, because we know it.' Heedless Blurter heard of (all this), and considered that Hwang-Tî knew how to express himself (on the subject).

2. (The operations of) Heaven and Earth proceed in the most admirable way, but they say nothing about them; the four seasons observe the clearest laws, but they do not discuss them ; all things have their complete and distinctive constitutions, but they say nothing about them.

The sages trace out the admirable operations of Heaven and Earth, and reach to and understand the distinctive constitutions of all things; and thus it is that the Perfect Man (is said to) do nothing and the Greatest Sage to originate nothing, such language showing that they look to Heaven and Earth as their model. Even they, with their spirit-like and most exquisite intelligence, as well as all the tribes that undergo their transformations, the dead and the living, the square and the round, do not understand their root and origin, but nevertheless they all from the oldest time by it preserve their being.

Vast as is the space included within the six cardinal points, it all (and all that it contains) lies within (this twofold root of Heaven and Earth); small as is an autumn hair, it is indebted to this for the completion of its form. All things beneath the sky, now rising, now descending, ever continue the same through this. The Yin and Yang, and the four seasons revolve and move by it, each in its proper order. Now it seems to be lost in obscurity, but it continues; now it seems to glide away, and have no form, but it is still spirit-like.

All things are nourished by it, without their knowing it. This is what is called the Root and Origin; by it we may obtain a view of what we mean by Heaven.

3. Nieh Khüeh asked about the Tâo from Phei-î, who replied, 'If you keep your body as it should be, and look only at the one thing, the Harmony of Heaven will come to you. Call in your knowledge, and make your measures uniform, and the spiritual (belonging to you) will come and lodge with you; the Attributes (of the Tâo) will be your beauty, and the Tâo (itself) will be your dwelling-place. You will have the simple look of a new-born calf, and will not seek to know the cause (of your being what you are).' Phei-î had not finished these words when the other dozed off into a sleep.

Phei-î was greatly pleased, and walked away, singing as he went,

'Like stump of rotten tree his frame,
Like lime when slaked his mind became. Real is his wisdom, solid, true,
Nor cares what's hidden to pursue.
0 dim and dark his aimless mind! No one from him can counsel find.
What sort of man is he?'

4. Shun asked (his attendant) Khang, saying, 'Can I get the Tâo and hold it as mine?' The reply was, 'Your body is not your own to hold;-- how then can you get and hold the Tâo?' Shun resumed, 'If my body be not mine to possess and hold, who holds it?' Khang said, 'It is the bodily form entrusted to you by Heaven and Earth. Life is not yours to hold. It is the blended harmony (of the Yin and Yang), entrusted to you by Heaven and Earth. Your nature, constituted as it is, is not yours to hold. It is entrusted to you by Heaven and Earth to act in accordance with it. Your grandsons and sons are not yours to hold. They are the exuviae entrusted to you by Heaven and Earth. Therefore when we walk, we should not know where

we are going; when we stop and rest, we should not know what to occupy ourselves with when we eat, we should not know the taste of our food;-- all is done by the strong Yang influence of Heaven and Earth'.

How then can you get (the Tâo), and hold it as your own?'

5. Confucius asked Lâo Tan, saying, 'Being at leisure to-day, I venture to ask you about the Perfect Tâo.' Lâo Tan replied, 'You must, as by fasting and vigil, clear and purge your mind, wash your spirit white as snow, and sternly repress your knowledge. The subject of the Tâo is deep, and difficult to describe;-- I will give you an outline of its simplest attributes.

'The Luminous was produced from the Obscure; the Multiform from the Unembodied; the Spiritual from the Tâo; and the bodily from the seminal essence. After this all things produced one another from their bodily organisations. Thus it is that those which have nine apertures are born from the womb, and those with eight from eggs. But their coming leaves no trace, and their going no monument; they enter by no door; they dwell in no apartment:-- they are in a vast arena reaching in all directions. They who search for and find (the Tâo) in this are strong in their limbs, sincere and far-reaching in their thinking, acute in their hearing, and clear in their seeing. They exercise their minds without being toiled; they respond to everything aright without regard to place or circumstance. Without this heaven would not be high, nor earth broad; the sun and moon would not move, and nothing would flourish:-- such is the operation of the Tâo.

'Moreover, the most extensive knowledge does not necessarily know it; reasoning will not make men wise in it;-- the sages have decided against both these methods. However you try to add to it, it admits of no increase; however you try to take from it, it admits of no diminution;-- this is what the sages maintain about it. How deep it is, like the sea! How grand it is, beginning again when it has come to an end! If it carried along and sustained all things, without being overburdened or weary, that would be like the way of the superior man, merely an external operation; when all things go to it, and find their dependence in it;-- this is the true character of the Tâo.

'Here is a man (born) in one of the middle states. He feels himself independent both of the Yin and Yang, and dwells between heaven and earth; only for the present a mere man, but he will return to his original source. Looking at him in his origin, when his life begins, we have (but) a gelatinous substance in which the breath is collecting. Whether his life be long or his death early, how short is the space between them! It is but the name for a moment of time, insufficient to play the part of a good

Yâo or a bad Kieh in.

'The fruits of trees and creeping plants have their distinctive characters, and though the relationships of men, according to which they are classified, are troublesome, the sage, when he meets with them, does not set himself in opposition to them, and when he has passed through them, he does not seek to retain them; he responds to them in their regular harmony according to his virtue; and even when he accidentally comes across any of them, he does so according to the Tâo. It was thus that the Tâo flourished, thus that the kings arose.

'Men's life between heaven and earth is like a white colt's passing a crevice, and suddenly disappearing. As with a plunge and an effort they all come forth; easily and quietly they all enter again. By a transformation they live, and by another transformation they die. Living things are made sad (by death), and mankind grieve for it; but it is (only) the removal of the bow from its sheath, and the emptying the natural satchel of its contents. There may be some confusion amidst the yielding to the change; but the intellectual and animal souls are taking their leave, and the body will follow them:-- This is the Great Returning home.

'That the bodily frame came from incorporeity, and will return to the same, is what all men in common know, and what those who are on their way to (know) it need not strive for. This is what the multitudes of men discuss together. Those whose (knowledge) is complete do not discuss it;-- such discussion shows that their (knowledge) is not complete. Even the most clear-sighted do not meet (with the Tâo);-- it is better to be silent than to reason about it. The Tâo cannot be heard with the ears;-- it is better to shut the ears than to try and hear it. This is what is called the Great Attainment.'

6. Tung-kwo Tsze asked Kwang-tsze, saying, 'Where is what you call the Tâo to be found?' Kwang-tsze replied, 'Everywhere.' The other said, 'Specify an instance of it. That will be more satisfactory.' ' It is here in this ant.' 'Give a lower instance.' 'It is in this panic grass.' 'Give me a still lower instance.' 'It is in this earthenware tile.' 'Surely that is the lowest instance?' 'It is in that excrement.' To this Tung-kwo Tsze gave no reply.

Kwang-tsze said, 'Your questions, my master, do not touch the fundamental point (of the Tâo). They remind me of the questions addressed by the superintendents of the market to the inspector about examining the value of a pig by treading on it, and testing its weight as the foot descends lower and lower on the body. You should not specify any particular thing. There is not a single thing without (the Tâo). So it is with the Perfect Tâo. And if we call it the Great (Tâo), it is just the same. There are the three terms,-- "Complete," "All-embracing," "the Whole." These names are different, but the reality (sought in them) is the same; referring to the One thing.

'Suppose we were to try to roam about in the palace of No-where;-- when met there, we might discuss (about the subject) without ever coming to an end. Or suppose we were to be together in (the region of) Non-action;-- should we say that (the Tâo was) Simplicity and Stillness? or Indifference and Purity? or Harmony and Ease? My will would be aimless. If it went nowhere, I should not know where it had got to; if it went and came again, I should not know where it had stopped; if it went on going and coming, I should not know when the process would end. In vague uncertainty should I be in the vastest waste. Though I entered it with the greatest knowledge, I should not know how inexhaustible it was. That which makes things what they are has not the limit which belongs to things, and when we speak of things being limited, we mean that they are so in themselves. (The Tâo) is the limit of the unlimited, and the boundlessness of the unbounded.

'We speak of fulness and emptiness; of withering and decay. It produces fulness and emptiness, but is neither fulness nor emptiness; it produces withering and decay, but is neither withering nor decay. It produces the root and branches, but is neither root nor branch; it produces accumulation and dispersion, but is itself neither accumulated nor dispersed.'

7. A-ho Kan and Shan Nang studied together under Lao-lung Kî. Shan Nang was leaning forward on his stool, having shut the door and gone to sleep in the day time. At midday A-ho Kan pushed open the door and entered, saying, 'Lao-lung is dead.' Shan Nang leant forward on his stool, laid hold of his staff and rose. Then he laid the staff aside with a clash, laughed and said, 'That Heaven knew how cramped and mean, how arrogant and assuming I was, and therefore he has cast me off, and is dead. Now that there is no Master to correct my heedless words, it is simply for me to die!' Yen Kang, (who had come in) to condole, heard these words, and said, 'It is to him who embodies the Tâo that the superior men everywhere cling. Now you who do not understand so much as the tip of an autumn hair of it, not even the ten-thousandth part of the Tâo, still know how to keep hidden your heedless words about it and die;-- how much more might he who embodied the Tâo do so! We look for it, and there is no form; we hearken for it, and there is no sound. When men try to discuss it, we call them dark indeed. When they discuss the Tâo, they misrepresent it.'

Hereupon Grand Purity asked Infinitude, saying, 'Do you know the Tâo?' 'I do not know it,' was the reply. He then asked Do-nothing, Who replied, 'I know it.' 'Is your knowledge of it determined by various points?' 'It is.' 'What are they?' Do-nothing said, 'I know that the Tâo may be considered noble, and may be considered mean, that it may be bound and compressed, and that it may be dispersed and diffused. These are the marks by which I know it.' Grand Purity took the words of those two, and asked No- beginning, saying, 'Such were their replies; which was right? and which was wrong? Infinitude's saying that he did not know it? or Do-nothing's saying that he knew it?' No-beginning said, 'The "I do not know it" was profound, and the "I know it" was shallow. The former had reference to its internal nature; the latter to its external conditions.' Grand Purity looked up and sighed, saying, 'Is "not to know it" then to know it? And is "to know it" not to know it? But who knows that he who does not know it (really) knows it?' No-beginning replied, 'The Tâo cannot be heard; what can be heard is not It. The Tâo cannot be seen; what can be seen is not It. The Tâo cannot be expressed in words; what can be expressed in words is not It. Do we know the Formless which gives form to form? In the same way the Tâo does not admit of being named.'

No-beginning (further) said, 'If one ask about the Tâo and another answer him, neither of them knows it. Even the former who asks has never learned anything about the Tâo. He asks what does not admit of being asked, and the latter answers where answer is impossible. When one asks what does not admit of being asked, his questioning is in (dire) extremity. When one answers where answer is impossible, he has no internal knowledge of the subject. When people without such internal knowledge wait to be questioned by others in dire extremity, they show that externally they see nothing of space and time, and internally know nothing of the Grand Commencement. Therefore they cannot cross over the Khwan-lun, nor roam in the Grand Void.'

8. Starlight asked Non-entity, saying, 'Master, do you exist? or do you not exist?' He got no answer to his question, however, and looked stedfastly to the appearance of the other, which was that of a deep void. All day long he looked to it, but could see nothing; he listened for it, but could hear nothing; he clutched at it, but got hold of nothing. Starlight then said, 'Perfect! Who can attain to this? I can (conceive the ideas of) existence and non-existence, but I cannot (conceive the ideas of) non-existing non-existence, and still there be a nonexisting existence. How is it possible to reach to this?'

9. The forger of swords for the Minister of War had reached the age of eighty, and had not lost a hair's- breadth of his ability. The Minister said

to him, 'You are indeed skilful, Sir. Have you any method that makes you so?' The man said, 'Your servant has (always) kept to his work. When I was twenty, I was fond of forging swords. I looked at nothing else. I paid no attention to anything but swords. By my constant practice of it, I came to be able to do the work without any thought of what I was doing. By length of time one acquires ability at any art; and how much more one who is ever at work on it! What is there which does not depend on this, and succeed by it?'

10. Zan Khiû asked Kung-nî, saying, 'Can it be known how it was before heaven and earth?' The reply was, 'It can. It was the same of old as now.' Zan Khiû asked no more and withdrew. Next day, however, he had another interview, and said, 'Yesterday I asked whether it could be known how it was before heaven and earth, and you, Master, said, "It can. As it is now, so it was of old." Yesterday, I seemed to understand you clearly, but to-day it is dark to me. I venture to ask you for an explanation of this.' Kung-nî said, 'Yesterday you seemed to understand me clearly, because your own spiritual nature had anticipated my reply. Today it seems dark to you, for you are in an unspiritual mood, and are trying to discover the meaning. (In this matter) there is no old time and no present; no beginning and no ending. Could it be that there were grandchildren and children before there were (other) grandchildren and children?'

Zan Khiû had not made any reply, when Kung-nî went on, 'Let us have done. There can be no answering (on your part). We cannot with life give life to death; we cannot with death give death to life. Do death and life wait (for each other)? There is that which contains them both in its one comprehension. Was that which was produced before Heaven and Earth a thing? That which made things and gave to each its character was not itself a thing. Things came forth and could not be before things, as if there had (previously) been things;-- as if there had been things (producing one another) without end. The love of the sages for others, and never coming to an end, is an idea taken from this.'

11. Yen Yüan asked Kung-nî, saying, 'Master, I have heard you say, "There should be no demonstration of welcoming; there should be no movement to meet;"-- I venture to ask in what way this affection of the mind may be shown.' The reply was, 'The ancients, amid (all) external changes, did not change internally; now-a-days men change internally, but take no note of external changes. When one only notes the changes of things, himself continuing one and the same, he does not change. How should there be (a difference between) his changing and not changing? How should he put himself in contact with (and come under the influence of) those external changes? He is sure, however, to keep his points

of contact with them from being many. The park of Shih-wei, the garden of Hwang-Tî, the palace of the Lord of Yü, and the houses of Thang and Wû;-- (these all were places in which this was done). But the superior men (so called, of later days), such as the masters of the Literati and of Mohism, were bold to attack each other with their controversies; and how much more so are the men of the present day! Sages in dealing with others do not wound them; and they who do not wound others cannot be wounded by them. Only he whom others do not injure is able to welcome and meet men.

'Forests and marshes make me joyful and glad; but before the joy is ended, sadness comes and succeeds to it. When sadness and joy come, I cannot prevent their approach; when they go, I cannot retain them. How sad it is that men should only be as lodging-houses for things, (and the emotions which they excite)! They know what they meet, but they do not know what they do not meet; they use what power they have, but they cannot be strong where they are powerless. Such ignorance and powerlessness is what men cannot avoid. That they should try to avoid what they cannot avoid, is not this also sad? Perfect speech is to put speech away; perfect action is to put action away; to digest all knowledge that is known is a thing to be despised.'

Kang-sang Khû.

1. Among the disciples of Lâo Tan there was a Kang-sang Khû, who had got a greater knowledge than the others of his doctrines, and took up his residence with it in the north at the hill of Wei-lêi. His servants who were pretentious and knowing he sent away, and his concubines who were officious and kindly he kept at a distance; living (only) with those who were boorish and rude, and employing (only) the bustling and ill-mannered. After three years there was great prosperity in Wei-lêi, and the people said to one another, 'When Mr. Kang-sang first came here, he alarmed us, and we thought him strange; our estimate of him after a short acquaintance was that he could not do us much good; but now that we have known him for years, we find him a more than ordinary benefit. Must he not be near being a sage? Why should you not unite in blessing him as the representative of our departed (whom we worship), and raise an altar to him as we do to the spirit of the grain?' Kang-sang heard of it, kept his face indeed to the south but was dissatisfied.

His disciples thought it strange in him, but he said to them, 'Why, my disciples, should you think this strange in me? When the airs of spring come forth, all vegetation grows; and, when the autumn arrives, all the previous fruits of the earth are matured. Do spring and autumn have these effects without any adequate cause? The processes of the Great Tâo have been in operation. I have heard that the Perfect man dwells idly in his apartment within its surrounding walls, and the people get wild and crazy, not knowing how they should repair to him. Now these small people of Wei-lêi in their opinionative way want to present their offerings to me, and place me among such men of ability and virtue. But am I a man to be set up as such a model? It is on this account that I am dissatisfied when I think of the words of Lâo Tan.'

2. His disciples said, 'Not so. In ditches eight cubits wide, or even twice as much, big fishes cannot turn their bodies about, but minnows and eels find them sufficient for them; on hillocks six or seven cubits high, large beasts cannot conceal themselves, but foxes of evil omen find it a good place for them. And moreover, honour should be paid to the wise, offices given to the able, and preference shown to the good and the beneficial. From of old Yâo and Shun acted thus;-- how much more may the people of Wei-lêi do so! 0 Master, let them have their way!'

Kang-sang replied, 'Come nearer, my little children. If a beast that could hold a carriage in its mouth leave its hill by itself, it will not escape the danger that awaits it from the net; or if a fish that could swallow a boat be left dry by the flowing away of the water, then (even) the ants are able to trouble it. Thus it is that birds and beasts seek to be as high as possible, and fishes and turtles seek to lie as deep as possible. In the same way men who wish to preserve their bodies and lives keep their persons concealed, and they do so in the deepest retirement possible. And moreover, what was there in those sovereigns to entitle them to your laudatory mention? Their sophistical reasonings (resembled) the reckless breaking down of walls and enclosures and planting the wild rubus and wormwood in their place; or making the hair thin before they combed it; or counting the grains of rice before they cooked them. They would do such things with careful discrimination; but what was there in them to benefit the world? If you raise the men of talent to office, you will create disorder; making the people strive with one another for promotion; if you employ men for their wisdom, the people will rob one another (of their reputation). These various things are insufficient to make the people good and honest. They are very eager for gain;-- a son will kill his father, and a minister his ruler (for it). In broad daylight men will rob, and at midday break through walls. I tell you that the root of the greatest disorder was planted in the times of Yâo and Shun. The branches of it will remain for a thousand ages; and after a thousand ages men will be found eating one another.'

3. (On this) Nan-yung Khû abruptly sat right up and said, 'What method can an old man like me adopt to become (the Perfect man) that you have described?' Kang-sang Tsze said, 'Maintain your body complete; hold your life in close embrace; and do not let your thoughts keep working anxiously:-- do this for three years, and you may become the man of whom I have spoken.' The other rejoined, 'Eyes are all of the same form, I do not know any difference between them:-- yet the blind have no power of vision. Ears are all of the same form; I do not know any difference between them:-- yet the deaf have no power of hearing. Minds are all of the same nature, I do not know any difference between them;-- yet the mad cannot make the minds of other men their own. (My) personality is indeed like (yours), but things seem to separate between us. I wish to find in myself what there is in you, but I am not able to do so. You have now said to me, "Maintain your body complete; hold your life in close embrace; and do not let your thoughts keep working anxiously." With all my efforts to learn your Way, (your words) reach only my ears.' Kang-sang replied, 'I can say nothing more to you,' and then he added, 'Small flies cannot transform the bean caterpillar; Yüeh fowls cannot hatch the eggs of geese, but Lû fowls can. It is not that the nature of these fowls is different; the ability in the one case and inability in the other arise from their different capacities as large and small. My ability is small and not sufficient to transform you. Why should you not go south and see Lâo-tsze?'

4. Nan-yung Khû hereupon took with him some rations, and after seven days and seven nights arrived at the abode of Lâo-tsze, who said to him, 'Are you come from Khû's?' 'I am,' was the reply. 'And why, Sir, have you come with such a multitude of attendants?' Nan-yung was frightened, and turned his head round to look behind him. Lâo-tsze said, 'Do you not understand my meaning?' The other held his head down and was ashamed, and then he lifted it up, and sighed, saying, 'I forgot at the moment what I should reply to your question, and in consequence I have lost what I wished to ask you.' 'What do you mean?' 'If I have not wisdom, men say that I am stupid, while if I have it, it occasions distress to myself. If I have not benevolence, then (I am charged) with doing hurt to others, while if I have it, I distress myself. If I have not righteousness, I (am charged with) injuring others, while if I have it, I distress myself. How can I escape from these dilemmas? These are the three perplexities that trouble me; and I wish at the suggestion of Khû to ask you about them.' Lâo-tsze replied, 'A little time ago, when I saw you and looked right into your eyes, I understood you, and now your words confirm the judgment which I formed. You look frightened and amazed. You have lost your parents, and are trying with a pole to find them at the (bottom of) the sea. You have gone astray; you are at your wit's end. You wish to recover your proper nature, and you know not what step to take first to find it. You are to be pitied!'

5. Nan-yung Khû asked to be allowed to enter (the establishment), and have an apartment assigned to him. (There) he sought to realise the qualities which he loved, and put away those which he hated. For ten days he afflicted himself, and then waited again on Lâo-tsze, who said to him, 'You must purify yourself thoroughly! But from your symptoms of distress, and signs of impurity about you, I see there still seem to cling to you things that you dislike. When the fettering influences from without become numerous, and you try to seize them (you will find it a difficult task); the better plan is to bar your inner man against their entrance. And when the similar influences within get intertwined, it is a difficult task to grasp (and hold them in check); the better plan is to bar the outer door against their exit. Even a master of the Tâo and its characteristics will not be able to control these two influences together, and how much less can one who is only a student of the Tâo do so!' Nan-yung Khû said, 'A certain villager got an illness, and when his neighbours asked about it, he was able to describe the malady, though it was one from which he had not suffered before. When I ask you about the Grand Tâo, it seems to me like drinking medicine which (only serves to) increase my illness. I should like to hear from you about the regular method of guarding the life;-- that will be sufficient for me.' Lâo-tsze replied, '(You ask me

about) the regular method of guarding the life;-- can you hold the One thing fast in your embrace? Can you keep from losing it? Can you know the lucky and the unlucky without having recourse to the tortoise-shell or the divining stalks? Can you rest (where you ought to rest)? Can you stop (when you have got enough)? Can you give over thinking of other men, and seek what you want in yourself (alone)? Can you flee (from the allurements of desire)? Can you maintain an entire simplicity? Can you become a little child? The child will cry all the day, without its throat becoming hoarse;-- so perfect is the harmony (of its physical constitution). It will keep its fingers closed all the day without relaxing their grasp;-- such is the concentration of its powers. It will keep its eyes fixed all day, without their moving;-- so is it unaffected by what is external to it. It walks it knows not whither; it rests where it is placed, it knows not why; it is calmly indifferent to things, and follows their current. This is the regular method of guarding the life.'

6. Nan-yung Khû said, 'And are these all the characteristics of the Perfect man?' Lâo-tsze replied, 'No. These are what we call the breaking up of the ice, and the dissolving of the cold. The Perfect man, along with other men, gets his food from the earth, and derives his joy from his Heaven (-conferred nature). But he does not like them allow himself to be troubled by the consideration of advantage or injury coming from men and things; he does not like them do strange things, or form plans, or enter on undertakings; he flees from the allurements of desire, and pursues his way with an entire simplicity. Such is the way by which he guards his life.' 'And is this what constitutes his perfection ?' 'Not quite. I asked you whether you could become a little child. The little child moves unconscious of what it is doing, and walks unconscious of whither it is going. Its body is like the branch of a rotten tree, and its mind is like slaked lime. Being such, misery does not come to it, nor happiness. It has neither misery nor happiness;-- how can it suffer from the calamities incident to men?'

7. He whose mind is thus grandly fixed emits a Heavenly light. In him who emits this heavenly light men see the (True) man. When a man has cultivated himself (up to this point), thenceforth he remains constant in himself. When he is thus constant in himself, (what is merely) the human element will leave him, but Heaven will help him. Those whom their human element has left we call the people of Heaven. Those whom Heaven helps we call the Sons of Heaven. Those who would by learning attain to this seek for what they cannot learn. Those who would by effort attain to this, attempt what effort can never effect. Those who aim by reasoning to reach it reason where reasoning has no place. To know to stop where they cannot arrive by means of knowledge is the highest attainment. Those

who cannot do this will be destroyed on the lathe of Heaven.

8. Where things are all adjusted to maintain the body; where a provision against unforeseen dangers is kept up to maintain the life of the mind; where an inward reverence is cherished to be exhibited (in all intercourse) with others;-- where this is done, and yet all evils arrive, they are from Heaven, and not from the men themselves. They will not be sufficient to confound the established (virtue of the character), or be admitted into the Tower of Intelligence. That Tower has its Guardian, who acts unconsciously, and whose care will not be effective, if there be any conscious purpose in it. If one who has not this entire sincerity in himself make any outward demonstration, every such demonstration will be incorrect. The thing will enter into him, and not let go its hold. Then with every fresh demonstration there will be still greater failure. If he do what is not good in the light of open day, men will have the opportunity of punishing him; if he do it in darkness and secrecy, spirits will inflict the punishment. Let a man understand this-- his relation both to men and spirits, and then he will do what is good in the solitude of himself.

He whose rule of life is in himself does not act for the sake of a name. He whose rule is outside himself has his will set on extensive acquisition. He who does not act for the sake of a name emits a light even in his ordinary conduct; he whose will is set on extensive acquisition is but a trafficker. Men see how he stands on tiptoe, while he thinks that he is overtopping others. Things enter (and take possession of) him who (tries to) make himself exhaustively (acquainted with them), while when one is indifferent to them, they do not find any lodgment in his person. And how can other men find such lodgment? But when one denies lodgment to men, there are none who feel attachment to him. In this condition he is cut off from other men. There is no weapon more deadly than the will;-- even Mû-yê was inferior to it. There is no robber greater than the Yin and Yang, from whom nothing can escape of all between heaven and earth. But it is not the Yin and Yang that play the robber;-- it is the mind that causes them to do so.

9. The Tâo is to be found in the subdivisions (of its subject); (it is to be found) in that when complete, and when broken up. What I dislike in considering it as subdivided, is that the division leads to the multiplication of it;-- and what I dislike in that multiplication is that it leads to the (thought of) effort to secure it. Therefore when (a man) comes forth (and is born), if he did not return (to his previous non- existence), we should have (only) seen his ghost; when he comes forth and gets this (return), he dies (as we say). He is extinguished, and yet has a real existence:-- (this is another way of saying that in life we have) only man's ghost. By taking

the material as an emblem of the immaterial do we arrive at a settlement of the case of man. He comes forth, but from no root; he reenters, but by no aperture. He has a real existence, but it has nothing to do with place; he has continuance, but it has nothing to do with beginning or end. He has a real existence, but it has nothing to do with place, such is his relation to space; he has continuance, but it has nothing to do with beginning or end, such is his relation to time; he has life; he has death; he comes forth; he enters; but we do not see his form;-- all this is what is called the door of Heaven. The door of Heaven is Non-Existence. All things come from non-existence. The (first) existences could not bring themselves into existence; they must have come from non-existence. And non-existence is just the same as non-existing. Herein is the secret of the sages.

10. Among the ancients there were those whose knowledge reached the extreme point. And what was that point? There were some who thought that in the beginning there was nothing. This was the extreme point, the completest reach of their knowledge, to which nothing could be added. Again, there were those who supposed that (in the beginning) there were existences, proceeding to consider life to be a (gradual) perishing, and death a returning (to the original state). And there they stopped, making, (however), a distinction between life and death. Once again there were those who said, 'In the beginning there was nothing; by and by there was life; and then in a little time life was succeeded by death. We hold that non-existence was the head, life the body, and death the os coccygis. But of those who acknowledge that existence and nonexistence, death and life, are all under the One Keeper, we are the friends.' Though those who maintained these three views were different, they were so as the different branches of the same ruling Family (of Khû),-- the Kâos and the Kings, bearing the surname of the lord whom they honoured as the author of their branch, and the Kiâs named from their appanage;-- (all one, yet seeming) not to be one.

The possession of life is like the soot that collects under a boiler. When that is differently distributed, the life is spoken of as different. But to say that life is different in different lives, and better in one than in another, is an improper mode of speech. And yet there may be something here which we do not know. (As for instance), at the lâ sacrifice the paunch and the divided hoofs may be set forth on separate dishes, but they should not be considered as parts of different victims; (and again), when one is inspecting a house, he goes over it all, even the adytum for the shrines of the temple, and visits also the most private apartments; doing this, and setting a different estimate on the different parts.

Let me try and speak of this method of apportioning one's approval:--

life is the fundamental consideration in it; knowledge is the instructor. From this they multiply their approvals and disapprovals, determining what is merely nominal and what is real. They go on to conclude that to themselves must the appeal be made in everything, and to try to make others adopt them as their model; prepared even to die to make good their views on every point. In this way they consider being employed in office as a mark of wisdom, and not being so employed as a mark of stupidity, success as entitling to fame, and the want of it as disgraceful. The men of the present day who follow this differentiating method are like the cicada and the little dove;-- there is no difference between them.

11. When one treads on the foot of another in the market-place, he apologises on the ground of the bustle. If an elder tread on his younger brother, he proceeds to comfort him; if a parent tread on a child, he says and does nothing. Hence it is said, 'The greatest politeness is to show no special respect to others; the greatest righteousness is to take no account of things; the greatest wisdom is to lay no plans; the greatest benevolence is to make no demonstration of affection; the greatest good faith is to give no pledge of sincerity.'

Repress the impulses of the will; unravel the errors of the mind; put away the entanglements to virtue; and clear away all that obstructs the free course of the Tâo. Honours and riches, distinctions and auster-ity, fame and profit; these six things produce the impulses of the will. Personal appearance and deportment, the desire of beauty and subtle reasonings, excitement of the breath and cherished thoughts; these six things produce errors of the mind. Hatred and longings, joy and anger, grief and delight; these six things are the entanglements to virtue. Refusals and approachments, receiving and giving, knowledge and ability; these six things obstruct the course of the Tâo. When these four conditions, with the six causes of each, do not agitate the breast, the mind is correct. Being correct, it is still; being still, it is pellucid; being pellucid, it is free from pre-occupation; being free from pre-occupation, it is in the state of inaction, in which it accomplishes everything.

The Tâo is the object of reverence to all the virtues. Life is what gives opportunity for the display of the virtues. The nature is the substantive character of the life. The movement of the nature is called action. When action becomes hypocritical, we say that it has lost (its proper attribute).

The wise communicate with what is external to them and are always laying plans. This is what with all their wisdom they are not aware of;-- they look at things askance. When the action (of the nature) is from external constraint, we have what is called virtue; when it is all one's own, we have what is called government. These two names seem to be opposite to each other, but in reality they are in mutual accord.

12. Î was skilful in hitting the minutest mark, but stupid in wishing men to go on praising him without end. The sage is skilful Heavenwards, but stupid manwards. It is only the complete man who can be both skilful Heavenwards and good manwards.

Only an insect can play the insect, only an insect show the insect nature. Even the complete man hates the attempt to exemplify the nature of Heaven. He hates the manner in which men do so, and how much more would he hate the doing so by himself before men!

When a bird came in the way of Î, he was sure to obtain it;-- such was his mastery with his bow. If all the world were to be made a cage, birds would have nowhere to escape to. Thus it was that Thang caged Î Yin by making him his cook, and that duke Mû of Khin caged Pâi-lî Hsî by giving the skins of five rams for him. But if you try to cage men by anything but what they like, you will never succeed.

A man, one of whose feet has been cut off, discards ornamental (clothes);-- his outward appearance will not admit of admiration. A criminal under sentence of death will ascend to any height without fear;-- he has ceased to think of life or death.

When one persists in not reciprocating the gifts (of friendship), he forgets all others. Having forgotten all others, he may be considered as a Heaven-like man. Therefore when respect is shown to a man, and it awakens in him no joy, and when contempt awakens no anger, it is only one who shares in the Heaven- like harmony that can be thus. When he would display anger and yet is not angry, the anger comes out in that repression of it. When he would put forth action, and yet does not do so, the action is in that not- acting. Desiring to be quiescent, he must pacify all his emotions; desiring to be spirit-like, he must act in conformity with his mind. When action is required of him, he wishes that it may be right; and it then is under an inevitable constraint. Those who act according to that inevitable constraint pursue the way of the sage.

Hsü Wû-kwei.

1. Hsü Wû-kwei having obtained through Nü Shang an introduction to the marquis Wû of Wei, the marquis, speaking to him with kindly sympathy, said, 'You are ill, Sir; you have suffered from your hard and laborious toils in the forests, and still you have been willing to come and see poor me.' Hsü Wû-kwei replied, 'It is I who have to comfort your lordship; what occasion have you to comfort me? If your lordship go on to fill up the measure of your sensual desires, and to prolong your likes and dislikes, then the condition of your mental nature will be diseased, and if you discourage and repress those desires, and deny your likings and dislikings, that will be an affliction to your ears and eyes (deprived of their accustomed pleasures);-- it is for me to comfort your lordship, what occasion have you to comfort me?' The marquis looked contemptuous, and made no reply.

After a little time, Hsü Wû-kwei said, 'Let me tell your lordship something:-- I look at dogs and judge of them by their appearance. One of the lowest quality seizes his food, satiates himself, and stops;-- he has the attributes of a fox. One of a medium quality seems to be looking at the sun. One of the highest quality seems to have forgotten the one thing,-- himself. But I judge still better of horses than I do of dogs. When I do so, I find that one goes straight forward, as if following a line; that another turns off, so as to describe a hook; that a third describes a square as if following the measure so called; and that a fourth describes a circle as exactly as a compass would make it. These are all horses of a state; but they are not equal to a horse of the kingdom. His qualities are complete. Now he looks anxious; now to be losing the way; now to be forgetting himself. Such a horse prances along, or rushes on, spurning the dust and not knowing where he is.' The marquis was greatly pleased and laughed.

When Hsü Wû-kwei came out, Nü Shang said to him, 'How was it, Sir, that you by your counsels produced such an effect on our ruler? In my counsellings of him, now indirectly, taking my subjects from the Books of Poetry, History, Rites, and Music; now directly, from the Metal Tablets, and the six Bow-cases, all calculated for the service (of the state), and to be of great benefit;-- in these counsellings, repeated times without number, I have never seen the ruler show his teeth in a smile:-- by what counsels have you made him so pleased to-day?' Hsü Wû-kwei replied, 'I only told him how I judged of dogs and horses by looking at their appearance.' 'So?' said Nü Shang, and the other rejoined, 'Have you not heard of the wanderer from Yüeh? when he had been gone from the state several days, he was glad when he saw any one whom he had seen in it; when he had been gone a month, he was glad when he saw any one whom he had known in it; and when he had been gone a round year, he was glad when he saw any one who looked like a native of it. The longer he was gone, the more longingly did he think of the people;-- was it not so? The men who withdraw to empty valleys, where the hellebore bushes stop up the little paths made by the weasels, as they push their way or stand amid the waste, are glad when they seem to hear the sounds of human footsteps; and how much more would they be so, if it were their brothers and relatives talking and laughing by their side! How long it is since the words of a True man were heard as he talked and laughed by our ruler's side!'

2. At (another) interview of Hsü Wû-kwei with the marquis Wû, the latter said, 'You, Sir, have been dwelling in the forests for a long time, living on acorns and chestnuts, and satiating yourself with onions and chives, without thinking of poor me. Now (that you are here), is it because you are old? or because you wish to try again the taste of wine and meat? or because (you wish that) I may enjoy the happiness derived from the spirits of the altars of the Land and Grain?' Hsü Wû-kwei replied, 'I was born in a poor and mean condition, and have never presumed to drink of your lordship's wine, or eat of your meat. My object in coming was to comfort your lordship under your troubles.' 'What? comfort me under my troubles?' 'Yes, to comfort both your lordship's spirit and body.' The marquis said, 'What do you mean?' His visitor replied, 'Heaven and Earth have one and the same purpose in the production (of all men). However high one man be exalted, he should not think that he is favourably dealt with; and however low may be the position of another, he should not think that he is unfavourably dealt with. You are indeed the one and only lord of the 10,000 chariots (of your state), but you use your dignity to embitter (the lives of) all the people, and to pamper your ears, eyes, nose, and mouth. But your spirit does not acquiesce in this.

The spirit (of man) loves to be in harmony with others and hates selfish indulgence'. This selfish indulgence is a disease, and therefore I would comfort you under it. How is it that your lordship more than others brings this disease on yourself?' The marquis said, 'I have wished to see you, Sir, for a long time. I want to love my people, and by the exercise of righteousness to make an end of war;-- will that be sufficient?' Hsü Wû-kwei replied, 'By no means. To love the people is the first step to injure them. By the exercise of righteousness to make an end of war is the root from which war is produced. If your lordship try to accomplish your object in this way, you are not likely to succeed. All attempts to accomplish what we think good (with an ulterior end) is a bad contrivance. Although your lordship practise benevolence and righteousness (as you propose), it will be no better than hypocrisy. You may indeed assume the (outward) form, but successful accomplishment will lead to (inward) contention, and the change thence arising will produce outward fighting. Your lordship also must not mass files of soldiers in the passages of your galleries and towers, nor have footmen and horsemen in the apartments about your altars. Do not let thoughts contrary to your success lie hidden in your mind; do not think of conquering men by artifice, or by (skilful) plans, or by fighting. If I kill the officers and people of another state, and annex its territory, to satisfy my selfish desires, while in my spirit I do not know whether the fighting be good, where is the victory that I gain? Your lordship's best plan is to abandon (your purpose). If you will cultivate in your breast the sincere purpose (to love the people), and so respond to the feeling of Heaven and Earth, and not (further) vex yourself, then your people will already have escaped death;-- what occasion will your lordship have to make an end of war?'

3. Hwang-Tî was going to see Tâ-kwei at the hill of Kü-Tshze. Fang Ming was acting as charioteer, and Khang Yü was occupying the third place in the carriage. Kang Zo and Hsî Phang went before the horses; and Khwan Hwun and Kû Khî followed the carriage. When they arrived at the wild of Hsiang-khang, the seven sages were all perplexed, and could find no place at which to ask the way. just then they met with a boy tending some horses, and asked the way of him. 'Do you know,' they said, 'the hill of Kü-tshze?' and he replied that he did. He also said that he knew where Tâ-kwei was living. 'A strange boy is this!' said Hwang-Tî. 'He not only knows the hill of Kü-tshze, but he also knows where Tâ-kwei is living. Let me ask him about the government of mankind.' The boy said, 'The administration of the kingdom is like this (which I am doing);-- what difficulty should there be in it? When I was young, I enjoyed myself roaming over all within the six confines of the world of space, and then I began to suffer from indistinct sight. A wise elder taught me, saying, "Ride in the chariot of the sun, and roam in the wild of Hsiang-Khang." Now the trouble in my eyes is a little better, and I am again enjoying myself roaming outside the six confines of the world of space. As to the government of the kingdom, it is like this (which I am doing);-- what difficulty should there be in it?' Hwang-Tî said, 'The administration of the world is indeed not your business, my son; nevertheless, I beg to ask you about it.' The little lad declined to answer, but on Hwang- Tî putting the question again, he said, 'In what does the governor of the kingdom differ from him who has the tending of horses, and who has only to put away whatever in him would injure the horses?'

Hwang-Tî bowed to him twice with his head to the ground, called him his 'Heavenly Master,' and withdrew.

4. If officers of wisdom do not see the changes which their anxious thinking has suggested, they have no joy; if debaters are not able to set forth their views in orderly style, they have no joy; if critical examiners find no subjects on which to exercise their powers of vituperation, they have no joy:-- they are all hampered by external restrictions.

Those who try to attract the attention of their age (wish to) rise at court; those who try to win the regard of the people count holding office a glory; those who possess muscular strength boast of doing what is difficult; those who are bold and daring exert themselves in times of calamity; those who are able swordmen and spearmen delight in fighting; those whose powers are decayed seek to rest in the name (they have gained); those who are skilled in the laws seek to enlarge the scope of government; those who are proficient in ceremonies and music pay careful attention to their deportment; and those who profess benevolence and righteousness value opportunities (for displaying them).

The husbandmen who do not keep their fields well weeded are not equal to their business, nor are traders who do not thrive in the markets. When the common people have their appropriate employment morning and evening, they stimulate one another to diligence; the mechanics who are masters of their implements feel strong for their work. If their wealth does not increase, the greedy are distressed; if their power and influence is not growing, the ambitious are sad.

Such creatures of circumstance and things delight in changes, and if they meet with a time when they can show what they can do, they cannot keep themselves from taking advantage of it. They all pursue their own way like (the seasons of) the year, and do not change as things do. They give the reins to their bodies and natures, and allow themselves to sink beneath (the pressure of) things, and all their lifetime do not come back (to their proper selves) is it not sad?

5. Kwang-tsze said, 'An archer, without taking aim beforehand, yet may hit the mark. If we say that he is a good archer, and that all the world may be Îs, is this allowable?' Hui-tsze replied, 'It is.' Kwang-tsze continued, 'All men do not agree in counting the same thing to be right, but every one maintains his own view to be right; (if we say) that all men may be Yâos, is this allowable?' Hui-tsze (again) replied, 'It is;' and Kwang-tsze went on, 'Very well; there are the literati, the followers of Mo (Tî), of Yang (Kû), and of Ping;-- making four (different schools). Including yourself, Master, there are five. Which of your views is really right? Or will you take the position of Lû Kü? One of his disciples said to him, "Master, I have got hold of your method. I can in winter heat the furnace under

my tripod, and in summer can produce ice." Lû Kü said, "That is only with the Yang element to call out the same, and with the Yin to call out the yin;-- that is not my method. I will show you what my method is." On this he tuned two citherns, placing one of them in the hall, and the other in one of the inner apartments. Striking the note Kung in the one, the same note vibrated in the other, and so it was with the note Kio; the two instruments being tuned in the same way. But if he had differently tuned them on other strings different from the normal arrangement of the five notes, the five-and-twenty strings would all have vibrated, without any difference of their notes, the note to which he had tuned them ruling and guiding all the others. Is your maintaining your view to be right just like this?'

Hui-tsze replied, 'Here now are the literati, and the followers of Mo, Yang, and Ping. Suppose that they have come to dispute with me. They put forth their conflicting statements; they try vociferously to put me down; but none of them have ever proved me wrong:-- what do you say to this?' Kwang-tsze said, 'There was a man of Khî who cast away his son in Sung to be a gatekeeper there, and thinking nothing of the mutilation he would incur; the same man, to secure one of his sacrificial vessels or bells, would have it strapped and secured, while to find his son who was lost, he would not go out of the territory of his own state:-- so forgetful was he of the relative importance of things. If a man of Khû, going to another state as a lame gate-keeper, at midnight, at a time when no one was nigh, were to fight with his boatman, he would not be abie to reach the shore, and he would have done what he could to provoke the boatman's animosity.'

6. As Kwang-tsze was accompanying a funeral, when passing by the grave of Hui-tsze, he looked round, and said to his attendants, 'On the top of the nose of that man of Ying there is a (little) bit of mud like a fly's wing.' He sent for the artisan Shih to cut it away. Shih whirled his axe so as to produce a wind, which immediately carried off the mud entirely, leaving the nose uninjured, and the (statue of) the man of Ying standing undisturbed. The ruler Yüan of Sung heard of the feat, called the artisan Shih, and said to him, 'Try and do the same thing on me.' The artisan said, 'Your servant has been able to trim things in that way, but the material on which I have worked has been dead for a long time.' Kwang-tsze said, 'Since the death of the Master, I have had no material to work upon. I have had no one with whom to talk.'

7. Kwan Kung being ill, duke Hwan went to ask for him, and said, 'Your illness, father Kung, is very severe; should you not speak out your mind to me? Should this prove the great illness, to whom will it be best for me to entrust my State?' Kwan Kung said, 'To whom does your grace wish to entrust it?' 'To Pâo Shû-yâ,' was the reply. 'He will not do. He is an admirable officer, pure and incorruptible, but with others who are not like himself he will not associate. And when he once hears of another man's faults, he never forgets them. If you employ him to administer the state, above, he will take the leading of your Grace, and, below, he will come into collision with the people;-- in no long time you will be holding him as an offender.' The duke said, 'Who, then, is the man?' The reply was, 'If I must speak, there is Hsî Phang;-- he will do. He is a man who forgets his own high position, and against whom those below him will not revolt. He is ashamed that he is not equal to Hwang-Tî, and pities those who are not equal to himself. Him who imparts of his virtue to others we call a sage; him who imparts of his wealth to others we call a man of worth. He who by his worth would preside over others, never succeeds in winning them; he who with his worth condescends to others, never but succeeds in winning them. Hsî Phang has not been (much) heard of in the state; he has not been (much) distinguished in his own clan. But as I must speak, he is the man for you.'

8. The king of Wû, floating about on the Kiang, (landed and) ascended the Hill of monkeys, which all, when they saw him, scampered off in terror, and hid themselves among the thick hazels. There was one, however, which, in an unconcerned way, swung about on the branches, displaying its cleverness to the king, who thereon discharged an arrow at it. With a nimble motion it caught the swift arrow, and the king ordered his attendants to hurry forward and shoot it; and thus the monkey was seized and killed. The king then, looking round, said to his friend Yen Pû-î, 'This monkey made a display of its artfulness, and trusted in its agility, to show me its arrogance;-- this it was which brought it to this fate. Take warning from it. Ah! do not by your looks give yourself haughty airs!' Yen Pû-î, when he returned home, put himself under the teaching of Tung Wû, to root up his pride. He put away what he delighted in and abjured distinction. In three years the people of the kingdom spoke of him with admiration.

9. Nan-po Tsze-khî was seated, leaning forward on his stool, and sighing gently as he looked up to heaven. (Just then) Yen Khang-tsze came in, and said, when he saw him, 'Master, you surpass all others. Is it right to make your body thus like a mass of withered bones, and your mind like so much slaked lime?' The other said, 'I formerly lived in a grotto on

a hill. At that time Thien Ho once came to see me, and all the multitudes of Khî congratulated him thrice (on his having found the proper man). I must first have shown myself, and so it was that he knew me; I must first have been selling (what I had), and so it was that he came to buy. If I had not shown what I possessed, how should he have known it; if I had not been selling (myself), how should he have come to buy me? I pity the men who lose themselves; I also pity the men who pity others (for not being known); and I also pity the men who pity the men who pity those that pity others. But since then the time is long gone by; (and so I am in the state in which you have found me).

10. Kung-nî, having gone to Khû, the king ordered wine to be presented to him. Sun Shû-âo stood, holding the goblet in his hand. Î-liâo of Shih-nan, having received (a cup), poured its contents out as a sacrificial libation, and said, 'The men of old, on such an occasion as this, made some speech.' Kung-nî said, 'I have heard of speech without words; but I have never spoken it; I will do so now. Î-liâo of Shih-nan kept (quietly) handling his little spheres, and the difficulties between the two Houses were resolved; Sun Shû- âo slept undisturbed on his couch, with his (dancer's) feather in his hand, and the men of Ying enrolled themselves for the war. I wish I had a beak three cubits long.'

In the case of those two (ministers) we have what is called 'The Way that cannot be trodden;' in (the case of Kung-nî) we have what is called 'the Argument without words.' Therefore when all attributes are comprehended in the unity of the Tâo, and speech stops at the point to which knowledge does not reach, the conduct is complete. But where there is (not) the unity of the Tâo, the attributes cannot (always) be the same, and that which is beyond the reach of knowledge cannot be exhibited by any reasoning. There may be as many names as those employed by the Literati and the Mohists, but (the result is) evil. Thus when the sea does not reject the streams that flow into it in their eastward course, we have the perfection of greatness. The sage embraces in his regard both Heaven and Earth; his beneficent influence extends to all tinder the sky; and we do not know from whom it comes. Therefore though when living one may have no rank, and when dead no honorary epithet; though the reality (of what he is) may not be acknowledged and his name not established; we have in him what is called 'The Great Man.'

A dog is not reckoned good because it barks well; and a man is not reckoned wise because be speaks skilfully;-- how much less can he be deemed Great! If one thinks he is Great, he is not fit to be accounted Great;-- how much less is he so from the practice of the attributes (of the Tâo)! Now none are so grandly complete as Heaven and Earth; but do they seek for anything to make them so grandly complete? He who knows this grand completion does not seek for it; he loses nothing and abandons nothing; he does not change himself from regard to (external) things; he turns in on himself, and finds there an inexhaustible store; he follows antiquity and does not feel about (for its lessons);-- such is the perfect sincerity of the Great Man.

11. Tsze-khî had eight sons. Having arranged them before him, he called Kiû-fang Yan, and said to him,

'Look at the physiognomy of my sons for me;-- which will be the fortunate one?' Yan said, 'Khwan is the fortunate one.' Tsze-khî looked startled, and joyfully said, 'In what way?' Yan replied, 'Khwan will share the meals of the ruler of a state to the end of his life.' The father looked uneasy, burst into tears, and said, 'What has my son done that he should come to such a fate?' Yan replied, 'When one shares the meals of the ruler of a state, blessings reach to all within the three branches of his kindred, and how much more to his father and mother! But you, Master, weep when you hear this;-- you oppose (the idea of) such happiness. It is the good fortune of your son, and you count it his misfortune.' Tsze-khî said, '0 Yan, what sufficient ground have you for knowing that this will be Khwan's good fortune? (The fortune) that is summed up in wine and flesh affects only the nose and the mouth, but you are not able to know how it will come about. I have never been a shepherd, and yet a ewe lambed in the south-west corner of my house. I have never been fond of hunting, and yet a quail hatched her young in the south-east corner. If these were not prodigies, what can be accounted such? Where I wish to occupy my mind with my son is in (the wide sphere of) heaven and earth; I wish to seek his enjoyment and mine in (the idea of) Heaven, and our support from the Earth. I do not mix myself up with him in the affairs (of the world); nor in forming plans (for his advantage); nor in the practice of what is strange. I pursue with him the perfect virtue of Heaven and Earth, and do not allow ourselves to be troubled by outward things. I seek to be with him in a state of undisturbed indifference, and not to practise what affairs might indicate as likely to be advantageous. And now there is to come to us this vulgar recompense. Whenever there is a strange realisation, there must have been strange conduct. Danger threatens;-- not through any sin of me or of my son, but as brought about, I apprehend, by Heaven. It is this which makes me weep!'

Not long after this, Tsze-khî sent off Khwan to go to Yen, when he was made prisoner by some robbers on the way. It would have been difficult to sell him if he were whole and entire, and they thought their easiest plan was to cut off (one of his) feet first. They did so, and sold him in Khî, where he became Inspector of roads for a Mr. Khû. Nevertheless he had flesh to eat till he died.

12. Nieh Khüeh met Hsü Yû (on the way), and said to him, 'Where, Sir, are you going to?' 'I am fleeing from Yâo,' was the reply. 'What do you mean?' 'Yâo has become so bent on his benevolence that I am afraid the world will laugh at him, and that in future ages men will be found eating one another. Now the people are collected together without difficulty. Love them, and they respond with affection; benefit them, and they come to you; praise them, and they are stimulated (to please you); make them to experience what they dislike, and they disperse. When the loving and benefiting proceed from benevolence and righteousness, those who forget the benevolence and righteousness, and those who make a profit of them, are the many. In this way the practice of benevolence and righteousness comes to be without sincerity and is like a borrowing of the instruments with which men catch birds. In all this the one man's seeking to benefit the world by his decisions and enactments (of such a nature) is as if he were to cut through (the nature of all) by one operation;-- Yâo knows how wise and superior men can benefit the world, but he does not also know how they injure it. It is only those who stand outside such men that know this.'

There are the pliable and weak; the easy and hasty; the grasping and crooked. Those who are called the pliable and weak learn the words of some one master, to which they freely yield their assent, being secretly pleased with themselves, and thinking that their knowledge is sufficient, while they do not know that they have not yet begun (to understand) a single thing. It is this which makes them so pliable and weak. The easy and hasty are like lice on a pig. The lice select a place where the bristles are more wide apart, and look on it as a great palace or a large park. The slits between the toes, the overlappings of its skin, about its nipples and its thighs,-- all these seem to them safe apartments and advantageous places;-- they do not know that the butcher one morning, swinging about his arms, will spread the grass, and kindle the fire, so that they and the pig will be roasted together. So do they appear and disappear with the place where they harboured:-- this is why they are called the easy and hasty.

Of the grasping and crooked we have an example in Shun. Mutton has no craving for ants, but ants have a craving for mutton, for it is rank. There was a rankness about the conduct of Shun, and the people were pleased with him. Hence when he thrice changed his residence, every one of them became a capital city. When he came to the wild of Tang, he had 100,000 families about him. Yâo having heard of the virtue and ability of Shun, appointed him to a new and uncultivated territory, saying, 'I look forward to the benefit of his coming here.' When Shun was appointed to this new territory, his years were advanced, and his intelligence was decayed;-- and yet he could not find a place of rest or a home. This is an example of being grasping and wayward.

Therefore (in opposition to such) the spirit-like man dislikes the flocking of the multitudes to him. When the multitudes come, they do not agree; and when they do not agree, no benefit results from their coming. Hence there are none whom he brings very near to himself, and none whom he keeps at a great distance. He keeps his virtue in close embrace, and warmly nourishes (the spirit of) harmony, so as to be in accordance with all men. This is called the True man. Even the knowledge of the ant he puts away; his plans are simply those of the fishes; even the notions of the sheep he discards. His seeing is simply that of the eye; his hearing that of the ear; his mind is governed by its general exercises. Being such, his course is straight and level as if marked out by a line, and its every change is in accordance (with the circumstances of the case).

13. The True men of old waited for the issues of events as the arrangements of Heaven, and did not by their human efforts try to take the place of Heaven. The True men of old (now) looked on success as life and on failure as death; and (now) on success as death and on failure as life. The operation of medicines will illustrate this:-- there are monk's-bane, the kieh-kang, the tribulus fruit, and china-root; each of these has the time and case for which it is supremely suitable; and all such plants and their suitabilities cannot be mentioned particularly. Kâu-kien took his station on (the hill of) Kwâi-khî with 3,000 men with their buff-coats and shields:-- (his minister) Kung knew how the ruined (Yüeh) might still be preserved, but the same man did not know the sad fate in store for himself. Hence it is said, 'The eye of the owl has its proper fitness; the leg of the crane has its proper limit, and to cut off any of it would distress (the bird).'
Hence (also) it is (further) said, 'When the wind passes over it, the volume of the river is diminished, and so it is when the sun passes over it. But let the wind and sun keep a watch together on the river, and it will not begin to feel that they are doing it any injury:-- it relies on its springs and flows on.' Thus, water does its part to the ground with undeviating exactness; and so does the shadow to the substance; and one thing to another. Therefore there is danger from the power of vision in the eyes, of hearing in the ears, and of the inordinate thinking of the mind; yea, there is danger from the exercise of every power of which man's constitution is the depository. When the danger has come to a head, it cannot be averted, and the calamity is perpetuated, and goes on increasing. The return from this (to a state of security) is the result of (great) effort, and success can be attained only after a long time; and yet men consider (their power of self-determination) as their precious possession:-- is it not sad?

It is in this way that we have the ruin of states and the slaughtering of the people without end; while no one knows how to ask how it comes about.

14. Therefore, the feet of man on the earth tread but on a small space, but going on to where he has not trod before, he traverses a great distance easily; so his knowledge is but small, but going on to what he does not already know, he comes to know what is meant by Heaven. He knows it as The Great Unity; The Great Mystery; The Great Illuminator; The Great Framer; The Great Boundlessness; The Great Truth; The Great Determiner. This makes his knowledge complete. As The Great Unity, he comprehends it; as The Great Mystery, he unfolds it; as the Great Illuminator, he contemplates it; as the Great Framer, it is to him the Cause of all; as the Great Boundlessness, all is to him its embodiment; as The Great Truth, he examines it; as The Great Determiner, he holds it fast. Thus Heaven is to him all; accordance with it is the brightest intelligence. Obscurity has in this its pivot; in this is the beginning. Such being the case, the explanation of it is as if it were no explanation; the knowledge of it is as if it were no knowledge. (At first) he does not know it, but afterwards he comes to know it. In his inquiries, he must not set to himself any limits, and yet he cannot be without a limit. Now ascending, now descending, then slipping from the grasp, (the Tâo) is yet a reality, unchanged now as in antiquity, and always without defect:-- may it not be called what is capable of the greatest display and expansion? Why should we not inquire into it? Why should we be perplexed about it? With what does not perplex let us explain what perplexes, till we cease to be perplexed. So may we arrive at a great freedom from all perplexity!

Tseh-yang.

1. Tseh-yang having travelled to Khû, Î Kieh spoke of him to the king, and then, before the king had granted him an interview, (left him, and) returned home. Tseh-yang went to see Wang Kwo, and said to him, 'Master, why do you not mention me to the king?' Wang Kwo replied, 'I am not so good a person to do that as Kung-yüeh Hsiû.' 'What sort of man is he?' asked the other, and the reply was, 'In winter he spears turtles in the Kiang, and in summer he rests in shady places on the mountain. When passers-by ask him (what he is doing there), he says, "This is my abode." Since Î Kieh was not able to induce the king to see you, how much less should I, who am not equal to him, be able to do so! Î Kieh's character is this:--he has no (real) virtue, but he has knowledge. If you do not freely yield yourself to him, but employ him to carry on his spirit-like influence (with you), you will certainly get upset and benighted in the region of riches and honours. His help will not be of a Virtuous character, but will go to make your virtue less;-- it will be like heaping on clothes in spring as a protection against cold, or bringing back the cold winds of winter as a protection against heat (in summer). Now the king of Khû is of a domineering presence and stern. He has no forgiveness for offenders, but is merciless as a tiger. It is only a man of subtle speech, or one of correct virtue, who can bend him from his purpose.

'But the sagely man, when he is left in obscurity, causes the members of his family to forget their poverty; and, when he gets forward to a position of influence, causes kings and dukes to forget their rank and emoluments, and transforms them to be humble. With the inferior creatures, he shares their pleasures, and they enjoy themselves the more; with other men, he rejoices in the fellowship of the Tâo, and preserves it in himself. Therefore though he may not speak, he gives them to drink of the harmony (of his spirit). Standing in association with them, he transforms them till they become in their feeling towards him as sons with a father. His wish is to return to the solitude of his own mind, and this is the effect of his occasional intercourse with them. So far-reaching is his influence on the minds of men; and therefore I said to you. "Wait for Kung-yüeh Hsiû."'

2. The sage comprehends the connexions between himself and others, and how they all go to constitute him of one body with them, and he does not know how it is so;-- he naturally does so. In fulfilling his constitution, as acted on and acting, he (simply) follows the direction of Heaven; and it is in consequence of this that men style him (a sage). If he were troubled

about (the insufficiency of) his knowledge, what he did would always be but small, and sometimes would be arrested altogether;-- how would he in this case be (the sage)? When (the sage) is born with all his excellence, it is other men who see it for him. If they did not tell him, he would not know that he was more excellent than others. And when he knows it, he is as if he did not know it; when he hears it, he is as if he did not hear it. His source of joy in it has no end, and men's admiration of him has no end;-- all this takes place naturally. The love of the sage for others receives its name from them. If they did not tell him of it, he would not know that he loved them; and when he knows it, he is as if he knew it not; when he hears it, he is as if he heard it not. His love of others never has an end, and their rest in him has also no end:-- all this takes place naturally.

3. When one sees at a distance his old country and old city, he feels a joyous satisfaction. Though it be full of mounds and an overgrowth of trees and grass, and when he enters it he finds but a tenth part remaining, still he feels that satisfaction. How much more when he sees what he saw, and hears what he heard before! All this is to him like a tower eighty cubits high exhibited in the sight of all men.

(The sovereign) Zan-hsiang was possessed of that central principle round which all things revolve, and by it he could follow them to their completion. His accompanying them had neither ending nor beginning, and was independent of impulse or time. Daily he witnessed their changes, and himself underwent no change; and why should he not have rested in this? If we (try to) adopt Heaven as our Master, we incapacitate ourselves from doing so. Such endeavour brings us under the power of things. If one acts in this way, what is to be said of him? The sage never thinks of Heaven nor of men. He does not think of taking the initiative, nor of anything external to himself. He moves along with his age, and does not vary or fail. Amid all the completeness of his doings, he is never exhausted. For those who wish to be in accord with him, what other course is there to pursue?

When Thang got one to hold for him the reins of government, namely, Man-yin Tang-hang, he employed him as his teacher. He followed his master, but did not allow himself to be hampered by him, and so he succeeded in following things to their completion. The master had the name; but that name was a superfluous addition to his laws, and the twofold character of his government was made apparent. Kung-ni's 'Task your thoughts to the utmost' was his expression of the duties of a master. Yung-khang said,
'Take the days away and there will be no year; without what is internal there will be nothing external.'

4. (King) Yung of Wei made a treaty with the marquis Thien Mâu (of Khî), which the latter violated. The king was enraged, and intended to send a man to assassinate him. When the Minister of War heard of it, he was ashamed, and said (to the king), 'You are a ruler of 10,000 chariots, and by means of a common man would avenge yourself on your enemy. I beg you to give me, Yen, the command of 200,000 soldiers to attack him for you. I will take captive his people and officers, halter (and lead off) his oxen and horses, kindling a fire within him that shall burn to his backbone. I will then storm his capital; and when he shall run away in terror, I will flog his back and break his spine.' Kî-Tsze heard of this advice, and was ashamed of it, and said (to the king), 'We have been raising the wall (of our capital) to a height of eighty cubits, and the work has been completed. If we now get it thrown down, it will be a painful toil to the convict builders. It is now seven years since our troops were called out, and this is the foundation of the royal sway. Yen would introduce disorder;-- he should not be listened to.' Hwâ-tsze heard of this advice, and, greatly disapproving of it, said (to the king), 'He who shows his skill in saying "Attack Khî!" would produce disorder; and he who shows his skill in saying "Do not attack it " would also produce disorder. And one who should (merely) say, "The counsellors to attack Khî and not to attack it would both produce disorder," would himself also lead to the same result.' The king said, 'Yes, but what am I to do?' The reply was, 'You have only to seek for (the rule of) the Tâo (on the subject).'

Hui-tsze, having heard of this counsel, introduced to the king Tâi Tsin-zan, who said, 'There is the creature called a snail; does your majesty know it?' 'I do.' 'On the left horn of the snail there is a kingdom which is called Provocation, and on the right horn another which is called Stupidity. These two kingdoms are continually striving about their territories and fighting. The corpses that lie on the ground amount to several myriads. The army of one may be defeated and put to flight, but in fifteen days it will return.' The king said, 'Pooh! that is empty talk!' The other rejoined, 'Your servant begs to show your majesty its real significance. When your majesty thinks of space-- east, west, north, and south, above and beneath-- can you set any limit to it?' 'It is illimitable,' said the king; and his visitor went on, 'Your majesty knows how to let your mind thus travel through the illimitable, and yet (as compared with this) does it not seem insignificant whether the kingdoms that communicate one with another exist or not?' The king replies, 'It does so;' and Tâi Tsin-zan said, finally, 'Among those kingdoms, stretching one after another, there is this Wei; in Wei there is this (city of) Liang; and in Liang there is your majesty. Can you make any distinction between yourself, and (the king of that kingdom of) Stupidity?' To this the king answered, 'There is no distinction,' and his visitor went out, while the king remained disconcerted and seemed to have lost himself.

When the visitor was gone, Hui-tsze came in and saw the king, who said, 'That stranger is a Great man. An (ordinary) sage is not equal to him.' Hui-tsze replied, 'If you blow into a flute, there come out its pleasant notes; if you blow into a sword-hilt, there is nothing but a wheezing sound. Yâo and Shun are the subjects of men's praises, but if you speak of them before Tâi Tsin-zan, there will be but the wheezing sound.'

5. Confucius, having gone to Khû, was lodging in the house of a seller of Congee at Ant-hill. On the roof of a neighbouring house there appeared the husband and his wife, with their servants, male and female. Tsze- lû said, 'What are those people doing, collected there as we see them?' Kung-nî replied, 'The man is a disciple of the sages. He is burying himself among the people, and hiding among the fields. Reputation has become little in his eyes, but there is no bound to his cherished aims. Though he may speak with his mouth, he never tells what is in his mind. Moreover, he is at variance with the age, and his mind disdains to associate with it;-- he is one who may be said to lie hid at the bottom of the water on the dry land. Is he not a sort of Î Liâo of Shih-nan?' Tsze-lû asked leave to go and call him, but Confucius said, 'Stop. He
knows that I understand him well. He knows that I am come to Khû, and thinks that I am sure to try and get the king to invite him (to court). He also thinks that I am a man swift to speak. Being such a man, he would feel ashamed to listen to the words of one of voluble and flattering tongue, and how much more to come himself and see his person! And why should we think that he will remain here?' Tsze-lû, however, went to see how it was, but found the house empty.

6. The Border-warden of Khang-wû, in questioning Tsze-lâo, said, 'Let not a ruler in the exercise of his government be (like the farmer) who leaves the clods unbroken, nor, in regulating his people, (like one) who recklessly plucks up the shoots. Formerly, in ploughing my corn-fields, I left the clods unbroken, and my recompense was in the rough 'unsatisfactory crops; and in weeding, I destroyed and tore up (many good plants), and my recompense was in the scantiness of my harvests. In subsequent years I changed my methods, ploughing deeply and carefully covering up the seed; and my harvests were rich and abundant, so that all the year I had more than I could eat.' When Kwang-tsze heard of his remarks, he said, 'Now-a- days, most men, in attending to their bodies and regulating their minds, correspond to the description of the Border-warden. They hide from themselves their Heaven(-given being); they leave (all care of) their (proper) nature; they extinguish their (proper) feelings; and they

leave their spirit to die:-- abandoning themselves to what is the general practice. Thus dealing with their nature like the farmer who is negligent of the clods in his soil, the illegitimate results of their likings and dislikings become their nature. The bushy sedges, reeds, and rushes, which seem at first to spring up to support our bodies, gradually eradicate our nature, and it becomes like a mass of running sores, ever liable to flow out, with scabs and ulcers, discharging in flowing matter from the internal heat. So indeed it is!'

7. Po Kü was studying with Lâo Tan, and asked his leave to go and travel everywhere. Lâo Tan said, 'Nay;-- elsewhere it is just as here.' He repeated his request, and then Lâo Tan said, 'Where would you go first?'

'I would begin with Khî,' replied the disciple. 'Having got there, I would go to look at the criminals (who had been executed). With my arms I would raise (one of) them up and set him on his feet, and, taking off my court robes, I would cover him with them, appealing at the same time to Heaven and bewailing his lot, while I said, "My son, my son, you have been one of the first to suffer from the great calamities that afflict the world."' (Lâo Tan) said, '(It is said), "Do not rob. Do not kill." (But) in the setting up of (the ideas of) glory and disgrace, we see the cause of those evils; in the accumulation of property and wealth, we see the causes of strife and contention. If now you set up the things against which men fret; if you accumulate what produces strife and contention among them; if you put their persons in such a state of distress, that they have no rest or ease, although you may wish that they should not come to the end of those (criminals), can your wish be realised?

'The superior men (and rulers) of old considered that the success (of their government) was to be found in (the state of) the people, and its failure to be sought in themselves; that the right might be with the people, and the wrong in themselves. Thus it was that if but a single person lost his life, they retired and blamed themselves. Now, however, it is not so. (Rulers) conceal what they want done, and hold those who do not know it to be stupid; they require what is very difficult, and condemn those who do not dare to undertake it; they impose heavy burdens, and punish those who are unequal to them; they require men to go far, and put them to death when they cannot accomplish the distance. When the people know that the utmost of their strength will be insufficient, they follow it up with deceit. When (the rulers) daily exhibit much hypocrisy, how can the officers and people not be hypocritical? Insufficiency of strength produces hypocrisy; insufficiency of knowledge produces deception; insufficiency of means produces robbery. But in this case against whom ought the robbery and theft to be charged?'

8. When Kü Po-yü was in his sixtieth year, his views became changed in the course of it. He had never before done anything but consider the views which he held to be right, but now he came to condemn them as wrong; he did not know that what he now called right was not what for fifty-nine years he had been calling wrong. All things have the life (which we know), but we do not see its root; they have their goings forth, but we do not know the door by which they depart. Men all honour that which lies within the sphere of their knowledge, but they do not know their dependence on what lies without that sphere which would be their (true) knowledge:-- may we not call their case one of great perplexity? Ah! Ah! there is no escaping from this dilemma. So it is! So it is!

9. Kung-nî asked the Grand Historiographer Tâ Thâo, (along with) Po Khang-khien and Khih-wei, saying, 'Duke Ling of Wei was so addicted to drink, and abandoned to sensuality, that he did not attend to the government of his state. Occupied in his pursuit of hunting with his nets and bows, he kept aloof from the meetings of the princes. In what was it that he showed his title to the epithet of Ling?' Tâ Thâo said, 'It was on account of those very things.' Po Khang-khien said, 'Duke Ling had three mistresses with whom he used to bathe in the same tub. (Once, however), when Shih-tsziû came to him with presents from the imperial court, he made his servants support the messenger in bearing the gifts. So dissolute was he in the former case, and when he saw a man of worth, thus reverent was he to him. It was on this account that he was styled "Duke Ling."' Khih-wei said, 'When duke Ling died, and they divined about burying him in the old tomb of his House, the answer was unfavourable; when they divined about burying him on Shâ-khiû, the answer was favourable. Accordingly they dug there to the depth of several fathoms, and found a stone coffin. Having washed and inspected it, they discovered an inscription, which said, "This grave will not be available for your posterity; Duke Ling will appropriate it for himself." Thus that epithet of Ling had long been settled for the duke. But how should those two be able to know this?'

10. Shâo Kih asked Thâi-kung Thiâo, saying, 'What do we mean by "The Talk of the Hamlets and Villages?"' The reply was, 'Hamlets and Villages are formed by the union-- say of ten surnames and a hundred names, and are considered to be (the source of) manners and customs. The differences between them are united to form their common character, and what is common to them is separately apportioned to form the differences. If you point to the various parts which make up the body of a horse, you do not have the horse; but when the horse is before you, and all its various parts stand forth (as forming the animal), you speak of "the horse." So it is that the mounds and hills are made to be the elevations that they are by accumulations of earth which individually are but low.

(So also rivers like) the Kiang and the Ho obtain their greatness by the union of (other smaller) waters with them. And (in the same way) the Great man exhibits the common sentiment of humanity by the union in himself of all its individualities. Hence when ideas come to him from without, though he has his own decided view, he does not hold it with bigotry; and when he gives out his own decisions, which are correct, the views of others do not oppose them. The four seasons have their different elemental characters, but they are not the partial gifts of Heaven, and so the year completes its course. The five official departments have their different duties, but the ruler does not partially employ any one of them, and so the kingdom is governed. (The gifts of) peace and war (are different), but the Great man does not employ the one to the prejudice of the other, and so the character (of his administration) is perfect. All things have their different constitutions and modes of actions, but the Tâo (which directs them) is free from all partiality, and therefore it has no name. Having no name, it therefore does nothing. Doing nothing, there is nothing which it does not do.

'Each season has its ending and beginning; each age has its changes and transformations; misery and happiness regularly alternate. Here our views are thwarted, and yet the result may afterwards have our approval; there we insist on our own views, and looking at things differently from others, try to correct them, while we are in error ourselves. The case may be compared to that of a great marsh, in which all its various vegetation finds a place, or we may look at it as a great hill, where trees and rocks are found on the same terrace. Such may be a description of what is intended by "The Talk of the Hamlets and Villages."'

Shâo Kih said, 'Well, is it sufficient to call it (an expression of) the Tâo?' Thâi-kung Thiâo said, 'It is not so. If we reckon up the number of things, they are not 10,000 merely. When we speak of them as "the Myriad Things," we simply use that large number by way of accommodation to denominate them. In this way Heaven and Earth are the greatest of all things that have form; the Yin and Yang are the greatest of all elemental forces. But the Tâo is common to them. Because of their greatness to use the Tâo or (Course) as a title and call it "the Great Tâo" is allowable. But what comparison can be drawn between it and "the Talk of the Hamlets and Villages?" To argue from this that it is a sufficient expression of the Tâo, is like calling a dog and a horse by the same name, while the difference between them is so great.'

11. Shâo Kih said, 'Within the limits of the four cardinal points, and the six boundaries of space, how was it that there commenced the production of all things?' Thâi-kung Thiâo replied, 'The Yin and Yang

reflected light on each other, covered each other, and regulated each the other; the four seasons gave place to one another, produced one another, and brought one another to an end. Likings and dislikings, the avoidings of this and movements towards that, then arose (in the things thus produced), in their definite distinctness; and from this came the separation and union of the male and female. Then were seen now security and now insecurity, in mutual change; misery and happiness produced each other; gentleness and urgency pressed on each other; the movements of collection and dispersion were established:-- these names and processes can be examined, and, however minute, can be recorded. The rules determining the order in which they follow one another, their mutual influence now acting directly and now revolving, how, when they are exhausted, they revive, and how they end and begin again; these are the properties belonging to things. Words can describe them and knowledge can reach to them; but with this ends all that can be said of things. Men who study the Tâo do not follow on when these operations end, nor try to search out how they began:-- with this all discussion of them stops.'

Shâo Kih said, 'Kî Kan holds that (the Tâo) forbids all action, and Kieh-tsze holds that it may perhaps allow of influence. Which of the two is correct in his statements, and which is one-sided in his ruling?' Thâi-kung Thiâo replied, 'Cocks crow and dogs bark;-- this is what all men know. But men with the greatest wisdom cannot describe in words whence it is that they are formed (with such different voices), nor can they find out by thinking what they wish to do. We may refine on this small point; till it is so minute that there is no point to operate on, or it may become so great that there is no embracing it. "Some one caused it;" "No one did it;" but we are thus debating about things; and the end is that we shall find we are in error. "Some one caused it;"-- then there was a real Being. "No one did it;"-- then there was mere vacancy. To have a name and a real existence,-- that is the condition of a thing. Not to have a name, and not to have real being;-- that is vacancy and no thing. We may speak and we may think about it, but the more we speak, the wider shall we be of the mark. Birth, before it comes, cannot be prevented; death, when it has happened, cannot be traced farther. Death and life are not far apart; but why they have taken place cannot be seen. That some one has caused them, or that there has been no action in the case are but speculations of doubt. When I look for their origin, it goes back into infinity; when I look for their end, it proceeds without termination. Infinite, unceasing, there is no room for words about (the Tâo). To regard it as in the category of things is the origin of the language that it is caused or that it is the result of doing nothing; but it would end as it began with things. The Tâo cannot have a (real) existence; if it has, it cannot be made to appear as if it had not. The name Tâo is a metaphor, used for the purpose of description. To say that it causes or does nothing is but to speak of one phase of things, and has nothing to do with the Great Subject. If words were sufficient for the purpose, in a day's time we might exhaust it; since they are not sufficient, we may speak all day, and only exhaust (the subject of) things. The Tâo is the extreme to which things conduct us. Neither speech nor silence is sufficient to convey the notion of it. Neither by speech nor by silence can our thoughts about it have their highest expression.

Wâi Wû, or 'What comes from Without.'

1. What comes from without cannot be determined beforehand. So it was that Lung-fang was killed; Pi- kan immolated; and the count of Kî (made to feign himself) mad, (while) O-lâi died, and Kieh and Kâu both perished. Rulers all wish their ministers to be faithful, but that faithfulness may not secure their confidence; hence Wû Yün became a wanderer along the Kiang, and Khang Hung died in Shû, where (the people) preserved his blood for three years, when it became changed into green jade. Parents all wish their sons to be filial, but that filial duty may not secure their love; hence Hsiâo-kî had to endure his sorrow, and Tsang Shan his grief.

When wood is rubbed against wood, it begins to burn; when metal is subjected to fire, it (melts and) flows. When the Yin and Yang act awry, heaven and earth are greatly perturbed; and on this comes the crash of thunder, and from the rain comes fire, which consumes great locust trees. (The case of men) is still worse. They are troubled between two pitfalls, from which they cannot escape. Chrysalis-like, they can accomplish nothing. Their minds are as if hung up between heaven and earth. Now comforted, now pitied, they are plunged in difficulties. The ideas of profit and of injury rub against each other, and produce in them a very great fire. The harmony (of the mind) is consumed in the mass of men. Their moonlike intelligence cannot overcome the (inward) fire. They thereupon fall away more and more, and the Course (which they should pursue) is altogether lost.

2. The family of Kwang Kâu being poor, he went to ask the loan of some rice from the Marquis Superintendent of the Ho, who said, 'Yes, I shall be getting the (tax-) money from the people (soon), and I will then lend you three hundred ounces of silver;-- will that do?' Kwang Kâu flushed with anger, and said, 'On the road yesterday, as I was coming here, I heard some one calling out. On looking round, I saw a goby in the carriage rut, and said to it, "Goby fish, what has brought you here?" The goby said, "I am Minister of Waves in the Eastern Sea. Have you, Sir, a gallon or a pint of water to keep me alive?" I replied, "Yes, I am going south to see the kings of Wû and Yüeh, and I will then lead a stream from the Western Kiang to meet you;-- will that do ?" The goby flushed with anger, and said, "I have lost my proper element, and I can here do nothing for myself; but if I could get a gallon or a pint of water, I should keep alive. Than do what you propose, you had better soon look for me in a stall of dry fish."'

3. A son of the duke of Zan, having provided himself with a great hook, a powerful black line, and fifty steers to be used as bait, squatted down on (mount) Kwâi Khî, and threw the line into the Eastern Sea. Morning after morning he angled thus, and for a whole year caught nothing. At the end of that time, a great fish swallowed the bait, and dived down, dragging the great hook with him. Then it rose to the surface in a flurry, and flapped with its fins, till the white waves rose like hills, and the waters were lashed into fury. The noise was like that of imps and spirits, and spread terror for a thousand lî. The prince having got such a fish, cut it in slices and dried them. From the Keh river to the east, and from Tshang-wû to the north, there was not one who did not eat his full from that fish; and in subsequent generations, story-tellers of small abilities have all repeated the story to one another with astonishment. (But) if the prince had taken his rod, with a fine line, and gone to pools and ditches, and watched for minnows and gobies, it would have been difficult for him to get a large fish. Those who dress up their small tales to obtain favour with the magistrates are far from being men of great understanding; and therefore one who has not heard the story of this scion of Zan is not fit to take any part in the government of the world;-- far is he from being so'.

4. Some literati, students of the Odes and Ceremonies, were breaking open a mound over a grave. The superior among them spoke down to the others, 'Day is breaking in the east; how is the thing going on?' The younger men replied, 'We have not yet opened his jacket and skirt, but there is a pearl in the mouth. As it is said in the Ode,

The bright, green grain
Is growing on the sides of the mound. While living, he gave nothing away;
Why, when dead, should he hold a pearl in his mouth?'"

Thereupon they took hold of the whiskers and pulled at the beard, while the superior introduced a piece of fine steel into the chin, and gradually separated the jaws, so as not to injure the pearl in the mouth.

5. A disciple of Lâo Lâi-tsze, while he was out gathering firewood, met with Kung-nî. On his return, he told (his master), saying, 'There is a man there, the upper part of whose body is long and the lower part short. He is slightly hump-backed, and his ears are far back. When you look at him, he seems occupied with the cares of all within the four seas; I do not know whose son he is.' Lâo Lâi-tsze said, 'It is Khiû; call him here;' and when Kung-nî came, he said to him, 'Khiû, put away your personal conceit, and airs of wisdom, and show yourself to be indeed a superior man.' Kung-nî bowed and was retiring, when he abruptly changed his

manner, and asked, 'Will the object I am pursuing be thereby advanced?' Lâo Lâi-tsze replied, 'You cannot bear the sufferings of this one age, and are stubbornly regardless of the evils of a myriad ages:-- is it that you purposely make yourself thus unhappy? or is it that you have not the ability to comprehend the case? Your obstinate purpose to make men rejoice in a participation of your joy is your life-long shame, the procedure of a mediocre man. You would lead men by your fame; you would bind them to you by your secret art. Than be praising Yâo and condemning Kieh, you had better forget them both, and shut up your tendency to praise. If you reflect on it, it does nothing but injury; your action in it is entirely wrong. The sage is full of anxiety and indecision in undertaking anything, and so he is always successful. But what shall I say of your conduct? To the end it is all affectation.'

6. The ruler Yüan of Sung (once) dreamt at midnight that a man with dishevelled hair peeped in on him at a side door and said, 'I was coming from the abyss of Tsai-lû, commissioned by the Clear Kiang to go to the place of the Earl of the Ho; but the fisherman Yü Tsü has caught me.' When the ruler Yüan awoke, he caused a diviner to divine the meaning (of the dream), and was told, 'This is a marvellous tortoise.' The ruler asked if among the fishermen there was one called Yü Tsü, and being told by his attendants that there was, he gave orders that he should be summoned to court. Accordingly the man next day appeared at court, and the ruler said, 'What have you caught (lately) in fishing?' The reply was, 'I have caught in my net a white tortoise, sievelike, and five cubits round.' 'Present the prodigy here,' said the ruler; and, when it came, once and again he wished to kill it, once and again he wished to keep it alive. Doubting in his mind (what to do), he had recourse to divination, and obtained the answer, 'To kill the tortoise for use in divining will be fortunate.' Accordingly they cut the creature open, and perforated its shell in seventy-two places, and there was not a single divining slip which failed.

Kung-nî said, 'The spirit-like tortoise could show itself in a dream to the ruler Yüan, and yet it could not avoid the net of Yü Tsü. Its wisdom could respond on seventy-two perforations without failing in a single divination, and yet it could not avoid the agony of having its bowels all scooped out. We see from this that wisdom is not without its perils, and spirit-like intelligence does not reach to everything. A man may have the greatest wisdom, but there are a myriad men scheming against him. Fishes do not fear the net, though they fear the pelican. Put away your small wisdom, and your great wisdom will be bright; discard your skilfulness, and you will become naturally skilful. A child when it is born needs no great master, and yet it becomes able to speak, living (as it does) among those who are able to speak.'

7. Hui-tsze said to Kwang-tsze, 'You speak, Sir, of what is of no use.'
The reply was, 'When a man knows what is not useful, you can then
begin to speak to him of what is useful. The earth for instance is certainly
spacious and great; but what a man uses of it is only sufficient ground
for his feet. If, however, a rent were made by the side of his feet, down to
the yellow springs, could the man still make use of it?' Hui-tsze said, 'He
could not use it,' and Kwang-tsze rejoined, 'Then the usefulness of what
is of no use is clear.'

8. Kwang-tsze said, 'If a man have the power to enjoy himself (in any
pursuit), can he be kept from doing so? If he have not the power, can
he so enjoy himself? There are those whose aim is bent on concealing
themselves, and those who are determined that their doings shall leave
no trace. Alas! they both shirk the obligations of perfect knowledge and
great virtue. The (latter) fall, and cannot recover themselves; the (former)
rush on like fire, and do not consider (what they are doing). Though men
may stand to each other in the relation of ruler and minister, that is but
for a time. In a changed age, the one of them would not be able to look
down on the other. Hence it is said, "The Perfect man leaves no traces
of his conduct."

'To honour antiquity and despise the present time is the characteristic of learners; but even the disciples of Khih-wei have to look at the
present age; and who can avoid being carried along by its course? It is
only the Perfect man who is able to enjoy himself in the world, and not
be deflected from the right, to accommodate himself to others and not
lose himself. He does not learn their lessons; he only takes their ideas
into consideration, and does not discard them as different from his own.

9. 'It is the penetrating eye that gives clear vision, the acute ear that
gives quick hearing, the discriminating nose that gives discernment of
odours, the practised mouth that gives the enjoyment of flavours, the
active mind that acquires knowledge, and the far-reaching knowledge that
constitutes virtue. In no case does the connexion with what is without
like to be obstructed; obstruction produces stoppage; stoppage, continuing without intermission, arrests all progress; and with this all injurious
effects spring up.

'The knowledge of all creatures depends on their breathing. But if
their breath be not abundant, it is not the fault of Heaven, which tries
to penetrate them with it, day and night without ceasing; but men notwithstanding shut their pores against it. The womb encloses a large and
empty space; the heart has its spontaneous and enjoyable movements. If
their apartment be not roomy, wife and mother-in-law will be bickering;

if the heart have not its spontaneous and enjoyable movements, the six faculties of perception will be in mutual collision. That the great forests, the heights and hills, are pleasant to men, is because their spirits cannot overcome (those distracting influences). Virtue overflows into (the love of) fame; (the love of) fame overflows into violence; schemes originate in the urgency (of circumstances); (the show of) wisdom comes from rivalry; the fuel (of strife) is produced from the obstinate maintenance (of one's own views); the business of offices should be apportioned in accordance with the approval of all. In spring, when the rain and the sunshine come seasonably, vegetation grows luxuriantly, and sickles and hoes begin to be prepared. More than half of what had fallen down becomes straight, and we do not know how.

10. 'Stillness and silence are helpful to those who are ill; rubbing the corners of the eyes is helpful to the aged; rest serves to calm agitation; but they are the toiled and troubled who have recourse to these things. Those who are at ease, and have not had such experiences, do not care to ask about them. The spirit-like man has had no experience of how it is that the sagely man keeps the world in awe, and so he does not inquire about it; the sagely man has had no experience of how it is that the man of ability and virtue keeps his age in awe, and so he does not inquire about it; the man of ability and virtue has had no experience of how it is that the superior man keeps his state in awe, and so he does not inquire about it. The superior man has had no experience of how it is that the small man keeps himself in agreement with his times that he should inquire about it.'

11. The keeper of the Yen Gate, on the death of his father, showed so much skill in emaciating his person that he received the rank of 'Pattern for Officers.' Half the people of his neighbourhood (in consequence) carried their emaciation to such a point that they died. When Yâo wished to resign the throne to Hsü Yû, the latter ran away. When Thang offered his to Wû Kwang, Wû Kwang became angry. When Kî Thâ heard it, he led his disciples, and withdrew to the river Kho, where the feudal princes came and condoled with him, and after three years, Shan Thû-tî threw himself into the water. Fishing-stakes are employed to catch fish; but when the fish are got, the men forget the stakes. Snares are employed to catch hares, but when the hares are got, men forget the snares. Words are employed to convey ideas; but when the ideas are apprehended, men forget the words. Fain would I talk with such a man who has forgot the words!

Yü Yen, or 'Metaphorical Language.'

1. Of my sentences nine in ten are metaphorical; of my illustrations seven in ten are from valued writers. The rest of my words are like the water that daily fills the cup, tempered and harmonised by the Heavenly element in our nature.

The nine sentences in ten which are metaphorical are borrowed from extraneous things to assist (the comprehension of) my argument. (When it is said, for instance), 'A father does not act the part of matchmaker for his own son,' (the meaning is that) 'it is better for another man to praise the son than for his father to do so.' The use of such metaphorical language is not my fault, but the fault of men (who would not otherwise readily understand me).

Men assent to views which agree with their own, and oppose those which do not so agree. Those which agree with their own they hold to be right, and those which do not so agree they hold to be wrong. The seven out of ten illustrations taken from valued writers are designed to put an end to disputations. Those writers are the men of hoary eld, my predecessors in time. But such as are unversed in the warp and woof, the beginning and end of the subject, cannot be set down as of venerable eld, and regarded as the predecessors of others. If men have not that in them which fits them to precede others, they are without the way proper to man, and they who are without the way proper to man can only be pronounced defunct monuments of antiquity.

Words like the water that daily issues from the cup, and are harmonised by the Heavenly Element (of our nature), may be carried on into the region of the unlimited, and employed to the end of our years. But without words there is an agreement (in principle). That agreement is not effected by words, and an agreement in words is not effected by it. Hence it is said, 'Let there be no words.' Speech does not need words. One may speak all his life, and not have spoken a (right) word; and one may not have spoken all his life, and yet all his life been giving utterance to the (right) words. There is that which makes a thing allowable, and that which makes a thing not allowable. There is that which makes a thing right, and that which makes a thing not right. How is a thing right? It is right because it is right. How is a thing wrong? It is wrong because it is wrong. How is a thing allowable? It is allowable because it is so. How is a thing not allowable? It is not allowable because it is not so. Things indeed have what makes them right, and what makes them allowable. There is nothing which has not its condition of right; nothing which has not its condition of allowability. But without the words of the (water-) cup in daily use, and harmonised by the Heavenly Element (in our nature), what one can continue long in the possession of these characteristics?

All things are divided into their several classes, and succeed to one another in the same way, though of different bodily forms. They begin and end as in an unbroken ring, though how it is they do so be not apprehended. This is what is called the Lathe of Heaven; and the Lathe of Heaven is the Heavenly Element in our nature.

2. Kwang-tsze said to Hui-tsze, 'When Confucius was in his sixtieth year, in that year his views changed. What he had before held to be right, he now ended by holding to be wrong; and he did not know whether the things which he now pronounced to be right were not those which he had for fifty-nine years held to be wrong.' Hui-tsze replied, 'Confucius with an earnest will pursued the acquisition of knowledge, and acted accordingly.' Kwang-tsze rejoined, 'Confucius disowned such a course, and never said that it was his. He said, "Man receives his powers from the Great Source (of his being), and he should restore them to their (original) intelligence in his life. His singing should be in accordance with the musical tubes, and his speech a model for imitation. When profit and righteousness are set before him, and his liking (for the latter) and dislike (of the former), his approval and disapproval, are manifested, that only serves to direct the speech of men (about him). To make men in heart submit, and not dare to stand up in opposition to him; to establish the fixed law for all under heaven:-- ah! ah! I have not attained to that."'

3. Tsang-tsze twice took office, and on the two occasions his state of mind was different. He said, 'While my parents were alive I took office, and though my emolument was only three fû (of grain), my mind was happy. Afterwards when I took office, my emolument was three thousand kung; but I could not share it with my parents, and my mind was sad.' The other disciples asked Kung-nî, saying, 'Such an one as Shan may be pronounced free from all entanglement:-- is he to be blamed for feeling as he did?' The reply was, 'But he was subject to entanglement. If he had been free from it, could he have had that sadness? He would have looked on his three fû and three thousand kung no more than on a heron or a mosquito passing before him.'

4. Yen Khang Tsze-yû said to Tung-kwo Tsze-khî, 'When I (had begun to) hear your instructions, the first year, I continued a simple rustic; the second year, I became docile; the third year, I comprehended (your teaching); the fourth year, I was (plastic) as a thing; the fifth year, I made

advances; the sixth year, the spirit entered (and dwelt in me); the seventh year, (my nature as designed by) Heaven was perfected; the eighth year, I knew no difference between death and life; the ninth year, I attained to the Great Mystery.

'Life has its work to do, and death ensues, (as if) the common character of each were a thing prescribed. Men consider that their death has its cause; but that life from (the operation of) the Yang has no cause. But is it really so? How does (the Yang) operate in this direction? Why does it not operate there?

'Heaven has its places and spaces which can be calculated; (the divisions of) the earth can be assigned bv men. But how shall we search for and find out (the conditions of the Great Mystery)? We do not know when and how (life) will end, but how shall we conclude that it is not determined (from without)? and as we do not know when and how it begins, how should we conclude that it is not (so) determined?

In regard to the issues of conduct which we deem appropriate, how should we conclude that there are no spirits presiding over them; and where those issues seem inappropriate, how should we conclude that there are spirits presiding over them?'

5. The penumbrae (once) asked the shadow, saying, 'Formerly you were looking down, and now you are looking up; formerly you had your hair tied up, and now it is dishevelled; formerly you were sitting, and now you have risen up; formerly you were walking, and now you have stopped: how is all this?' The shadow said, 'Venerable Sirs, how do you ask me about such small matters? These things all belong to me, but I do not know how they do so. I am (like) the shell of a cicada or the cast-off skin of a snake;-- like them, and yet not like them. With light and the sun I make my appearance; with darkness and the night I fade away. Am not I dependent on the substance from which I am thrown? And that substance is itself dependent on something else! When it comes, I come with it; when it goes, I go with it. When it comes under the influence of the strong Yang, I come under the same. Since we are both produced by that strong Yang, what occasion is there for you to question me?'

6. Yang Tsze-kü had gone South to Phei, while Lâo Tan was travelling in the west in Khin. (He thereupon) asked (Lâo-tsze) to come to the border (of Phei), and went himself to Liang, where he met him. Lâo-tsze stood in the middle of the way, and, looking up to heaven, said with a sigh, 'At first I thought that you might be taught, but now I see that you cannot be.' Yang Tsze-kü made no reply; and when they came to their lodging-house, he brought in water for the master to wash his hands and rinse his mouth, along with a towel and comb. He then took off his shoes outside the door, went forward on his knees, and said, 'Formerly, your disciple wished to ask you, Master, (the reason of what you said); but you were walking, and there was no opportunity, and therefore I did not presume to speak. Now there is an opportunity, and I beg to ask why you spoke as you did.' Lâo-tsze replied, 'Your eyes are lofty, and you stare;-- who would live with you? The purest carries himself as if he were soiled; the most virtuous seems to feel himself defective.' Yang Tsze-kü looked abashed and changed countenance, saying, 'I receive your commands with reverence.'

When he first went to the lodging-house, the people of it met him and went before him. The master of it carried his mat for him, and the mistress brought the towel and comb. The lodgers left their mats, and the cook his fire-place (as he passed them). When he went away, the others in the house would have striven with him about (the places for) their mats.

Zang Wang, or 'Kings who have wished to resign the Throne.'

1. Yâo proposed to resign the throne to Hsü Yü, who would not accept it. He then offered it to Tsze-kâu Kih-fû, but he said, 'It is not unreasonable to propose that I should occupy the throne, but I happen to be suffering under a painful sorrow and illness. While I am engaged in dealing with it, I have not leisure to govern the kingdom.' Now the throne is the most important of all positions, and yet this man would not occupy it to the injury of his life; how much less would he have allowed any other thing to do so! But only he who does not care to rule the kingdom is fit to be entrusted with it.

Shun proposed to resign the throne to Tsze-kâu Kih-po, who declined in the very same terms as Kih-fû had done. Now the kingdom is the greatest of all concerns, and yet this man would not give his life in exchange for the throne. This shows how they who possess the Tâo differ from common men.

Shun proposed to resign the throne to Shan Küan, who said, 'I am a unit in the midst of space and time. In winter I wear skins and furs; in summer, grass-cloth and linen; in spring I plough and sow, my strength being equal to the toil; in autumn I gather in my harvest, and am prepared to cease from labour and eat. At sunrise I get up and work; at sunset I rest. So do I enjoy myself between heaven and earth, and my mind is content:-- why should I have anything to do with the throne? Alas! that you, Sir, do not know me better!' Thereupon he declined the proffer, and went away, deep among the hills, no man knew where.

Shun proposed to resign the throne to his friend, a farmer of Shih-hû. The farmer, however, said (to himself), 'How full of vigor does our lord show himself, and how exuberant is his strength! If Shun with all his powers be not equal (to the task of government, how should I be so?).' On this he took his wife on his back, led his son by the hand, and went away to the sea-coast, from which to the end of his life he did not come back.

When Thâi-wang Than-fû was dwelling in Pin, the wild tribes of the North attacked him. He tried to serve them with skins and silks, but they were not satisfied. He tried to serve them with dogs and horses, but they were not satisfied, and then with pearls and jade, but they were not satisfied. What they sought was his territory. Thâi-wang Than-fû said (to his people), 'To dwell with the elder brother and cause the younger brother to be killed, or with the father and cause the son to be killed,-- this is what I cannot bear to do. Make an effort, my children, to remain here. What difference is there between being my subjects, or the subjects of those wild people? And I have heard that a man does not use that which he employs for nourishing his people to injure them.' Thereupon he took his staff and switch and left, but the people followed him in an unbroken train, and he established a (new) state at the foot of mount Khî. Thus Thâi- wang Than-fû might be pronounced one who could give its (due) honour to life. Those who are able to do so, though they may be rich and noble, will not, for that which nourishes them, injure their persons; and though they may be poor and mean, will not, for the sake of gain, involve their bodies (in danger). The men of the present age who occupy high offices and are of honourable rank all lose these (advantages) again, and in the prospect of gain lightly expose their persons to ruin:-- is it not a case of delusion?

The people of Yüeh three times in succession killed their ruler, and the prince Sâu, distressed by it, made his escape to the caves of Tan, so that Yüeh was left without a ruler. The people sought for the prince, but could not find him, till (at last) they followed him to the cave of Tan. The prince was not willing to come out to them, but they smoked him out with moxa, and made him mount the royal chariot. As he took hold of the strap, and mounted the carriage, he looked up to heaven, and called out, '0 Ruler, 0 Ruler, could you not have spared me this?' Prince Sâu did not dislike being ruler;-- he disliked the evil inseparable from being so. It may be said of him that he would not for the sake of a kingdom endanger his life; and this indeed was the reason why the people of Yüeh wanted to get him for their ruler.

2. Han and Wei were contending about some territory which one of them had wrested from the other. Tsze-hwâ Tsze went to see the marquis Kâo-hsi (of Han), and, finding him looking sorrowful, said, 'Suppose now that all the states were to sign an agreement before you to the effect that "Whoever should with his left hand carry off (the territory in dispute) should lose his right hand, and whoever should do so with his right hand should lose his left hand, but that, nevertheless, he who should carry it off was sure to obtain the whole kingdom;" would your lordship feel yourself able to carry it off?' The marquis said, 'I would not carry it off,' and Tsze-hwâ rejoined, 'Very good. Looking at the thing from this point of view, your two arms are of more value to you than the whole kingdom. But your body is of more value than your two arms, and Han is of much less value than the whole kingdom. The territory for which you are now contending is further much less important than Han:-- your lordship, since you feel so much concern for your body, should not be endangering

your life by indulging your sorrow.'

The marquis Kâo-hsî said, 'Good! Many have given me their counsel about this matter; but I never heard what you have said.' Tsze-hwâ Tsze may be said to have known well what was of great importance and what was of little.

3. The ruler of Lû, having heard that Yen Ho had attained to the Tâo, sent a messenger, with a gift of silks, to prepare the way for further communication with him. Yen Ho was waiting at the door of a mean house, in a dress of coarse hempen cloth, and himself feeding a cowl. When the messenger arrived, Yen Ho himself confronted him. 'Is this,' said the messenger, 'the house of Yen Ho?' 'It is,' was the reply; and the other was presenting the silks to him, when he said, 'I am afraid you heard (your instructions) wrongly, and that he who sent you will blame you. You had better make sure.' The messenger on this returned, and made sure that he was right; but when he came back, and sought for Yen Ho, he was not to be found.

Yes; men like Yen Ho do of a truth dislike riches and honours. Hence it is said, 'The true object of the Tâo is the regulation of the person. Quite subordinate to this is its use in the management of the state and the clan; while the government of the kingdom is but the dust and refuse of it.' From this we may see that the services of the Tîs and Kings are but a surplusage of the work of the sages, and do not contribute to complete the person or nourish the life. Yet the superior men of the present age will, most of them, throw away their lives for the sake of their persons, in pursuing their (material) objects;-- is it not cause for grief? Whenever a sage is initiating any movement, he is sure to examine the motive which influences him, and what he is about to do. Here, however, is a man, who uses a pearl like that of the marquis of Sui to shoot a bird at a distance of 10,000 feet. All men will laugh at him; and why? Because the thing which he uses is of great value, and what he wishes to get is of little. And is not life of more value than the pearl of the marquis of Sui?

4. Tsze Lieh-tsze was reduced to extreme poverty, and his person had a hungry look. A visitor mentioned the case to Tsze-yang, (the premier) of Kang, saying, 'Lieh Yü-khâu, I believe, is a scholar who has attained to the Tâo. Is it because our ruler does not love (such) scholars, that he should be living in his state in such poverty?' Tsze-yang immediately ordered an officer to send to him a supply of grain. When Lieh-tsze saw the messenger, he bowed to him twice, and declined the gift, on which the messenger went away. On Lieh-tsze's going into the house, his wife looked to him and beat her breast, saying, 'I have heard that the wife and

children of a possessor of the Tâo all enjoy plenty and ease, but now we look starved. The ruler has seen his error, and sent you a present of food, but you would not receive it;-- is it appointed (for us to suffer thus)?' Tsze Lieh-tsze laughed and said to her, 'The ruler does not himself know me. Because of what some one said to him, he sent me the grain; but if another speak (differently) of me to him, he may look on me as a criminal. This was why I did not receive the grain!

In the end it did come about, that the people, on an occasion of trouble and disorder, put Tsze-yang to death.

5. When king Kâo of Khû lost his kingdom, the sheep-butcher Yüeh followed him in his flight. When the king (recovered) his kingdom and returned to it, and was going to reward those who had followed him, on coming to the sheep-butcher Yüeh, that personage said, 'When our Great King lost his kingdom, I lost my sheep-killing. When his majesty got back his kingdom, I also got back my sheep-killing. My income and rank have been recovered; why speak further of rewarding me?' The king, (on hearing of this reply), said, 'Force him (to take the reward);' but Yüeh said, 'It was not through any crime of mine that the king lost his kingdom, and therefore I did not dare to submit to the death (which would have been mine if I had remained in the capital). And it was not through any service of mine that he recovered his kingdom, and therefore I do not dare to count myself worthy of any reward from him.'

The king (now) asked that the butcher should be introduced to him, but Yüeh said, 'According to the law of Khû, great reward ought to be given to great service, and the recipient then be introduced to the king; but now my wisdom was not sufficient to preserve the kingdom, nor my courage sufficient to die at the hands of the invaders. When the army of Wû entered, I was afraid of the danger, and got out of the way of the thieves;-- it was not with a distinct purpose (of loyalty) that I followed the king. And now he wishes, in disregard of the law, and violations of the conditions of our social compact, to see me in court;-- this is not what I would like to be talked of through the kingdom.' The king said to Tsze-khî, the Minister of War, 'The position of the sheep-butcher Yüeh is low and mean, but his setting forth of what is right is very high; do you ask him for me to accept the place of one of my three most distinguished nobles.' (This being communicated to Yüeh), he said, 'I know that the place of such a distinguished noble is nobler than a sheep-butcher's stall, and that the salary of 10,000 kung is more than its profits. But how should I, through my greed of rank and emolument, bring on our ruler the name of an unlawful dispensation of his gifts? I dare not respond to your wishes, but desire to return to my stall as the sheep-butcher.' Accordingly he did not accept (the proffered reward).

6. Yüan Hsien was living in Lû. His house, whose walls were only a few paces round, looked as if it were thatched with a crop of growing grass; its door of brushwood was incomplete, with branches of a mulberry tree for its side-posts; the window of each of its two apartments was formed by an earthenware jar (in the wall), which was stuffed with some coarse serge. It leaked above, and was damp on the ground beneath; but there he sat composedly, playing on his guitar. Tsze-kung, in an inner robe of purple and an outer one of pure white, riding in a carriage drawn by two large horses, the hood of which was too high to get into the lane (leading to the house), went to see him. Yüan Hsien, in a cap made of bark, and slippers without heels, and with a stalk of hellebore for a staff, met him at the door. 'Alas! Master,' said Tsze-kung, 'that you should be in such distress!' Yüan Hsien answered him, 'I have heard that to have no money is to be poor, and that not to be able to carry one's learning into practice is to be distressed. I am poor but not in distress.' Tsze-kung shrank back, and looked ashamed, on which the other laughed and said, 'To act with a view to the world's (praise); to pretend to be public-spirited and yet be a partisan; to learn in order to please men; to teach for the sake of one's own gain; to conceal one's wickedness under the garb of benevolence and righteousness; and to be fond of the show of chariots and horses:-- these are things which Hsien cannot bear to do.'

Tsang-tsze was residing in Wei. He wore a robe quilted with hemp, and had no outer garment; his countenance looked rough and emaciated; his hands and feet were horny and callous; he would be three days without lighting a fire; in ten years he did not have a new suit; if he put his cap on straight, the strings would break; if he drew tight the overlap of his robe, his elbow would be seen; in putting on his shoes, the heels would burst them. Yet dragging his shoes along, he sang the 'Sacrificial Odes of Shang' with a voice that filled heaven and earth as if it came from a bell or a sounding stone. The Son of Heaven could not get him to be a minister; no feudal prince could get him for his friend. So it is that he who is nourishing his mind's aim forgets his body, and he who is nourishing his body discards all thoughts of gain, and he who is carrying out the Tâo forgets his own mind.

Confucius said to Yen Hui, 'Come here, Hui. Your family is poor, and your position is low; why should you not take office?' Hui replied, 'I have no wish to be in office. Outside the suburban district I possess fields to the extent of fifty acres, which are sufficient to supply me with congee; and inside it I have ten acres, which are sufficient to supply me with silk and flax. I find my pleasure in playing on my lute, and your doctrines, Master, which I study, are sufficient for my enjoyment; I do not wish to take office.' Confucius looked sad, changed countenance, and said, "How good is the mind of Hui! I have heard that he who is contented will not entangle himself with the pursuit of gain, that he who is conscious of having gained (the truth) in himself is not afraid of losing other things, and that he who cultivates the path of inward rectification is not ashamed though he may have no official position. I have long been preaching this; but to-day I see it realised in Hui:-- this is what I have gained.'

7. Prince Mâu of Kung-shan spoke to Kan-tsze, saying, 'My body has its place by the streams and near the sea, but my mind dwells at the court of Wei;-- what have you to say to me in the circumstances?' Kan-tsze replied, 'Set the proper value on your life. When one sets the proper value on his life, gain seems to him unimportant.' The prince rejoined, 'I know that, but I am not able to overcome (my wishes).' The reply was, 'If you cannot master yourself (in the matter), follow (your inclinations so that) your spirit may not be dissatisfied. When you cannot master yourself, and try to force yourself where your spirit does not follow, this is what is called doing yourself a double injury; and those who so injure themselves are not among the long-lived.'

Mâu of Wei was the son of a lord of ten thousand chariots. For him to live in retirement among crags and caves was more difficult than for a scholar who had not worn the dress of office. Although he had not attained to the Tâo, he may be said to have had some idea of it.

8. When Confucius was reduced to extreme distress between Khan and Tshâi, for seven days he had no cooked meat to eat, but only some soup of coarse vegetables without any rice in it. His countenance wore the appearance of great exhaustion, and yet he kept playing on his lute and singing inside the house. Yen Hui (was outside), selecting the vegetables, while Tsze-lû and Tsze-kung were talking together, and said to him, 'The Master has twice been driven from Lû; he had to flee from Wei; the tree (beneath which he rested) was cut down in Sung; he was reduced to extreme distress in Shang and Kâu; he is held in a state of siege here between Khan and Tshâi; any one who kills him will be held guiltless; there is no prohibition against making him a prisoner. And yet he keeps playing and singing, thrumming his lute without ceasing.
Can a superior man be without the feeling of shame to such an extent as this?' Yen Hui gave them no reply, but went in and told (their words) to Confucius, who pushed aside his lute, and said, 'Yû and Tshze are small men. Call them here, and I will explain the thing to them.'

When they came in, Tsze-lû said, 'Your present condition may be called one of extreme distress.' Confucius replied, 'What words are these!

When the Superior man has free course with his principles, that is what we call his success; when such course is denied, that is what we call his failure. Now I hold in my embrace the principles of benevolence and righteousness, and with them meet the evils of a disordered age;-- where is the proof of my being in extreme distress? Therefore looking inwards and examining myself, I have no difficulties about my principles; though I encounter such difficulties (as the present), I do not lose my virtue. It is when winter's cold is come, and the hoar-frost and snow are falling, that we know the vegetative power of the pine and cypress. This strait between Khan and Tshâi is fortunate for me.' He then took back his lute so that it emitted a twanging sound, and began to play and sing. (At the same time) Tsze-lû, hurriedly, seized a shield, and began to dance, while Tsze-kung said, 'I did not know (before) the height of heaven nor the depth of the earth.'

The ancients who had got the Tâo were happy when reduced to extremity, and happy when having free course. Their happiness was independent of both these conditions. The Tâo, and its characteristics!-- let them have these and distress and success come to them as cold and heat, as wind and rain in the natural order of things. Thus it was that Hsü Yû. found pleasure on the north of the river Ying, and that the earl of Kung enjoyed himself on the top of mount (Kung).

9. Shun proposed to resign the throne to his friend, the Northerner Wû-kâi, who said, 'A strange man you are, 0 sovereign! You (first) lived among the channeled fields, and then your place was in the palace of Yâo. And not only so:-- you now further wish to extend to me the stain of your disgraceful doings. I am ashamed to see you.' And on this he threw himself into the abyss of Khing-lang.

When Thang was about to attack Kieh, he took counsel with Pien Sui, who said, 'It is no business of mine.' Thang then said, 'To whom should I apply?' And the other said, 'I do not know.' Thang then took counsel with Wû Kwang, who gave the same answer as Pien Sui; and when asked to whom he should apply, said in the same way, 'I do not know.' 'Suppose,' Thang then said, 'I apply to Î Yin, what do you say about him?' The reply was, 'He has a wonderful power in doing what is disgraceful, and I know nothing more about him!'

Thang thereupon took counsel with Î Yin, attacked Kieh, and overcame him, after which he proposed to resign the throne to Pien Sui, who declined it, saying, 'When you were about to attack Kieh, and sought counsel from me, you must have supposed me to be prepared to be a robber. Now that you have conquered Kieh, and propose to resign the throne to me, you must consider me to be greedy. I have been born in an age of disorder, and a man without principle twice comes, and tries to extend to me the stain of his disgraceful proceedings!-- I cannot bear to hear the repetition of his proposals.' With this he threw himself into the Kâu water and died.

Thang further made proffer of the throne to Wû Kwang, saying, 'The wise man has planned it; the martial man has carried it through; and the benevolent man should occupy it:-- this was the method of antiquity. Why should you, Sir, not take the position?' Wû Kwang refused the proffer, saying, 'To depose the sovereign is contrary to right; to kill the people is contrary to benevolence. When another has encountered the risks, if I should accept the gain of his adventure, I should violate my disinterestedness. I have heard it said, "If it be not right for him to do so, one should not accept the emolument; in an age of unprincipled (government), one should not put foot on the soil (of the) country:"-- how much less should

I accept this position of honour! I cannot bear to see you any longer.' And with this he took a stone on his back, and drowned himself in the Lü water.

10. Formerly, at the rise of the Kâu dynasty, there were two brothers who lived in Kû-kû, and were named Po-î and Shû-khî. They spoke together and said, 'We have heard that in the west there is one who seems to rule according to the Right Way; let us go and see.' (Accordingly) they came to the south of (mount) Khî; and when king Wû heard of them, he sent (his brother) Shû Tan to see them, and make a covenant with them, engaging that their wealth should be second (only to that of the king), and that their offices should be of the first rank, and instructing him to bury the covenant with the blood of the victim after they had smeared the corners of their mouths with it. The brothers looked at each other and laughed, saying, 'Ah! How strange! This is not what we call the Right Way. Formerly, when Shan Nang had the kingdom, he offered his sacrifices at the proper seasons and with the utmost reverence, but without praying for any blessing. Towards men he was leal-hearted and sincere, doing his utmost in governing them, but without seeking anything for himself. When it was his pleasure to use administrative measures, he did so; and a sterner rule when he thought that would be better. He did not by the ruin of others establish his own power; he did not exalt himself by bringing others low; he did not, when the time was opportune, seek his own profit. But now Kâu, seeing the disorder of Yin, has suddenly taken the government into its hands; with the high it has taken counsel, and with those below employed bribes; it relies on its troops to maintain the terror of its might; it makes covenants over victims to prove its good faith; it vaunts its proceedings to please the masses; it kills and attacks

for the sake of gain:-- this is simply overthrowing disorder and changing it for tyranny. We have heard that the officers of old, in an age of good government, did not shrink from their duties, and in an age of disorder did not recklessly seek to remain in office. Now the kingdom is in a state of darkness; the virtue of Kâu is decayed. Than to join with it and lay our persons in the dust, it is better for us to abandon it, and maintain the purity of our conduct.'

The two princes then went north to the hill of Shâu-yang, where they died of starvation. If men such as they, in the matter of riches and honours, can manage to avoid them, (let them do so); but they must not depend on their lofty virtue to pursue any perverse course, only gratifying their own tendencies, and not doing service in their time:-- this was the style of these two princes.

Tâo Kih, or 'The Robber Kih.'

1. Confucius was on terms of friendship with Liû-hsiâ Kî, who had a brother named Tâo Kih. This Tâo Kih had 9,000 followers, who marched at their will through the kingdom, assailing and oppressing the different princes. They dug through walls and broke into houses; they drove away people's cattle and horses; they carried off people's wives and daughters. In their greed to get, they forgot the claims of kinship, and paid no regard to their parents and brethren. They did not sacrifice to their ancestors. Wherever they passed through the country, in the larger states the people guarded their city walls, and in the smaller the people took to their strongholds. All were distressed by them.

Confucius spoke to Liû-hsiâ Kî, saying, 'Fathers should be able to Jay down the law to their sons, and elder to instruct their younger brothers. If they are unable to do so, they do not fulfil the duties of the relationships which they sustain. You, Sir, are one of the most talented officers of the age, and your younger brother is this Robber Kih. He is a pest in the kingdom, and you are not able to instruct him better; I cannot but be ashamed of you, and I beg to go for you and give him counsel.' Liû-hsiâ Kî replied, 'You say, Sir, that fathers must be able to lay down the law to their sons, and elder to instruct their younger brothers, but if sons will not listen to the orders of their fathers, nor the younger receive the lessons of their elder brothers, though one may have your powers of persuasion, what is to be done? And, moreover, Kih is a man whose mind is like a gushing fountain, and his will like a whirlwind; he is strong enough to resist all enemies, and clever enough to gloss over his wrong-doings. If you agree with him, he is glad; if you oppose him, he is enraged; and he readily meets men with the language of abuse. You must not go to him.'

Confucius, however, did not attend to this advice. With Yen Hui as his charioteer, and Tsze-kung seated on the right, he went to see Tâo Kih, whom he found with his followers halted on the south of Thâi-shan, and mincing men's livers, which he gave them to eat. Confucius alighted from his carriage, and went forward, till he saw the usher, to whom he said, 'I, Khung Khiû of Lû, have heard of the general's lofty righteousness,' bowing twice respectfully to the man as he said so. The usher went in and announced the visitor. But when Tâo Kih heard of the arrival, he flew into a great rage; his eyes became like blazing stars, and his hair rose up and touched his cap. 'Is not this fellow,' said he, 'Khung Khiû, that artful hypocrite of Lû? Tell him from me, "You invent speeches and babble away, appealing without ground to (the examples of) Wan and Wû. The ornaments on your cap are as many as the branches of a tree, and your girdle is (a piece of skin) from the ribs of a dead ox, The more you talk, the more nonsense you utter. You get your food without (the labour of) ploughing, and your clothes without (that of) weaving. You wag your lips and make your tongue a drum-stick. You arbitrarily decide what is right and what is wrong, thereby leading astray the princes throughout the kingdom, and making its learned scholars not occupy their thoughts with their proper business. You recklessly set up your filial piety and fraternal duty, and curry favour with the feudal princes, the wealthy and the noble. Your offence is great; your crime is very heavy. Take yourself off home at once. If you do not do so, I will take your liver, and add it to the provision for to-day's food.'"

But Confucius sent in another message, saying, 'I enjoy the good will of (your brother) Kî, and I wish and hope to tread the ground beneath your tent.' When the usher had communicated this message, Tâo Kih said, 'Make him come forward.' On this Confucius hastened forwards. Declining to take a mat, he drew hastily back, and bowed twice to Tâo Kih, who in a great rage stretched his legs apart, laid his hand on his sword, and with glaring eyes and a voice like the growl of a nursing tigress, said, 'Come forwards, Khiû. If what you say be in accordance with my mind, you shall live; but, if it be contrary to it, you shall die.' Confucius replied, 'I have heard that everywhere under the sky there are three (most excellent) qualities. To be naturally tall and large, to be elegant and handsome without a peer, so that young and old, noble and mean, are pleased to look upon him;-- this is the highest of those qualities. To comprehend both heaven and earth in his wisdom, and to be able to speak eloquently on all subjects;-- this is the middle one of them. To be brave and courageous, resolute and daring, gathering the multitudes round him, and leading on his troops;-- this is the lowest of them. Whoever possesses one of these qualities is fit to stand with his face to the south, and style himself a Prince. But you, General, unite in yourself all the three. Your person is eight cubits and two inches in height; there is a brightness about your face and a light in your eyes; your lips look as if stained with vermilion; your teeth are like rows of precious shells; your voice is attuned to the musical tubes, and yet you are named "The Robber Kih." I am ashamed of you, General, and cannot approve of you. If you are inclined to listen to me, I should like to go as your commissioner to Wû and Yüeh in the south; to Khî and Lû in the north; to Sung and Wei in the cast; and to Tsin and Khû in the west. I will get them to build for you a great city several hundred lî in size, to establish under it towns containing several hundred thousands of inhabitants, and honour you there as a feudal lord. The kingdom will see you begin your career afresh; you will cease from your wars and disband your soldiers; you will collect and nourish your brethren, and along with them offer the sacrifices to your ancestors:-- this will be a course befitting a sage and an officer of ability, and will fulfil the wishes of the whole kingdom.'

'Come forward, Khiû,' said Tâo Kih, greatly enraged. 'Those who can be persuaded by considerations of gain, and to whom remonstrances may be addressed with success, are all ignorant, low, and ordinary people. That I am tall and large, elegant and handsome, so that all who see me are pleased with me;-- this is an effect of the body left me by my parents. Though you were not to praise me for it, do I not know it myself? And I have heard that he who likes to praise men to their face will also like to speak ill of them behind their back. And when you tell me of a great wall and a multitudinous people, this is to try to persuade me by considerations of gain, and to cocker me as one of the ordinary people. But how could such advantages last for long? Of all great cities there is none so great as the whole kingdom, which was possessed by Yâo and Shun, while their descendants (now) have not so much territory as would admit an awl. Thang and Wû were both set up as the Sons of Heaven, but in after ages (their posterity) were cut off and extinguished;-- was not this because the gain of their position was so great a prize?

Tâo Kih, or 'The Robber Kih.' (cont.)

1. (cont.) 'And moreover I have heard that anciently birds and beasts were numerous, and men were few, so that they lived in nests in order to avoid the animals. In the daytime they gathered acorns and chestnuts, and in the night they roosted on the trees; and on account of this they are called the people of the Nest-builder. Anciently the people did not know the use of clothes. In summer they collected great stores of faggots, and in winter kept themselves warm by means of them; and on account of this they are called the people who knew how to take care of their lives. In the age of Shan Nang, the people lay down in simple innocence, and rose up in quiet security. They knew their mothers, but did not know their fathers. They dwelt along with the elks and deer. They ploughed and ate; they wove and made clothes; they had no idea of injuring one another:-- this was the grand time of Perfect virtue. Hwang-Tî, however, was not able to perpetuate this virtuous state. He fought with Khih-yû in the wild of Ko-lû till the blood flowed over a hundred lî. When Yâo and Shun arose, they instituted their crowd of ministers. Thang banished his lord. King Wû killed Kâu. Since that time the strong have oppressed the weak, and the many tyrannised over the few. From Thang and Wû downwards, (the rulers) have all been promoters of disorder and confusion. You yourself now cultivate and inculcate the ways of Wan and Wû; you handle whatever subjects are anywhere discussed for the instruction of future ages. With your peculiar robe and narrow girdle, with your deceitful speech and hypocritical conduct, you delude the lords of the different states, and are seeking for riches and honours. There is no greater robber than you are;-- why does not all the world call you the Robber Khiû, instead of styling me the Robber Kih?

'You prevailed by your sweet speeches on Tsze-lû, and made him your follower; you made him put away his high cap, lay aside his long sword, and receive your instructions, so that all the world said, "Khung Khiû is able to arrest violence and repress the wrong-doer;" but in the end, when Tsze-lû wished to slay the ruler of Wei, and the affair proved unsuccessful, his body was exhibited in pickle over the eastern gate of the capital;-- so did your teaching of him come to nothing.

'Do you call yourself a scholar of talent, a sage? Why, you were twice driven out of Lû; you had to run away from Wei; you were reduced to extremity in Khî; you were held in a state of siege between Khan and Tshâi; there is no resting-place for your person in the kingdom; your instructions brought Tsze-lû to pickle. Such have been the misfortunes (attending your course). You have done no good either for yourself or for others;-- how can your doctrines be worth being thought much of?

'There is no one whom the world exalts so much as it does Hwang-Tî, and still he was not able to perfect his virtue, but fought in the wilderness of Ko-lû, till the blood flowed over a hundred lî. Yâo was not kind to his son. Shun was not filial. Yü was paralysed on one side. Thang banished his sovereign. King Wû smote Kâu. King Wan was imprisoned in Yû-lî. These are the six men of whom the world thinks the most highly, yet when we accurately consider their history, we see that for the sake of gain they all disallowed their true (nature), and did violence to its proper qualities and tendencies:-- their conduct cannot be thought of but with deep shame.

'Among those whom the world calls men of ability and virtue were (the brothers) Po-Î and Shû-khî. They declined the rule of Kû-kû, and died of starvation on the hill of Shâu-yang, leaving their bones and flesh unburied. Pâo Tsiâo vaunted his conduct, and condemned the world, but he died with his arms round a tree. When Shan-thû Tî's remonstrances were not listened to, he fastened a stone on his back, and threw himself into the Ho, where he was eaten by the fishes and turtles. Kieh Tsze-thui was the most devoted (of followers), and cut a piece from his thigh as food for duke Wan. But when the duke afterwards overlooked him (in his distribution of favours), he was angry, and went away, and was burned to death with a tree in his arms. Wei Shang had made an appointment with a girl to meet him under a bridge; but when she did not come, and the water rose around him, he would not go away, and died with his arms round one of the pillars. (The deaths of) these four men were not different from those of the dog that is torn in pieces, the pig that is borne away by a current, or the beggar (drowned in a ditch) with his alms-gourd in his hand. They were all caught as in a net by their (desire for) fame, not caring to nourish their life to its end, as they were bound to do.

'Among those whom the world calls faithful ministers there have been none like the prince Pî-kan and Wû Tsze-hsü. But Tsze-hsü's (dead) body was cast into the Kiang, and the heart of Pî-kan was cut out. These two were what the world calls loyal ministers, but the end has been that everybody laughs at them. Looking at all the above cases, down to those of Tsze-hsü and Pî-kan, there is not one worthy to be honoured; and as to the admonitions which you, Khiû, wish to impress on me, if you tell me about the state of the dead, I am unable to know anything about it; if you tell me about the things of men (alive), they are only such as I have stated, what I have heard and know all about. I will now tell you, Sir, my views about the condition of man. The eyes wish to look on beauty; the ears to hear music; the mouth to enjoy flavours; the will to be gratified.

The greatest longevity man can reach is a hundred years; a medium longevity is eighty years; the lowest longevity is sixty. Take away sickness, pining, bereavement, mourning, anxieties, and calamities, the times when, in any of these, one can open his mouth and laugh, are only four or five days in a month. Heaven and earth have no limit of duration, but the death of man has its (appointed) time. Take the longest amount of a limited time, and compare it with what is unlimited, its brief existence is not different from the passing of a crevice by one of king Mû's horses. Those who cannot gratify their will and natural aims, and nourish their appointed longevity, are all unacquainted with the (right) Way (of life). I cast from me, Khiû, all that you say. Be quick and go. Hurry back and say not a word more. Your Way is only a wild recklessness, deceitful, artful, vain, and hypocritical. It is not available to complete the true (nature of man); it is not worth talking about!'

Confucius bowed twice, and hurried away. He went out at the door, and mounted his carriage. Thrice he missed the reins as he tried to take hold of them. His eyes were dazed, and he could not see; and his colour was that of slaked lime. He laid hold of the cross-bar, holding his head down, and unable to draw his breath. When he got back, outside the east gate of (the capital of) Lû, he encountered Liû-hsiâ Kî, who said to him, 'Here you are, right in the gate. For some days I have not seen you. Your carriage and horses are travel-stained;-- have you not been to see Tâo Kih?' Confucius looked up to heaven, sighed, and said, 'Yes.' The other went on, 'And did he not set himself in opposition to all your views, as I said he would do?' 'He did. My case has been that of the man who cauterised himself without being ill. I rushed away, stroked the tiger's head, played with his whiskers, and narrowly escaped his mouth.'

2. Tsze-kang asked Mân Kâu-teh, saying, 'Why do you not pursue a (righteous) course? Without such a course you will not be believed in; unless you are believed in, you will not be employed in office; and if not employed in office, you will not acquire gain. Thus, if you look at the matter from the point of reputation, or estimate it from the point of gain, a righteous course is truly the right thing. If you discard the thought of reputation and gain, yet when you think over the thing in your own mind, you will see that the scholar should not be a single day without pursuing a (righteous) course.' Mân Kâu-teh said, 'He who has no shame becomes rich, and he in whom many believe becomes illustrious. Thus the greatest fame and gain would seem to spring from being without shame and being believed in. Therefore if you look at the matter from the point of reputation, or estimate it from the point of gain, to be believed in is the right thing. If you discard the thought of fame and gain, and think over the thing in your own mind, you will see that the scholar in the course

which he pursues is (simply) holding fast his Heavenly (nature, and gaining nothing).'

Tsze-kang said, 'Formerly Kieh and Kâu each enjoyed the honour of being the sovereign, and all the wealth of the kingdom was his; but if you now say to a (mere) money-grabber, "Your conduct is like that of Kieh or Kâu," he will look ashamed, and resent the imputation:-- (these two sovereigns) are despised by the smallest men. Kung-nî and Mo Tî (on the other hand) were poor, and common men; but if you say to a Prime Minister that his conduct is like that of Kung-nî or Mo Tî, then he will be put out and change countenance, and protest that he is not worthy (to be so spoken of):-- (these two philosophers) are held to be truly noble by (all) scholars. Thus it is that the position of sovereign does not necessarily connect with being thought noble, nor the condition of being poor and of common rank with being thought mean. The difference of being thought noble or mean arises from the conduct being good or bad.' Mân KAu-teh replied, 'Small robbers are put in prison; a great robber becomes a feudal lord; and in the gate of the feudal lord your righteous scholars will be found. For instance, Hsiâo-po, the duke Hwan, killed his elder brother, and took his sister-in-law to himself, and yet Kwan Kung became his minister; and Thien Khang, styled Khang-tsze, killed his ruler, and usurped the state, and yet Confucius received a present of silks from him. In their discussions they would condemn the men, but in their conduct they abased themselves before them. In this way their words and actions must have been at war together in their breasts;-- was it not a contradiction and perversity? As it is said in a book, "Who is bad? and who is good? The successful is regarded as the Head, and the unsuccessful as the Tail."'

Tsze-kang said, 'If you do not follow the usual course of what is held to be right, but observe no distinction between the near and remote degrees of kin, no difference between the noble and the mean, no order between the old and the young, then how shall a separation be made of the fivefold arrangement (of the virtues), and the six parties (in the social organisation)?' Mân Kâu-teh replied, 'Yâo killed his eldest son, and Shun banished his half-brother':-- did they observe the rules about the different degrees of kin? Thang deposed Kieh; king Wû overthrew Kâu:-- did they observe the righteousness that should obtain between the noble and the mean? King Kî took the place of his elder brother, and the duke of Kâu killed his:-- did they observe the order that should obtain between the elder and the younger? The Literati make hypocritical speeches; the followers of Mo hold that all should be loved equally:-- do we find in them the separation of the fivefold arrangement (of the virtues), and the six parties (in the social organisation)? And further, you, Sir, are all for reputation, and I am all for gain; but where the actual search for reputation and gain may not be in accordance with principle and will not bear to be examined in the light of the right way, let me and you refer the matter to-morrow to the decision of Wû-yo.'

(This Wû-yo) said, 'The small man pursues after wealth; the superior man pursues after reputation. The way in which they change their feelings and alter their nature is different; but if they were to cast away what they do, and replace it with doing nothing, they would be the same. Hence it is said, "Do not be a small man;-- return and pursue after the Heavenly in you. Do not be a superior man;-- follow the rule of the Heavenly in you. Be it crooked, be it straight, view the thing in the light of Heaven as revealed in you. Look all round on every side of it, and as the time indicates, cease your endeavours. Be it right, be it wrong, hold fast the ring in yourself in which all conditions converge. Alone by yourself, carry out your idea; ponder over the right way. Do not turn your course; do not try to complete your righteousness. You will fail in what you do. Do not haste to be rich; do not follow after your perfection. If you do, you will lose the heavenly in you."

'Pî-kan had his heart cut out; Tsze-hsü had his eyes gouged out:-- such were the evil consequences of their loyalty. The upright person bore witness against his father; Wei Shang was drowned:-- such were the misfortunes of good faith. Pao-tsze stood till he was dried up; Shan-tsze would not defend himself:-- such were the injuries brought on by disinterestedness. Confucius did not see his mother; Khwang-tsze did not see his father:-- such were the failures of the righteous. These are instances handed down from former ages, and talked about in these later times. They show us how superior men, in their determination to be correct in their words and resolute in their conduct, paid the penalty of these misfortunes, and were involved in these distresses.'

3. Mr. Dissatisfied asked Mr. Know-the-Mean, saying, 'There is no man after all who does not strive for reputation and pursue after gain. When men are rich, then others go to them. Going to them, they put themselves beneath them. In that position they do honour to them as nobler than themselves. But to see others taking that position and doing honour to us is the way to prolong life, and to secure the rest of the body and the satisfaction of the mind. You alone, Sir, however, have no idea of this. Is it that your knowledge is deficient? Is it that you have the knowledge, but want the strength to carry it into practice? Or is it that your mind is made up to do what you consider right, and never allow yourself to forget it?' Know-the-Mean replied, 'Here now is this man judging of us, his contemporaries, and living in the same neighbourhood as himself, that we consider ourselves scholars who have abjured all vulgar ways and risen above the world. He is entirely without the thought of submitting

to the rule of what is right. He therefore studies ancient times and the present, and the differing questions about the right and wrong, and agrees with the vulgar ideas and influences of the age, abandoning what is most important and discarding what is most honourable, in order to be free to act as he does. But is he not wide of the mark when he thinks that this is the way to promote long life, and to secure the rest of the body and the satisfaction of the mind? He has his painful afflictions and his quiet repose, but he does not inquire how his body is so variously affected; he has his apprehensive terrors, and his happy joys, but he does not inquire how his mind has such different experiences. He knows how to pursue his course, but he does not know why he does so. Even if he had the dignity of the Son of Heaven, and all the wealth of the kingdom were his, he would not be beyond the reach of misfortunes and evils.' Dissatisfied rejoined, 'But riches are in every way advantageous to man. With them his attainment of the beautiful and mastery of every art become what the perfect man cannot obtain nor the sagely man reach to; his appropriation of the bravery and strength of others enables him to exercise a powerful sway; his availing himself of the wisdom and plans of others makes him be accounted intelligent and discriminating; his taking advantage of the virtues of others makes him be esteemed able and good. Though he may not be the holder of a state, he is looked to with awe as a ruler and father. Moreover, music, beauty, with the pleasures of the taste and of power, are appreciated by men's minds and rejoiced in without any previous learning of them; the body reposes in them without waiting for the example of others. Desire and dislike, avoidance and pursuit, do not require any master;-- this is the nature of man. Though the world may condemn one's indulgence of them, who can refrain from it?' Know-the-Mean replied, 'The action of the wise is directed for the good of the people, but they do not go against the (proper) rule and degree. Therefore when they have enough, they do not strive (for more); they have no further object, and so they do not seek for one. When they have not enough, they will seek for it; they will strive for it in every quarter, and yet not think of themselves as greedy. If they have (already) a superfluity, they will decline (any more); they will decline the throne, and yet not think of themselves as disinterested:-- the conditions of disinterestedness and greediness are (with them) not from the constraint of anything external. Through their exercise of introspection, their power may be that of the sovereign, but they will not in their nobility be arrogant to others; their wealth may be that of the whole kingdom, but they will not in their possession of it make a mock of others. They estimate the evils to which they are exposed, and are anxious about the reverses which they may experience. They think how their possessions may be injurious to their nature, and therefore they will decline and not accept them;-- but not because they seek for reputation and praise.

'Yâo and Shun were the sovereigns, and harmony prevailed. It did so, not because of their benevolence towards the people;-- they would not, for what was (deemed) admirable, injure their lives. Shan Küan and Hsü Yü might have been the sovereigns, but they would not receive the throne;-- not that they declined it without purpose, but they would not by its occupancy injure themselves. These all followed after what was advantageous to them, and declined what was injurious, and all the world celebrates their superiority. Thus, though they enjoy the distinction, they did what they did, not for the sake of the reputation and praise.)'

Dissatisfied (continued his argument), saying, 'In thus thinking it necessary for their reputation, they bitterly distressed their bodies, denied themselves what was pleasant, and restricted themselves to a bare sustenance in order to sustain their life; but so they had life-long distress, and long-continued pressure till their death arrived.' Know-the-Mean replied, 'Tranquil ease is happiness; a superfluity is injurious:-- so it is with all things, and especially it is so, where the superfluity is of wealth. The ears of the rich are provided with the music of bells, drums, flageolets and flutes; and their mouths are stuffed with the flesh of fed beasts and with wine of the richest flavour; so are their desires satisfied, till they forget their proper business:-- theirs may be pronounced a condition of disorder. Sunk deeply in their self- sufficiency, they resemble individuals ascending a height with a heavy burden on their backs:-- their condition may be pronounced one of bitter suffering. They covet riches, thinking to derive comfort from them; they covet power, and would fain monopolise it; when quiet and retired, they are drowned in luxurious indulgence; their persons seem to shine, and they are full of boasting:-- they may be said to be in a state of disease. In their desire to be rich and striving for gain, they fill their stores, and, deaf to all admonition, refuse to desist from their course. They are even more elated, and hold on their way:-- their conduct may be pronounced disgraceful. When their wealth is amassed till they cannot use it, they clasp it to their breasts and will not part with it; when their hearts are distressed with their very fulness, they still seek for more and will not desist:-- their condition may be said to be sad. In-doors they are apprehensive of pilfering and begging thieves, and out-of-doors they are afraid of being injured by plundering robbers; in-doors they have many chambers and partitions, and out-of-doors they do not dare to go alone: they may be said to be in a state of (constant) alarm.
'These six conditions are the most deplorable in the world, but they forget them all, and have lost their faculty of judgment. When the evil comes, though they begged it with all the powers of their nature, and by the sacrifice of all their wealth, they could not bring back one day of untroubled peace. When they look for their reputation, it is not to be

seen; when they seek for their wealth, it is not to be got. To task their thoughts, and destroy their bodies, striving for (such an end as) this;-- is it not a case of great delusion ?'

Yüeh Kien, or 'Delight in the Sword-fight.'

Formerly, king Wan of Kâo delighted in the sword-fight. More than three thousand men, masters of the weapon, appeared as his guests, lining the way on either side of his gate, and fighting together before him day and night. Over a hundred of them would die or be (severely) wounded in the course of a year, but he was never weary of looking on (at their engagements), so fond was he of them. The thing continued for three years, when the kingdom began to decay, and other states to plan measures against it.

The crown-prince Khwei was distressed, and laid the case before his attendants, saying, 'If any one can persuade the king, and put an end to these swordsmen, I will give him a thousand ounces of silver.' His attendants said, '(Only) Kwang-tsze is able to do this.' Thereupon the prince sent men with a thousand ounces of silver to offer to Kwang-tsze, who, however, would not accept them, but went with the messengers. When he saw the prince, he said, '0 prince, what have you to say to Kâu, and why would you give me the silver?' The prince replied, 'I have heard that you, master, are sagacious and sage. I sent you respectfully the thousand ounces of silver, as a prelude to the silks and other gifts. But as you decline to receive them, how dare I now tell you (what I wished from you)?' Kwang-tsze rejoined, 'I have heard, 0 prince, that what you wanted me for was to wean the king from what is his delight. Suppose that in trying to persuade his Majesty I should offend him, and not fulfil your expectation, I shall be punished with death; and could I then enjoy this silver? Or suppose that I shall succeed in persuading his Majesty, and accomplish what you desire, what is there in the kingdom of Kâo that I might ask for which I would not get?'

The crown-prince said, 'Yes; but my (father), the king, will see none but swordsmen.' Kwang-tsze replied, 'I know; but I am expert in the use of the sword.' 'That is well,' observed the prince; 'but the swordsmen whom his Majesty sees all have their hair in a tangle, with whiskers projecting out. They wear slouching caps with coarse and unornamented tassels, and their coats are cut short behind. They have staring eyes, and talk about the hazards of their game. The king is delighted with all this; but now you are sure to present yourself to him in your scholar's dress, and this will stand greatly in the way of your success.'

Kwang-tsze said, 'I will then, with your leave, get me a swordsman's dress.' This was ready in three days, and when he appeared in it before the prince, the latter went with him to introduce him to the king, who then drew his sword from its scabbard and waited for him. When Kwang-tsze entered the door of the hall, he did not hurry forward, nor, when he saw the king, did he bow. The king asked him, 'What do you want to teach me, Sir, that you have got the prince to mention you beforehand?' The reply was, 'I have heard that your Majesty is fond of the sword-fight, and therefore I have sought an interview with you on the ground of (my skill in the use of) the sword.' 'What can you do with your sword against an opponent?'

'Let me meet with an opponent every ten paces, my sword would deal with him, so that I should not be stopped in a march of a thousand lî.' The king was delighted with him, and said, 'You have not your match in the kingdom.' Kwang-tsze replied, 'A good swordsman first makes a feint (against his opponent), then seems to give him an advantage, and finally gives his thrust, reaching him before he can return the blow. I should like to have an opportunity to show you my skill.' The king said, 'Stop (for a little), Master. Go to your lodging, and wait for my orders. I will make arrangements for the play, and then call you.'

The king accordingly made trial of his swordsmen for seven days, till more than sixty of them were killed, or (severely) wounded. He then selected five or six men, and made them bring their swords and take their places beneath the hall, after which he called Kwang-tsze, and said to him, 'To-day I am going to make (you and) these men show what you can do with your swords.' 'I have long been looking for the opportunity,' replied Kwang-tsze. The king then asked him what would be the length of the sword which he would use; and he said, 'Any length will suit me, but I have three swords, any one of which I will use, as may please your Majesty. Let me first tell you of them, and then go to the arena.' 'I should like to hear about the three swords,' said the king; and Kwang-tsze went on, 'There is the sword of the Son of Heaven; the sword of a feudal prince; and the sword of a common man.'

'What about the sword of the Son of Heaven?'

'This sword has Yen-khî and Shih-khang for its point; Khî and (Mount) Tâi for its edge; Tsin and Wei for its back; Kâu and Sung for its hilt; Han and Wei for its sheath. It is embraced by the wild tribes all around; it is wrapped up in the four seasons; it is bound round by the Sea of Po; and its girdle is the enduring hills. It is regulated by the five elements; its wielding is by means of Punish ments and Kindness; its unsheathing is like that of the Yin and Yang; it is held fast in the spring and summer; it is put in action in the autumn and winter. When it is thrust forward, there is nothing in front of it; when lifted up, there is nothing above it; when laid down, there is nothing below it; when wheeled round, there is nothing left on any side of it; above, it cleaves the floating clouds; and below, it penetrates to every division of the earth. Let this sword be once used, and the princes are all reformed, and the whole kingdom submits. This is the sword of the Son of Heaven.'

King Wan looked lost in amazement, and said again, 'And what about the sword of a feudal lord?' (Kwang- tsze) replied, 'This sword has wise and brave officers for its point; pure and disinterested officers for its edge; able and honourable officers for its back; loyal and sage officers for its hilt; valiant and eminent officers for its sheath. When this sword is thrust directly forward, as in the former case, there is nothing in front of it; when directed upwards, there is nothing above it; when laid down, there is nothing below it; when wheeled round, there is nothing on any side of it. Above, its law is taken from the round heaven, and is in accordance with the three luminaries; below, its law is taken from the square earth, and is in accordance with the four seasons; between, it is in harmony with the minds of the people, and in all the parts of the state there is peace. Let this sword be once used, and you seem to hear the crash of the thunder-peal. Within the four borders there are none who do not respectfully submit, and obey the orders of the ruler. This is the sword of the feudal lord.'

'And what about the sword of the common man?' asked the king (once more). (Kwang-tsze) replied, 'The sword of the common man (is wielded by) those who have their hair in a tangle, with whiskers projecting out; who wear slouching caps with coarse and unornamented tassels, and have their coats cut short behind; who have staring eyes, and talk (only) about the hazards (of their game). They hit at one another before you. Above, the sword slashes through the neck; and below, it scoops out the liver and lungs. This is the sword of the common man. (The users of it) are not different from fighting cocks; any morning their lives are brought to an end; they are of no use in the affairs of the state. Your Majesty occupies the seat of the Son of Heaven, and that you should be so fond of the swordsmanship of such common men, is unworthy, as I venture to think, of your Majesty.'

On this the king drew Kwang-tsze with him, and went up to the top of the hall, where the cook set forth a meal, which the king walked round three times (unable to sit down to it). Kwang-tsze said to him, 'Sit down quietly, Great King, and calm yourself. I have said all I wished to say about swords.' King Wan, thereafter, did not quit the palace for three months, and the swordsmen all killed themselves in their own rooms.

Yü-fû, or 'The Old Fisherman.'

Confucius, rambling in the forest of Tsze-wei, stopped and sat down by the Apricot altar. The disciples began to read their books, while he proceeded to play on his lute, singing as he did so. He had not half finished his ditty when an old fisherman stepped down from his boat, and came towards them. His beard and eyebrows were turning white; his hair was all uncombed; and his sleeves hunc, idly down. He walked thus up from the bank, till he got to the dry ground, when he stopped, and, with his left hand holding one of his knees, and the right hand at his chin, listened. When the ditty was finished, he beckoned to Tsze- kung and Tsze-lû, who both responded and went to him. Pointing to Confucius, he said, 'Who is he?' Tsze- lû replied, 'He is the Superior Man of Lû.' 'And of what family is he?' 'He is of the Khung family.' 'And what is the occupation of this Mr. Khung?' To this question Tsze-lû gave no reply, but Tsze-kung replied, 'This scion of the Khung family devotes himself in his own nature to leal-heartedness and sincerity; in his conduct he manifests benevolence and righteousness; he cultivates the ornaments of ceremonies and music; he pays special attention to the relationships of society; above, he would promote loyalty to the hereditary lords; below, he seeks the transformation of all classes of the people; his object being to benefit the kingdom:-- this is what Mr. Khung devotes himself to.'

The stranger further asked, 'Is he a ruler possessed of territory?' 'No,' was Tsze-kung's reply. 'Is he the assistant of any prince or king?' 'No;' and on this the other began to laugh and to retrace his steps, saying as he went, 'Yes, benevolence is benevolence! But I am afraid he will not escape (the evils incident to humanity). By embittering his mind and toiling his body, he is imperilling his true (nature)! Alas! how far removed is he from the proper way (of life)!'

Tsze-kung returned, and reported (what the man had said) to Confucius, who pushed his lute aside, and arose, saying, 'Is he not a sage?' and down the slope he went in search of him. When he reached the edge of the lake, there was the fisherman with his pole, dragging the boat towards him. Turning round and seeing Confucius, he came back towards him and stood up. Confucius then drew back, bowed to him twice, and went forward. 'What do you want with me, Sir?' asked the stranger. The reply was, 'A little while ago, my Master, you broke off the thread of your remarks and went away. Inferior to you, I do not know what you wished to say, and have ventured here to wait for your instructions, fortunate if I may but hear the sound of your words to complete the assistance that you can give me!' 'Ah!' responded the stranger, 'how great is your love of learning!'

Confucius bowed twice, and then rose up, and said, 'Since I was young, I have cultivated learning till I am now sixty-nine years old; but I have not had an opportunity of hearing the perfect teaching; dare I but listen to you with a humble and unprejudiced mind?' The stranger replied, 'Like seeks to like, and (birds) of the same note respond to one another;-- this is a rule of Heaven. Allow me to explain what I am in possession of, and to pass over (from its standpoint) to the things which occupy you. What you occupy yourself with are the affairs of men. When the sovereign, the feudal lords, the great officers, and the common people, these four classes, do what is correct (in their several positions), we have the beauty of good order; and when they leave their proper duties, there ensues the greatest disorder. When the officials attend to their duties, and the common people are anxiously concerned about their business, there is no encroachment on one another's rights.

'Fields running to waste; leaking rooms; insufficiency of food and clothing; taxes unprovided for; want of harmony among wives and concubines; and want of order between old and young;-- these are the troubles of the common people.

'Incompetency for their charges; inattention to their official business; want of probity in conduct; carelessness and idleness in subordinates; failure of merit and excellence; and uncertainty of rank and emolument:-- these are the troubles of great officers.

'No loyal ministers at their courts; the clans in their states rebellious; want of skill in their mechanics; articles of tribute of bad quality; late appearances at court in spring and autumn; and the dissatisfaction of the sovereign:-- these are the troubles of the feudal lords.

'Want of harmony between the Yin and Yang; unseasonableness of cold and heat, affecting all things injuriously; oppression and disorder among the feudal princes, their presuming to plunder and attack one another, to the injury of the people; ceremonies and music ill-regulated; the resources for expenditure exhausted or deficient; the social relationships uncared for; and the people abandoned to licentious disorder:-- these are the troubles of the Son of Heaven and his ministers.

'Now, Sir, you have not the high rank of a ruler, a feudal lord, or a minister of the royal court, nor are you in the inferior position of a great minister, with his departments of business, and yet you take it on you to regulate ceremonies and music, and to give special attention to the relationships of society, with a view to transform the various classes of the people:-- is it not an excessive multiplication of your business?

'And moreover men are liable to eight defects, and (the conduct of) affairs to four evils; of which we must by all means take account.

'To take the management of affairs which do not concern him is called monopolising. To bring forward a subject which no one regards is called loquacity. To lead men on by speeches made to please them is called sycophancy. To praise men without regard to right or wrong is called flattery. To be fond of speaking of men's wickedness is called calumny. To part friends and separate relatives is called mischievousness. To praise a man deceitfully, or in the same way fix on him the character of being bad, is called depravity. Without reference to their being good or bad, to agree with men with double face, in order to steal a knowledge of what they wish, is called being dangerous. Those eight defects produce disorder among other men and injury to one's self. A superior man will not make a friend of one who has them, nor will an intelligent ruler make him his minister.

'To speak of what I called the four evils:-- To be fond of conducting great affairs, changing and altering what is of long-standing, to obtain for one's self the reputation of meritorious service, is called ambition; to claim all wisdom and intrude into affairs, encroaching on the work of others, and representing it as one's own, is called greediness; to see his errors without changing them, and to go on more resolutely in his own way when remonstrated with, is called obstinacy; when another agrees with himself, to approve of him, and, however good he may be, when he disagrees, to disapprove of him, is called boastful conceit. These are the four evils. When one can put away the eight defects, and allow no course to the four evils, he begins to be capable of being taught.'

Confucius looked sorrowful and sighed. (Again) he bowed twice, and then rose up and said, 'I was twice driven from Lû. I had to flee from Wei; the tree under which I rested was cut down in Sung; I was kept in a state of siege between Khan and Tshâi. I do not know what errors I had committed that I came to be misrepresented on these four occasions (and suffered as I did).' The stranger looked grieved (at these words), changed countenance, and said, 'Very difficult it is, Sir, to make you understand. There was a man who was frightened at his shadow and disliked to see his footsteps, so that he ran to escape from them. But the more frequently he lifted his feet, the more numerous his footprints were; and however fast he ran, his shadow did not leave him. He thought he was going too slow, and ran on with all his speed without stopping, till his strength was exhausted and he died. He did not know that, if he had stayed in a shady place, his shadow would have disappeared, and that if he had remained still, he would have lost his footprints:-- his stupidity was excessive! And you, Sir, exercise your judgment on the questions about benevolence and righteousness; you investigate the points where agreement and difference touch; you look at the changes from movement to rest and from rest to movement; you have mastered the rules of receiving and giving; you have defined the feelings of liking and disliking; you have harmonised the limits of joy and anger:-- and yet you have hardly been able to escape (the troubles of which you speak). If you earnestly cultivated your own person, and carefully guarded your (proper) truth, simply rendering to others what was due to them, then you would have escaped such entanglements. But now, when you do not cultivate your own person, and make the cultivation of others your object, are you not occupying yourself with what is external?'

Confucius with an air of sadness said, 'Allow me to ask what it is that you call my proper Truth.' The stranger replied, 'A man's proper Truth is pure sincerity in its highest degree;-- without this pure sincerity one cannot move others. Hence if one (only) forces himself to wail, however sadly he may do so, it is not (real) sorrow; if he forces himself to be angry, however he may seem to be severe, he excites no awe; if he forces himself to show affection, however he may smile, he awakens no harmonious reciprocation. True grief, without a sound, is yet sorrowful; true anger, without any demonstration, yet awakens awe; true affection, without a smile, yet produces a harmonious reciprocation. Given this truth within, it exercises a spiritual efficacy without, and this is why we count it so valuable. In our relations with others, it appears according to the requirements of each case:-- in the service of parents, as gentle, filial duty; in the service of rulers, as loyalty and integrity; in festive drinking, as pleasant enjoyment; in the performance of the mourning rites, as sadness and sorrow. In loyalty and integrity, good service is the principal thing; in festive drinking, the enjoyment; in the mourning rites, the sorrow; in the service of parents, the giving them pleasure. The beauty of the service rendered (to a ruler) does not require that it always be performed in one way; the service of parents so as to give them pleasure takes no account of how it is done; the festive drinking which ministers enjoyment does not depend on the appliances for it; the observance of the mourning rites with the proper sorrow asks no questions about the rites themselves. Rites are prescribed for the practice of the common people; man's proper Truth is what he has received from Heaven, operating spontaneously, and unchangeable. Therefore the sages take their law from Heaven, and prize their (proper) Truth, without submitting to the restrictions of custom. The stupid do the reverse of this. They are unable to take their law from Heaven, and are influenced by other men; they do not know how to prize the proper Truth (of their nature), but are under the dominion of ordinary things, and change according to the customs (around them):-- always, consequently, incomplete. Alas for you, Sir, that you were early steeped in the hypocrisies of men, and have been so late in hearing about the Great Way!'

(Once more), Confucius bowed twice (to the fisherman), then rose again, and said, 'That I have met you to-day is as if I had the happiness of getting to heaven. If you, Master, are not ashamed, but will let me be as your servant, and continue to teach me, let me venture to ask where your dwelling is. I will then beg to receive your instructions there, and finish my learning of the Great Way.' The stranger replied, 'I have heard the saying, "If it be one with whom you can walk together, go with him to the subtlest mysteries of the Tâo. If it be one with whom you cannot walk together and he do not know the Tâo, take care that you do not associate with him, and you will yourself incur no responsibility." Do your utmost, Sir. I must leave you, I must leave you!' With this he shoved off his boat, and went away among the green reeds.

Yen Yüan (now) returned to the carriage, where Tsze-lû handed to him the strap; but Confucius did not look round, (continuing where he was), till the wavelets were stilled, and he did not hear the sound of the pole, when at last he ventured to (return and) take his seat. Tsze-lû, by his side in the carriage, asked him, saying, 'I have been your servant for a long time, but I have never seen you, Master, treat another with the awe and reverence which you have now shown. I have seen you in the presence of a Lord of ten thousand chariots or a Ruler of a thousand, and they have never received you in a different audience-room, or treated you but with the courtesies due to an equal, while you have still carried yourself with a reserved and haughty air; but to-day this old fisherman has stood erect in front of you with his pole in his hand, while you, bent from your loins in the form of a sounding-stone, would bow twice before you answered him;-- was not your reverence of him excessive? Your disciples will all think it strange in you, Master. Why did the old fisherman receive such homage from you?'

Confucius leant forward on the cross-bar of the carriage, heaved a sigh, and said, 'Difficult indeed is it to change you, 0 Yû! You have been trained in propriety and righteousness for long, and yet your servile and mean heart has not been taken front you. Come nearer, that I may speak fully to you. If you meet one older than yourself, and do not show him respect, you fail in propriety. If you see a man of superior wisdom and goodness, and do not honour him, you want the great characteristic of humanity. If that (fisherman) did not possess it in the highest degree, how could he make others submit to him? And if their submission to him be not sincere, they do not attain to the truth (of their nature), and inflict a lasting injury on their persons. Alas! there is no greater calamity to man than the want of this characteristic; and you, 0 Yû, you alone, would take such want on yourself

'Moreover, the Tâo is the course by which all things should proceed. For things to fail in this is death; to observe it, is life. To oppose it in practice is ruin; to conform it, is success. Therefore wherever the sagely man finds the Tâo, he honours it. And that old fisherman to-day might be said to possess it;-- dared I presume not to show him reverence?'

Lieh Yü-khâu.

1. Lieh Yü-khâu had started to go to Khî, but came back when he was half-way to it. He met Po-hwan Wû-zan, who said, 'Why have you come back?' His reply was, 'I was frightened.' 'What frightened you?' 'I went into ten soup-shops to get a meal, and in five of them the soup was set before me before (I had paid for it).' 'But what was there in that to frighten you?' (Lieh-tsze) said, 'Though the inward and true purpose be not set forth, the body like a spy gives some bright display of it. And this outward demonstration overawes men's minds, and makes men on light grounds treat one as noble or as aged, from which evil to him will be produced. Now vendors of soup supply their commodity simply as a matter of business, and however much they may dispose of, their profit is but little, and their power is but slight; and yet they treated me as I have said:-- how much more would the lord of ten thousand chariots do so! His body burdened with (the cares of his) kingdom, and his knowledge overtasked by its affairs, he would entrust those affairs to me, and exact from me the successful conduct (of its government). It was this which frightened me.' Po-hwan Wû-zan replied, 'Admirable perspicacity! But if you carry yourself as you do, men will flock to you for protection.'

Not long after, Po-hwan Wû-zan went (to visit Lieh-tsze), and found the space outside his door full of shoes. There he stood with his face to the north, holding his staff upright, and leaning his chin on it till the skin was wrinkled. After standing so for some time, and without saying a word, he was going away, when the door-keeper went in, and told Lieh-tsze. The latter (immediately) took up his shoes, and ran barefoot after the visitor. When he overtook him at the (outer) gate, he said, 'Since you, Sir, have come, are you going away without giving me some medicine?' The other replied, 'It is of no use. I did tell you that men would flock to you, and they do indeed do so. It is not that you can cause men to flock to you, but you cannot keep them from not so coming;-- of what use is (all my warning)? What influences them and makes them glad is the display of your extraordinary (qualities); but you must also be influenced in your turn, and your proper nature be shaken, and no warning can be addressed to you. Those who associate with you do not admonish you of this. The small words which they speak are poison to a man. You perceive it not; you understand it not;-- how can you separate yourself from them?

'The clever toil on, and the wise are sad. Those who are without ability seek for nothing. They eat to the full, and wander idly about. They drift like a vessel loosed from its moorings, and aimlessly wander about.'

233

2. A man of Kang, called Hwan, learned his books in the neighbour-hood of Khiû-shih, and in no longer time than three years became a Confucian scholar, benefiting the three classes of his kindred as the Ho extends its enriching influence for nine lî. He made his younger brother study (the principles of) Mo, and then they two-- the scholar and the Mohist-- disputed together (about their respective systems), and the father took the side of the younger. After ten years Hwan killed himself. (By and by) he appeared to his father in a dream, saying, 'It was I who made your son become a Mohist; why did You not recognise that good service? I am become (but) the fruit of a cypress in autumn.' But the Creator, in apportioning the awards of men, does not recompense them for their own doings, but recompenses them for the (use of the) Heavenly in them. It was thus that Hwan's brother was led to learn Mohism. When this Hwan thought that it was he who had made his brother different from what he would have been, and proceeded to despise his father, he was like the people of Khî, who, while they drank from a well, tried to keep one another from it. Hence it is said, 'Now-a-days all men are Hwans.' From this we perceive that those who possess the characteristics (of the Tâo) consider that they do not know them; how much more is it so with those who possess the Tâo itself! The ancients called such (as Hwan) 'men who had escaped the punishment of Heaven.'

3. The sagely man rests in what is his proper rest; he does not rest in what is not so;-- the multitude of men rest in what is not their proper rest; they do not rest in their proper rest.

4. Kwang-tsze said, 'To know the Tâo is easy; not to say (that you know it) is difficult. To know it and not to speak of it is the way to attain to the Heavenly; to know and to speak of it, is the way to show the Human. The ancients pursued the Heavenly (belonging to them), and not the Human.'

5. Kû Phing-man learned how to slaughter the dragon from Kih-lî Yî, expending (in doing so) all his wealth of a thousand ounces of silver. In three years he became perfect in the art, but he never exercised his skill.

6. The sage looks on what is deemed necessary as unnecessary, and therefore is not at war (in himself). The mass of men deem what is unnec-essary to be necessary, and therefore they are often at war (in themselves). Therefore those who pursue this method of (internal) war, resort to it in whatever they seek for. But reliance on such war leads to ruin.

7. The wisdom of the small man does not go beyond (the minutiae of) making presents and writing memoranda, wearying his spirits out in what

is trivial and mean. But at the same time he wishes to aid in guiding to (the secret of) the Tâo and of (all) things in the incorporeity of the Grand Unity. In this way he goes all astray in regard to (the mysteries of) space and time. The fetters of embodied matter keep him from the knowledge of the Grand Beginning. (On the other hand), the perfect man directs the energy of his spirit to what was before the Beginning, and finds pleasure in the mysteriousness belonging to the region of nothingness. He is like the water which flows on without the obstruction of matter, and expands into the Grand Purity.

Alas for what you do, (0 men)! You occupy yourselves with things trivial as a hair, and remain ignorant of the Grand Rest!

8. There was a man of Sung, called Tshâo Shang, who was sent by the king of Sung on a mission to Khin. On setting out, he had several carriages with him; and the king (of Khin) was so pleased with him that he gave him another hundred. When he returned to Sung, he saw Kwang-tsze, and said to him, 'To live in a narrow lane of a poor mean hamlet, wearing sandals amid distress of poverty, with a weazen neck and yellow face;-- that is what I should find it difficult to do. But as soon as I come to an understanding with the Lord of a myriad carriages, to find myself with a retinue of a hundred carriages,-- that is wherein I excel.' Kwang-tsze replied, 'When the king of Khan is ill, the doctor whom he calls to open an ulcer or squeeze a boil receives a carriage; and he who licks his piles receives five. The lower the service, the more are the carriages given. Did you, Sir, lick his piles? How else should you have got so many carriages? Begone!'

9. Duke Âi of Lû asked Yen Ho, saying, 'If I employ Kung-nî as the support of my government, will the evils of the state be thereby cured?' The reply was, '(Such a measure) would be perilous! It would be full of hazard! Kung-nî, moreover, will try to ornament a feather and paint it; in the conduct of affairs he uses flowery speeches. A (mere) branch is to him more admirable (than the root); he can bear to misrepresent their nature in instructing the people, and is not conscious of the unreality of his words. He receives (his inspiration) from his own mind, and rules his course from his own spirit:-- what fitness has he to be set over the people? Is such a man suitable for you (as your minister)? Could you give to him the nourishment (of the people)? You would do so by mistake (but not on purpose, for a time, but not as a permanency). To make the people leave what is real, and learn what is hypocritical-- that is not the proper thing to be shown to them; if you take thought for future ages, your better plan will be to give up (the idea of employing Confucius). What makes government difficult, is the dealing with men without forgetting yourself;

this is not according to the example of Heaven in diffusing its benefits. Merchants and traffickers are not to be ranked (with administrative officers) if on an occasion you so rank them, the spirits (of the people) do not acquiesce in your doing so. The instruments of external punishment are made of metal and wood; those of internal punishment are agitation (of the mind) and (the sense of) transgression. When small men become subject to the external punishment, the (instruments of) metal and wood deal with them; when they become liable to the internal punishments, the Yin and Yang consume them. It is only the true man who can escape both from the external and internal punishment.'

10. Confucius said, 'The minds of men are more difficult of approach than (the position defended by) mountains and rivers, and more difficult to know than Heaven itself. Heaven has its periods of spring and autumn, of winter and summer, and of morning and evening; but man's exterior is thickly veiled, and his feelings lie deep. Thus the demeanour of some is honest-like, and yet they go to excess (in what is mean); others are really gifted, and yet look to be without ability; some seem docile and impressible, but yet they have far-reaching schemes; others look firm, and yet may be twisted about; others look slow, and yet they are hasty. In this way those who hasten to do what is right as if they were thirsty will anon hurry away from it as if it were fire. Hence the superior man looks at them when employed at a distance to test their fidelity, and when employed near at hand to test their reverence. By employing them on difficult services, he tests their ability; by questioning them suddenly, he tests their knowledge; by appointing them a fixed time, he tests their good faith; by entrusting them with wealth, he tests their benevolence; by telling them of danger, he tests their self-command in emergencies; by making them drunk, he tests their tendencies; by placing them in a variety of society, he tests their chastity:-- by these nine tests the inferior man is discovered.'

11. When Khâo-fû, the Correct, received the first grade of official rank, he walked with head bowed down; on receiving the second, with bent back; on receiving the third, with body stooping, he ran and hurried along the wall:-- who would presume not to take him as a model? But one of those ordinary men, on receiving his first appointment, goes along with a haughty stride; on receiving his second, he looks quite elated in his chariot; and on receiving the third, he calls his uncles by their personal names;-- how very different from Hsü (Yû) in the time (of Yâo of) Thang!

Of all things that injure (men) there is none greater than the practising of virtue with the purpose of the mind, till the mind becomes supercilious. When it becomes so, the mind (only) looks inwards (on itself), and such looking into itself leads to its ruin. This evil quality has five forms, and the chief of them is that which is the central. What do we mean by the central quality? It is that which appears in a man's loving (only) his own views, and reviling whatever he does not do (himself).

Limiting (men's advance), there are eight extreme conditions; securing (that advance), there are three things necessary; and the person has its six repositories. Elegance; a (fine) beard; tallness; size; strength; beauty; bravery; daring; and in all these excelling others:-- (these are the eight extreme conditions) by which advance is limited. Depending on and copying others; stooping in order to rise; and being straitened by the fear of not equalling others:-- these are the three things that lead to advancing. Knowledge seeking to reach to all that is external; bold movement producing many resentments; benevolence and righteousness leading to many requisitions; understanding the phenomena of life in an extraordinary degree; understanding all knowledge so as to possess an approach to it; understanding the great condition appointed for him, and following it, and the smaller conditions, and meeting them as they occur:-- (these are the six repositories of the person).

12. There was a man who, having had an interview with the king of Sung, and been presented by him with ten carriages, showed them boastfully to Kwang-tsze, as if the latter had been a boy. Kwang-tsze said to him, 'Near the Ho there was a poor man who supported his family by weaving rushes (to form screens). His son, when diving in a deep pool, found a pearl worth a thousand ounces of silver. The father said, "Bring a stone, and break it in pieces. A pearl of this value must have been in a pool nine khung deep, and under the chin of the Black Dragon. That you were able to get it must have been owing to your finding him asleep. Let him awake, and the consequences to you will not be small!" Now the kingdom of Sung is deeper than any pool of nine khung, and its king is fiercer than the Black Dragon. That you were able to get the chariots must have been owing to your finding him asleep. Let him awake, and you will be ground to powder.'

13. Some (ruler) having sent a message of invitation to him, Kwang-tsze replied to the messenger, 'Have you seen, Sir, a sacrificial ox? It is robed with ornamental embroidery, and feasted on fresh grass and beans. But when it is led into the grand ancestral temple, though it wished to be (again) a solitary calf, would that be possible for it?'

14. When Kwang-tsze was about to die, his disciples signified their wish to give him a grand burial. 'I shall have heaven and earth,' said he, 'for my coffin and its shell; the sun and moon for my two round symbols

of jade; the stars and constellations for my pearls and jewels; and all things assisting as the mourners.

Will not the provisions for my burial be complete? What could you add to them?' The disciples replied, 'We are afraid that the crows and kites will eat our master.' Kwang-tsze rejoined, 'Above, the crows and kites will eat me; below, the mole-crickets and ants will eat me:-- to take from those and give to these would only show your partiality.'

The attempt, with what is not even, to produce what is even will only produce an uneven result; the attempt, with what is uncertain, to make the uncertain certain will leave the uncertainty as it was. He who uses only the sight of his eyes is acted on by what he sees; it is the (intuition of the) spirit, that gives the assurance of certainty. That the sight of the eyes is not equal to that intuition of the spirit is a thing long acknowledged. And yet stupid people rely on what they see, and will have it to be the sentiment of all men;-- all their success being with what is external:-- is it not sad?

Thien Hsiâ.

1. The methods employed in the regulation of the world are many; and (the employers of them) think each that the efficiency of his own method leaves nothing to be added to it.

But where is what was called of old 'the method of the Tâo?' We must reply, 'It is everywhere.' But then whence does the spiritual in it come down? and whence does the intelligence in it come forth? There is that which gives birth to the Sage, and that which gives his perfection to the King:-- the origin of both is the One.

Not to be separate from his primal source constitutes what we call the Heavenly man; not to be separate from the essential nature thereof constitutes what we call the Spirit-like man; not to be separate from its real truth constitutes what we call the Perfect man.

To regard Heaven as his primal Source, Its Attributes as the Root (of his nature), and the Tâo as the Gate (by which he enters into this inheritance), (knowing also) the prognostics given in change and transformation, constitutes what we call the Sagely man.

To regard benevolence as (the source of all) kindness, righteousness as (the source of all) distinctions, propriety as (the rule of) all conduct, and music as (the idea of) all harmony, thus diffusing a fragrance of gentleness and goodness, constitutes what we call the Superior man.

To regard laws as assigning the different (social) conditions, their names as the outward expression (of the social duties), the comparison of subjects as supplying the grounds of evidence, investigation as conducting to certainty, so that things can be numbered as first, second, third, fourth (and so on):-- (this is the basis of government). Its hundred offices are thus arranged; business has its regular course; the great matters of clothes and food are provided for; cattle are fattened and looked after; the (government) stores are filled; the old and weak, orphans and solitaries, receive anxious consideration:-- in all these ways is provision made for the nourishment of the people.

How complete was (the operation of the Tâo) in the men of old! It made them the equals of spiritual beings, and subtle and all-embracing as heaven and earth. They nourished all things, and produced harmony all under heaven. Their beneficent influence reached to all classes of the people. They understood all fundamental principles, and followed them out to their graduated issues; in all the six directions went their penetration, and in the four quarters all things were open to them. Great and small, fine and coarse;-- all felt their presence and operation. Their intelligence, as seen in all their regulations, was handed down from age to age in their old laws, and much of it was still to be found in the Historians. What of it was in the Shih, the Shû, the Lî, and the Yo, might be learned from the scholars of Tsâu and Lû, and the girdled members of the various courts. The Shih describes what should be the aim of the mind; the Shû, the course of events; the Lî is intended to direct the conduct; the Yo, to set forth harmony; the Yî, to show the action of the Yin and Yang; and the Khun Khiû, to display names and the duties belonging to them.

Some of the regulations (of these men of old), scattered all under heaven, and established in our Middle states, are (also) occasionally mentioned and described in the writings of the different schools.

There ensued great disorder in the world, and sages and worthies no longer shed their light on it. The Tâo and its characteristics ceased to be regarded as uniform. Many in different places got one glimpse of it, and plumed themselves on possessing it as a whole. They might be compared to the ear, the eye, the nose, or the mouth. Each sense has its own faculty, but their different faculties cannot be interchanged. So it was with the many branches of the various schools. Each had its peculiar excellence, and there was the time for the use of it; but notwithstanding no one covered or extended over the whole (range of truth). The case was that of the scholar of a corner who passes his judgment on all the beautiful in heaven and earth, discriminates the principles that underlie all things, and attempts to estimate the success arrived at by the ancients. Seldom is it that such an one can embrace all the beautiful in heaven and earth, or rightly estimate the ways of the spiritual and intelligent; and thus it was that the Tâo, which inwardly forms the sage and externally the king, became obscured and lost its clearness, became repressed and lost its development. Every one in the world did whatever he wished, and was the rule to himself. Alas! the various schools held on their several ways, and could not come back to the same point, nor agree together.

The students of that later age unfortunately did not see the undivided purity of heaven and earth, and the great scheme of truth held by the ancients. The system of the Tâo was about to be torn in fragments all under a the sky.

2. To leave no example of extravagance to future generations; to show no wastefulness in the use of anything; to make no display in the degree of their (ceremonial) observances; to keep themselves (in their expenditure) under the restraint of strict and exact rule, so as to be prepared for

occurring emergencies;-- such regulations formed part of the system of the Tâo in antiquity, and were appreciated by Mo Tâ, and (his disciple) Khin Hwa-lî. When they heard of such ways, they were delighted with them; but they enjoined them in excess, and followed them themselves too strictly. (Mo) made the treatise 'Against Music,' and enjoined the subject of another, called 'Economy in Expenditure,' on his followers. He would have no singing in life, and no wearing of mourning on occasions of death. He inculcated Universal Love, and a Common Participation in all advantages, and condemned Fighting. His doctrine did not admit of Anger. He was fond also of Learning, and with it all strove not to appear different from others. Yet he did not agree with the former kings, but attacked the ceremonies and music of the ancients.

Hwang-Tî had his Hsien-khih; Yâo, his Tâ Kang; Shun, his Tâ Shâo; Yü, his Tâ Hsiâ; Thang, his Tâ Hû; king Wan, his music of the Phi-yung; and king Wû and the duke of Kâu made the Wû.

In the mourning rites of the ancients, the noble and mean had their several observances, the high and low their different degrees. The coffin of the Son of Heaven was sevenfold; of a feudal lord, fivefold; of a great officer, threefold; of other officers, twofold. But now Mo-tsze alone, would have no singing during life, and no wearing of mourning after death. As the rule for all, he would have a coffin of elaeococca wood, three inches thick, and without any enclosing shell. The teaching of such lessons cannot be regarded as affording a proof of his love for men; his practising them in his own case would certainly show that he did not love himself; but this has not been sufficient to overthrow the views of Mo-tsze. Notwithstanding, men will sing, and he condemns singing; men will wail, and he condemns wailing; men will express their joy, and he condemns such expression:-- is this truly in accordance with man's nature? Through life toil, and at death niggardliness:-- his way is one of great unkindliness. Causing men sorrow and melancholy, and difficult to be carried into practice, I fear it cannot be regarded as the way of a sage. Contrary to the minds of men everywhere, men will not endure it. Though Mo-tsze himself might be able to endure it, how can the aversion of the world to it be overcome? The world averse to it, it must be far from the way of the (ancient) kings.

Mo-tsze, in praise of his views, said, 'Anciently, when Yü was draining off the waters of the flood, he set free the channels of the Kiang and the Ho, and opened communications with them from the regions of the four Î and the nine provinces. The famous hills with which he dealt were 300, the branch streams were 3000, and the smaller ones innumerable. With his own hands he carried the sack and wielded the spade, till he had united all the streams of the country (conducting them to the sea). There was no hair left on his legs from the knee to the ankle. He bathed his hair in the violent wind, and combed it in the pelting rain, thus marking out the myriad states. Yü was a great sage, and thus he toiled in the service of the world.' The effect of this is that in this later time most of the Mohists wear skins and dolychos cloth, with shoes of wood or twisted hemp, not stopping day or night, but considering such toiling on their part as their highest achievement. They say that he who cannot do this is acting contrary to the way of Yü, and not fit to be a Mohist.

The disciples of Khin of Hsiang-lî, the followers of the various feudal lords; and Mohists of the south, such as Khû Hû, Ki Khih, and Tang Ling-tsze, all repeated the texts of Mo, but they differed in the objections which they offered to them, and in their deceitful glosses they called one another Mohists of different schools. They had their disputations, turning on 'what was hard,' and 'what was white,' what constituted 'sameness' and what 'difference,' and their expressions about the difference between 'the odd' and 'the even,' with which they answered one another. They regarded their most distinguished member as a sage, and wished to make him their chief, hoping that he would be handed down as such to future ages. To the present day these controversies are not determined.

The idea of Mo Tî and Khin Hwa-lî was good, but their practice was wrong. They would have made the Mohists of future ages feel it necessary to toil themselves, till there was not a hair on their legs, and still be urging one another on; (thus producing a condition) superior indeed to disorder, but inferior to the result of good government. Nevertheless, Mo-tsze was indeed one of the best men in the world, which you may search without finding his equal. Decayed and worn (his person) might be, but he is not to be rejected,-- a scholar of ability indeed!

3. To keep from being entangled by prevailing customs; to shun all ornamental attractions in one's self; not to be reckless in his conduct to others; not to set himself stubbornly against a multitude; to desire the peace and repose of the world in order to preserve the lives of the people; and to cease his action when enough had been obtained for the nourishment of others and himself, showing that this was the aim of his mind;-- such a scheme belonged to the system of the Tâo in antiquity, and it was appreciated by Sung Hsing and Yin Wan.

When they heard of such ways, they were delighted with them. They made the Hwa-shan cap, and wore it as their distinguishing badge. In their intercourse with others, whatever their differences might be, they began by being indulgent to them. Their name for 'the Forbearance of the Mind' was 'the Action of the Mind.' By the warmth of affection they sought the harmony of joy, and to blend together all within the four seas; and their wish was to plant this everywhere as the chief thing to be pursued. They endured insult without feeling it a disgrace; they sought to save the people from fighting; they forbade aggression and sought to hush the weapons of strife, to save their age from war. In this way they went everywhere, counselling the high and instructing the low. Though the world might not receive them, they only insisted on their object the more strongly, and would not abandon it. Hence it is said, 'The high and the low might be weary of them, but they were strong to show themselves.'

Notwithstanding all this, they acted too much out of regard to others, and too little for themselves. It was as if they said, 'What we request and wish is simply that there may be set down for us five pints of rice;-- that will be enough.' But I fear the Master would not get his fill from this; and the disciples, though famishing, would still have to be mindful of the world, and, never stopping day or night, have to say, 'Is it necessary I should preserve my life? Shall I scheme how to exalt myself above the master, the saviour of the age?'

It was moreover as if they said, 'The superior man does not censoriously scrutinize (the faults of others); he does not borrow from others to supersede his own endeavours; when any think that he is of no use to the world, he knows that their intelligence is inferior to his own; he considers the prohibition of aggression and causing the disuse of arms to be an external achievement, and the making his own desires to be few and slight to be the internal triumph.' Such was their discrimination between the great and the small, the subtle and the coarse; and with the attainment of this they stopped.

4. Public-spirited, and with nothing of the partizan; easy and compliant, without any selfish partialities; capable of being led, without any positive tendencies; following in the wake of others, without any double mind; not looking round because of anxious thoughts; not scheming in the exercise of their wisdom; not choosing between parties, but going along with all;-- all such courses belonged to the Tâoists of antiquity, and they were appreciated by Phang Mang, Thien Phien, and Shan Tâo. When they heard of such ways, they were delighted with them. They considered that the first thing for them to do was to adjust the controversies about different things. They said, 'Heaven can cover, but it cannot sustain; Earth can contain, but it cannot cover. The Great Tâo embraces all things, but It does not discriminate between them.'

They knew that all things have what they can do and what they cannot do. Hence it is said, 'If you select, you do not reach all; if you teach some things, you must omit the others; but the Tâo neglects none.' Therefore Shan Tâo discarded his knowledge and also all thought of himself, acting only where he had no alternative, and pursued it as his course to be indifferent and pure in his dealings with others. He said that the best knowledge was to have no knowledge, and that if we had a little knowledge it was likely to prove a dangerous thing. Conscious of his unfitness, he undertook no charge, and laughed at those who valued ability and virtue. Remiss and evasive, he did nothing, and disallowed the greatest sages which the world had known. Now with a hammer, now with his hand, smoothing all corners, and breaking all bonds, he accommodated himself to all conditions. He disregarded right and wrong, his only concern being to avoid trouble; he learned nothing from the wise and thoughtful, and took no note of the succession of events, thinking only of carrying himself with a lofty disregard of everything. He went where he was pushed, and followed where he was led, like a whirling wind, like a feather tossed about, like the revolutions of a grindstone.

What was the reason that he appeared thus complete, doing nothing wrong? that, whether in motion or at rest, he committed no error, and could be charged with no transgression? Creatures that have no knowledge are free from the troubles that arise from self-assertion and the entanglements that spring from the use of knowledge. Moving and at rest, they do not depart from their proper course, and all their life long they do not receive any praise. Hence (Shan Tâo) said, 'Let me come to be like a creature without knowledge. Of what use are the (teachings of the) sages and worthies?' But a clod of earth never fails in the course (proper for it), and men of spirit and eminence laughed together at him, and said, 'The way of Shan Tâo does not describe the conduct of living men; that it should be predicable only of the dead is strange indeed!'

It was just the same with Thien Phien. He learned under Phang Mang, but it was as if he were not taught at all. The master of Phang Mang said, 'The Tâoist professors of old came no farther than to say that nothing was absolutely right and nothing absolutely wrong.' His spirit was like the breath of an opposing wind; how can it be described in words? But he was always contrary to (the views of) other men, which he would not bring together to view, and he did not escape shaving the corners and bonds (of which I have spoken). What he called the Tâo was not the true Tâo, and what he called the right was really the wrong.

Phang Mang, Thien Phien, and Shan Tâo did not in fact know the Tâo; but nevertheless they had heard in a general way about it.

5. To take the root (from which things spring) as the essential (part),

and the things as its coarse (embodiment); to see deficiency in accumulation; and in the solitude of one's individuality to dwell with the spirit-like and intelligent;-- such a course belonged to the Tâo of antiquity, and it was appreciated by Kwan Yin and Lâo Tan. When they heard of such ways, they were delighted with them. They built their system on the assumption of an eternal non-existence, and made the ruling idea in it that of the Grand Unity. They made weakness and humility their mark of distinction, and considered that by empty vacuity no injury could be sustained, but all things be preserved in their substantiality.

Kwan Yin says, 'To him who does not dwell in himself the forms of things show themselves as they are.

His movement is like that of water; his stillness is like that of a mirror; his response is like that of the echo. His tenuity makes him seem to be disappearing altogether; he is still as a clear (lake), harmonious in his association with others, and he counts gain as loss. He does not take precedence of others, but follows them.' Lâo Tan says, 'He knows his masculine power, but maintains his female weakness,-- becoming the channel into which all streams flow. He knows his white purity, but keeps his disgrace,-- becoming the valley of the world. Men all prefer to be first; he alone chooses to be last, saying, "I will receive the offscourings of the world." Men all choose fulness; he alone chooses emptiness. He does not store, and therefore he has a superabundance; he looks solitary, but has a multitude around him. In his conducting of himself he is easy and leisurely and wastes nothing. He does nothing, and laughs at the clever and ingenious. Men all seek for happiness, but he feels complete in his imperfect condition, and says, "Let me only escape blame." He regards what is deepest as his root, and what is most restrictive as his rule; and says, "The strong is broken; the sharp and pointed is blunted." He is always generous and forbearing with others, and does not encroach on any man;-- this may be pronounced the height (of perfection).'

O Kwan Yin, and Lâo Tan, ye were among the greatest men of antiquity; True men indeed!

6. That the shadowy and still is without bodily form; that change and transformation are ever proceeding, but incapable of being determined. What is death? What is life? What is meant by the union of Heaven and Earth? Does the spiritual intelligence go away? Shadowy, where does it go? Subtle, whither does it proceed? All things being arranged as they are, there is no one place which can be fitly ascribed to it. Such were the questions belonging to the scheme of Tâo in antiquity, and they were appreciated by Kwang Kâu. When he heard of such subjects, he was delighted with them. (He discussed them), using strange and mystical expressions,

wild and extravagant words, and phrases to which no definite meaning could be assigned. He constantly indulged his own wayward ideas, but did not make himself a partisan, nor look at them as peculiar to himself. Considering that men were sunk in stupidity and could not be talked to in dignified style, he employed the words of the cup of endless application, with important quotations to substantiate the truth, and an abundance of corroborative illustrations. He chiefly cared to occupy himself with the spirit-like operation of heaven and earth, and did not try to rise above the myriads of things. He did not condemn the agreements and differences of others, so that he might live in peace with the prevalent views. Though his writings may seem to be sparkling trifles, there is no harm in amusing one's self with them; though his phraseology be ever-varying, its turns and changes are worth being looked at;-- the fulness and completeness of his ideas cannot be exhausted. Above he seeks delight in the Maker; below, he has a friendly regard to those who consider life and death as having neither beginning nor end. As regards his dealing with the Root (origin of all things), he is comprehensive and great, opening up new views, deep, vast, and free. As regards the Author and Master (the Great Tâo Itself), be may be pronounced exact and correct, carrying our thoughts to range and play on high. Nevertheless on the subject of transformation, and the emancipation of that from (the thraldom of) things, his principles are inexhaustible, and are not derived from his predecessors. They are subtle and obscure, and cannot be fully explained.

7. Hui Shih had many ingenious notions. His writings would fill five carriages; but his doctrines were erroneous and contradictory, and his words were wide of their mark. Taking up one thing after another, he would say:-- 'That which is so great that there is nothing outside it may be called the Great One; and that which is so small that there is nothing inside it maybe called the Small One.' 'What has no thickness and will not admit of being repeated is 1000 lî in size.' 'Heaven may be as low as the earth.' 'A mountain may be as level as a marsh.' ' The sun in the meridian may be the sun declining.' 'A creature may be born to life and may die at the same time.' '(When it is said that) things greatly alike are different from things a little alike, this is what is called making little of agreements and differences; (when it is said that) all things are entirely alike or entirely different, this is what is called making much of agreements and differences.' 'The south is unlimited and yet has a limit.' 'I proceed to Yueh to-day and came to it yesterday.' 'Things which are joined together can be separated.' 'I know the centre of the world;-- it is north of Yen or south of Yueh.' 'If all things be regarded with love, heaven and earth are of one body (with me).'

Hui Shih by such sayings as these made himself very conspicuous throughout the kingdom, and was considered an able debater. All other debaters vied with one another and delighted in similar exhibitions. (They would say), 'There are feathers in an egg.' 'A fowl has three feet.' 'The kingdom belongs to Ying.' 'A dog might have been (called) a sheep.' 'A tadpole has a tail.' 'Fire is not hot.' 'A mountain gives forth a voice.' 'A wheel does not tread on the ground.' 'The eye does not see.' 'The finger indicates, but needs not touch, (the object).' 'Where you come to may not be the end.' 'The tortoise is longer than the snake.' 'The carpenter's square is not square.' 'A compass should not itself be round.' 'A chisel does not surround its handle.' 'The shadow of a flying bird does not (itself) move.' 'Swift as the arrowhead is, there is a time when it is neither flying nor at rest.' 'A dog is not a hound.' 'A bay horse and a black ox are three.' 'A white dog is black.' 'A motherless colt never had a mother.' 'If from a stick a foot long you every day take the half of it, in a myriad ages it will not be exhausted.'-- It was in this way that the debaters responded to Hui Shih, all their lifetime, without coming to an end.

Hwan Twan and Kung-sun Lung were true members of this class. By their specious representations they threw a glamour over men's minds and altered their ideas. They vanquished men in argument, but could not subdue their minds, only keeping them in the enclosure of their sophistry. Hui Shih daily used his own knowledge and the arguments of others to propose strange theses to all debaters;-- such was his practice. At the same time he would talk freely of himself, thinking himself the ablest among them, and saying, 'In heaven or earth who is my match?' Shih maintained indeed his masculine energy, but he had not the art (of controversy).

In the south there was a man of extraordinary views, named Hwang Liâo, who asked him how it was that the sky did not fall nor the earth sink, and what was the cause of wind, rain, and the thunder's roll and crash. Shih made no attempt to evade the questions, and answered him without any exercise of thought, talking about all things, without pause, on and on without end; yet still thinking that his words were few, and adding to them the strangest observations. He thought that to contradict others was a real triumph, and wished to make himself famous by over-coming them; and on this account he was not liked by the multitude of debaters. He was weak in real attainment, though he might seem strong in comparison with others, and his way was narrow and dark. If we look at Hui Shih's ability from the standpoint of Heaven and Earth, it was only like the restless activity of a mosquito or gadfly; of what service was it to anything?
To give its full development to any one capacity is a good thing, and he who does so is in the way to a higher estimation of the Tâo; but Hui Shih could find no rest for himself in doing this. He diffused himself

over the world of things without satiety, till in the end he had only the reputation of being a skilful debater. Alas! Hui Shih, with all his talents, vast as they were, made nothing out; he pursued all subjects and never came back (with success). It was like silencing an echo by his shouting, or running a race with his shadow. Alas!

www.ingramcontent.com/pod-product-compliance
Lightning Source LLC
Chambersburg PA
CBHW050223270326
41914CB00003BA/548

* 9 7 8 1 9 4 0 8 4 9 5 2 2 *